PRENTICE HALL STUDIES
IN INTERNATIONAL RELATIONS
ENDURING QUESTIONS IN CHANGING TIMES

CHARLES W. KEGLEY, JR., *SERIES EDITOR*

In the era of globalization in the twenty-first century, people cannot afford to ignore the impact of international relations on their future. From the value of one's investments to the quality of the air one breathes, international relations matter. The instantaneous spread of communications throughout the world is making for the internationalization of all phenomena, while the distinction between the domestic and the foreign, the public and the private, and the national and the international is vanishing. Globalization is an accelerating trend that is transforming how virtually every field of study in the social sciences is being investigated and taught.

Contemporary scholarship has made bold advances in understanding the many facets of international relations. It has also laid a firm foundation for interpreting the major forces and factors that are shaping the global future.

To introduce the latest research findings and theoretical commentary, a new publication series has been launched. *Prentice Hall Studies in International Relations: Enduring Questions in Changing Times* presents books that focus on the issues, controversies, and trends that are defining the central topics dominating discussion about international relations.

U.S. FOREIGN POLICY AND INTERNATIONAL POLITICS
GEORGE W. BUSH, 9/11, AND THE GLOBAL-TERRORIST HYDRA

M. KENT BOLTON
California State University, San Marcos

UPPER SADDLE RIVER, NEW JERSEY 07458

Library of Congress Cataloging-in-Publication Data

Bolton, M. Kent.
  U.S. foreign policy and international politics: George W. Bush, 9/11, and the global-terrorist hydra/M. Kent Bolton.
     p. cm.—(Prentice Hall studies in international relations)
  Includes bibliographical references and index.
  ISBN 0-13-117439-8
  1. United States—Foreign relations—2001- . 2. September 11 Terrorist Attacks, 2001—Influence. 3. War on Terrorism, 2001- . 4. Terrorism. 5. World politics—1995–2005. 6. International relations. I. Title. II. Series.

  E902.B65 2004
    327.73'009'0511—dc22

                                                                    2004015994

Editorial Director: Charlyce Jones Owen
Acquisitions Editor: Glenn Johnston
Editorial Assistant: Suzanne Remore
Marketing Manager: Kara Kindstrom
Marketing Assistant: Jennifer Lang
Prepress and Manufacturing Buyer: Sherry Lewis
Interior Design: John P. Mazzola
Cover Art Director: Jayne Conte
Cover Design: Kiwi Design
Composition/Full-Service Project Management: Kari Callaghan Mazzola and John P. Mazzola
Printer/Binder: Phoenix Color Corp.
Cover Printer: Phoenix Color Corp.

This book was set in 10/12 Electra.

Pearson Education LTD.
Pearson Education Singapore, Pte. Ltd
Pearson Education, Canada, Ltd
Pearson Education–Japan
Pearson Education Australia PTY, Limited

Pearson Education North Asia Ltd
Pearson Educación de Mexico, S.A. de C.V.
Pearson Education Malaysia, Pte. Ltd
Pearson Education, Upper Saddle River, NJ

10 9 8 7 6 5 4 3 2 1
ISBN 0-13-117439-8

I dedicate this book to my parents,
who instilled in me an intellectual curiosity, occasionally to their chagrin.

I also dedicate it to my family: Lyn, Karisa, and Kris.
Without their help, support, and understanding,
this never would have been possible.

CONTENTS

PREFACE

In spring 2002 I was on sabbatical leave. A few months previously, the traumatic events of 9/11 occurred—an attack that one could intuitively feel would affect U.S. foreign policy—making this project a compelling one. Additionally, upon returning from sabbatical I was scheduled to teach U.S. foreign policy. Thus was the confluence of events resulting in this book.

This project was conceived as an opportunity for students to participate in and experience research firsthand. It was also conceived as a continuation of my research interests, broadly known as comparative foreign-policy analysis. I was first introduced to comparative foreign-policy studies during my doctoral studies (at Ohio State University), and my research program has since centered on said subspecialty of international politics and foreign-policy studies.* The 9/11 terrorist attacks presented a unique opportunity to study a timely topic in great detail, combine it with my existing research program, and involve students in examining whether, in fact, 9/11 demonstrably changed U.S. foreign policy, a thesis that seemed self-evident.

Multiple reasons made this project so compelling. First, the 9/11 attacks struck me as a seminal event that might change the entire direction of U.S. foreign policy. Being scheduled to teach foreign policy upon completion of sabbatical served to increase the event's relevance. Second, one of the texts I have used for years in

---

*M. Kent Bolton, "Pas de Trois," *Conflict Management and Peace Science* 18, no. 2 (2001), pp. 175–212; M. Kent Bolton, "Domestic Sources of Vietnam's Foreign Policy," in *Vietnam's Foreign Policy in Transition*, ed. Carlyle Thayer and Ramses Amer (Singapore: Institute of Southeast Asian Studies, 1999); M. Kent Bolton, "Vietnam Crucible," in *Third World–United States Relations in the New World Order*, ed. A. Grammy and Kaye Bragg (New York: NOVA Science Publishers, 1996).

teaching foreign policy is Charles Kegley and Eugene Wittkopf's *American Foreign Policy: Pattern and Process.* ** One of their main theses is that from the late 1940s to the early 1990s U.S. foreign policy is appropriately described as resistant to change. They argue that change in U.S. foreign policy occurs only slowly and incrementally, irrespective of which party occupies the White House, which party controls Congress, and even during certain dramatic changes in America's external environment. Given these facts, the obvious question became: Does the Kegley-Wittkopf thesis still hold following 9/11? Or, as I began to believe, was 9/11 a decisive event that would change U.S. foreign policy substantively, and that would persist over time? Third, 9/11 presented a rare opportunity to combine an existing research program with classroom pedagogy—a challenge many professors wish to accomplish but do so less frequently than desirable.

A brief note concerning methodology and data collection, respectively, is in order. The method used to assess whether, and if so how, 9/11 affected U.S. foreign policy is the comparative foreign-policy analysis framework first described by James Rosenau ("pre-theories") and subsequently used by Kegley and Wittkopf in the latters' *American Foreign Policy: Pattern and Process.* Data were collected and filed in terms of clusters of exogenous variables specified by said construct. Thus it made sense organizationally to collect data and present them separately, initially, then address interactions between them as process, as do Kegley and Wittkopf.

At the beginning of this research, a conscious decision to limit the sources from which to collect data was made. The very nature of assessing trends in U.S. foreign policy normally requires examining such trends over time. For this project, however, time defined data collection: *viz.*, data collected from 9/11 through the summer of 2002. Thus, a caveat is appropriate: The conclusions contained herein are necessarily tentative. Another reason for limiting data collection is sheer amount of data. Typically, scholarly research projects attempt to gather every source available. For present purposes, the task would be too daunting given the project's effective time frame. To cite one example, if one conducts a Lexis-Nexis search, limiting the potential domain to U.S. newspapers using the words "terror" and either "September 11" or "9/11" (even for a short time frame, say 2001), too many hits are generated for the service to display.

Instead, the following method of data collection was employed. Specifically, data collection consisted of examining four preeminent U.S. newspapers (the *Los Angeles Times*, the *Christian Science Monitor*, the *New York Times* and the *Washington Post*) for articles on U.S. foreign policy. Data collection was less than systematic, initially. It was not until December 2001 that this project coalesced into its present form. As a result, systematic data collection of articles from these newspapers did not begin until December. Prior to December, data collection consisted of a somewhat selective collection of articles from my local paper, the *Los Angeles*

**Charles W. Kegley, Jr. and Eugene R. Wittkopf, *American Foreign Policy: Pattern and Process*, 5th ed. (New York: St. Martin's Press, 1996).

Times, with the rationale that said articles would be useful in teaching future U.S. foreign-policy classes.

Once systematic collection began, the aforementioned newspapers were searched daily, specifically their Web editions, for relevant articles, columns, and op-ed articles. When an article was found that was in any way connected to U.S. foreign policy, however marginally, as it related to President Bush's war on terror, global terrorism, "evildoers," and so forth, it was saved. Each article was categorized as one or more of the following inputs: external-systemic, societal, governmental, role, and individual. Occasionally, an additional source was consulted, though very infrequently and on an *ad hoc* basis. For instance, the reader will note that a relatively small number of reports, polls, weekly publications, and government sources are in the endnotes of each chapter. Often, for instance, presidential speeches were taken from the White House Web Site rather than newspapers. Another example is "The Global War on Terrorism: The First 100 Days," produced by the Coalition Information Centers, as well as the Patriot Act, though both are used sparingly. Both Reuters and Associated Press Web Sites provided a small number of citations, as did an occasional article from the *Far Eastern Economic Review*, *Newsweek*, and *Time*.

In the time since this book was written, much has happened to confirm the general thesis promulgated in this text. While beyond the current scope, a select few examples will be considered in the conclusion chapter, Chapter 7. As of this writing, my initial impression that 9/11 would indeed represent a fundamental, substantive, and enduring juncture in U.S. foreign policy has been borne out time and again. Alas, only when additional terrorist plots are implemented against the United States (and its allies) or such plots are foiled with the details filtering out to the public will one know definitively just how fundamental a turning point in U.S. foreign policy 9/11 represents. As recent reports have made clear, most experts believe it to be a matter of when rather than a matter of if such plots will occur.

ACKNOWLEDGMENTS

I would like to express gratitude to the Sabbatical Committee at California State University, San Marcos (CSUSM), and its members for their support. The time necessary to complete this manuscript would have been virtually impossible without the generous support of the aforementioned persons. I also want to thank the following reviewers for their helpful comments: Stephen R. Rock, Vassar College; William F. Kelly, Auburn University; Charles T. Barber, University of Southern Indiana; and Alpo Rusi, University of Lapland. Finally, I wish to thank my family for their forbearance as I researched this project and for the time during which they gave me wide latitude to write this manuscript. Only they know how truly crucial their support was during this project.

M. Kent Bolton

INTRODUCTION

Few would argue that U.S. foreign policy specifically and international politics generally are static enterprises. Clearly, countless stimuli affect U.S. foreign policy, the principal policymakers charged with formulating it, and international politics on a daily basis. If one accepts the notion that myriad stimuli confront policymakers daily, the natural question arises as to whether the policymakers' responses constitute a constantly changing output or a relatively stable output. In attempting to understand U.S. foreign policy and international politics, for example, does one consider U.S. foreign-policy output as something that changes day to day or, conversely, something that is relatively stable over time? It is more than a mere academic question. If the former, students of U.S. foreign policy are faced with a Herculean task: assessing daily how U.S. foreign policy and international politics have changed from the previous day. If the latter, one's task is somewhat simpler: namely, to identify the patterns and processes over specific periods or eras of U.S. foreign policy and international politics.

Consider the following U.S foreign-policy events over the course of the past sixty years. In considering each, ask yourself whether the result of the event was a specific, identifiable, substantive change in U.S. foreign policy. First, consider Japan's surprise attack of Pearl Harbor in December of 1941. Consider, next, the beginning of the Cold War. Specifically, think of the post–World War II series of events that collectively comprised the Cold War's commencement: (1) the Turkey-Greece crises (1946–1947); (2) the Berlin Airlift crisis (1948); (3) the fleeing of the American-sponsored Kuomintang (KMT or Nationalists) to Formosa (Taiwan) and the resultant creation of the Communist Peoples' Republic of China (PRC) in 1949; and (4) the invasion of South Korea by Soviet-PRC sponsored, Communist North Korea (1950). Now consider more recent yet equally memorable U.S. foreign-policy events. For instance, recall the Tet Offensive during the Vietnam War in January 1968.

Recall the Yom Kippur war (1973) in which Israel was invaded by several of its Arab neighbors eventually resulting in what nearly became a nuclear clash between the United States, on the one hand, and the Soviet Union on the other. Next, consider the fall of Saigon in spring 1975. During the Reagan Administration's tenure, recall the administration's reaction to the Soviet Union's downing of Korean Airline KAL 007 (fall 1983). Much more recently, consider Iraq's invasion of Kuwait (1990) resulting first in *Operation Desert Shield* followed by *Operation Desert Storm*. Consider, just a few short years later, the discovery in the early-to-mid 1990s of North Korea's nuclear weapons program. Finally, consider the trauma to America of the multiple terrorist attacks on the World Trade Center and the Pentagon on a day few Americans will ever forget, September 11, 2001.

Each of the aforementioned foreign-policy episodes represented a potential turning point in U.S. foreign policy. Each caused varying degrees of trauma to the American public. Each affected the U.S. foreign-policy bureaucracy and its decision-makers in varying degrees. It appears, however, that only a relatively few of the aforementioned foreign-policy episodes resulted in demonstrable and sustained changes in U.S. foreign-policy output: its goals, values, strategies, and so forth. *Why?*

Japan's attack of Pearl Harbor, for instance, was a monumental wakeup call to America's policymakers and public. The attack on Pearl Harbor constituted an assault on America's then widely held isolationist ethos. Despite the "infamy" with which President Franklin Roosevelt characterized the attack as well as the material damage caused by Japan, the result was ultimately quite positive. America formally entered World War II on the side of the Allies and emerged from the war, some four years later, as one of the world's two superpowers, forever changing America's view of itself in international politics as well as the world's view of America.

The series of events associated with the commencement of the Cold War similarly had a momentous impact on U.S. foreign policy. The results included President Truman promulgating the Truman Doctrine—committing the United States to protecting potential targets of "wars of liberation" abroad—the U.S. Congress passing the 1947 National Security Act (a statute that created the National Security Council, the Defense Department, the Central Intelligence Agency, and so forth) and, importantly, the United States jettisoning some one-hundred and seventy years of isolationism and replacing it with a policy of globalism or internationalism. These results, in turn, set U.S. foreign policy on a course of containment of Communism for the next fifty years.

Finally, though the effects of 9/11 are still not entirely clear, they already include America forsaking fifty years of containment of Communism, and what one might charitably call "benign" internationalism. U.S. foreign policy has been set on a dramatic new trajectory. Said trajectory—though still relatively new—includes what the president has described as new and "unique internationalism," and what others describe as "neo-interventionism." Further, 9/11—rather as the beginning of the Cold War led to the Truman Doctrine—has served as the midwife to the Bush Doctrine, a policy that notifies the world's actors that they are either with the United States in its fight against global terrorism or they are against the United States.

It makes clear that each country will be treated accordingly. Additionally, the results of 9/11 include a new operational policy, what the Bush administration terms its policy of "preemption." (As will be discussed later, a more accurate characterization of said policy would be "prevention.") Moreover, one result of 9/11 is a policy, thus far implemented twice, known as regime change. Last, but clearly not least, 9/11 has apparently resulted in America supplanting a forty-plus-year policy instrument of mutually assured destruction (MAD) or deterrence. Considered together, these changes constitute substantive changes.

Again, *why?* Why do some foreign-policy events result in demonstrable and enduring changes in U.S. foreign policy while others result in the *status quo ante*, or at most incremental change? A simple metaphor of U.S. foreign policy that is often used as a representation of process is the simple stimulus-response model — namely, *stimuli-response* where the response is some foreign-policy outcome (sometimes symbolized as S:R). A slightly more complex representation of the same process introduces the "black box" between the stimuli and resultant responses (see Figure 1.1).

The black box typically contains a broad array of important decision-making variables that may be activated depending upon the nature of the threat, type of regime or government, leadership attributes, and a host of other potential variables. Given the previously enumerated U.S. foreign-policy events, the relevance of this model is twofold: (1) Why do some stimuli result in demonstrable changes in U.S. foreign-policy outcomes? (2) What variables inside the black box are integral to substantive changes in U.S. foreign-policy outcomes versus the variables that tend to result in continuity (or incremental change)?

Foreign-policy events are a complex function of various inputs resulting in outputs. Some foreign policy events are, for lack of a better description, "routine" and result in the foreign-policy bureaucracy responding slowly and deliberatively. Others are better characterized as international or foreign-policy "crises." During routine foreign-policy events, the bureaucracy frequently trumps individual decision-makers (the president and his top advisors); during crises, individuals occasionally have the opportunity to circumvent the bureaucracy and set U.S. foreign policy on a new direction before the larger bureaucracy can respond. Pearl Harbor, the beginning of the Cold War, and 9/11 are all of the latter category.

Before examining the effects of 9/11 on U.S. foreign policy, however, a brief but important discussion of change versus continuity in foreign policy output and, specifically, how some notable international relations and/or foreign policy texts have handled the issue is worthwhile. Some scholars only treat the issue as of secondary or

FIGURE 1.1   STIMULUS-RESPONSE MODEL

tertiary importance while others treat it as critical to understanding foreign policy and international politics. In either case it is often integrally linked to the particular author's/scholar's terms of reference: how one defines important concepts and definitions; the variables one identifies as critical to foreign policy and international relations; the theory or theories ones uses, and so forth.

Many U.S. foreign policy and/or international politics textbooks address — implicitly in some cases, explicitly in others — the issue of whether or not foreign policy output is best characterized as a process resulting in frequent changes, what we shall call "discontinuity" (each new administration, each new session of Congress, and so forth). By contrast, others argue U.S. foreign policy is best characterized as a process resulting in "continuity" or incremental change in output. The seminal *Strategies of Containment*, by John Lewis Gaddis, for example, examines various changes in America's Soviet containment policies over the course of the Cold War. In making his case, Professor Gaddis notes that variables like Soviet behavior, degree of partisanship, specific presidential characteristics, and more all affected U.S. foreign policy. The results, according to Gaddis, were *changes* in America's strategy of containment — some changes esoteric, other changes rather more dramatic. Richard A. Melanson's *American Foreign Policy since the Vietnam War* argues the discontinuity thesis as well. He identifies the foreign-policy consensus that existed in the United States from around 1947 until the mid-1960s. He argues, however, that the trauma of the Vietnam War caused each subsequent president (Nixon onward) consciously to alter his "grand strategies," "strategic objectives," and "tactics" among other things. Hence, Melanson *implicitly* argues that since the Vietnam War, U.S. foreign policy is best described as subject to frequent change, or discontinuity.[1]

After teaching foreign policy for some ten years this author has found that most students intuitively accept the discontinuity thesis: Foreign policy does change frequently; certainly from president to president if not from Congress to Congress or more frequently. Anecdotally, upon polling students over several years, it is an overwhelming sentiment. For example, when asked if students think there were demonstrable differences in U.S. foreign policy under the Carter administration versus the Reagan administration, the response in the affirmative is invariably nearly unanimous.

By contrast, in *American Foreign Policy: Pattern and Process*, authors Kegley and Wittkopf argue that there has existed remarkable and understandable continuity in U.S. foreign policy from 1947 through the 1990s — remarkable inasmuch as it is somewhat counterintuitive, understandable given the multiple inputs that go into the foreign-policy process. Using James Rosenau's "pre-theories" construct, the authors examine five categories or clusters of foreign-policy inputs: *external* (what Rosenau called *systemic*), *societal*, *governmental*, *individual*, and *role*.[2] Kegley and Wittkopf effectively argue that individual presidents (and top advisors) have relatively little effect on U.S. foreign policy during normal times. They do allow for exceptions: principally foreign-policy crises, when time is of the essence and during which the larger foreign-policy bureaucracy may well be circumvented. They further argue that role and role theory — the office shapes the individual rather than the reverse—is a constraining influence on change in foreign policy. Similarly, the sheer size of the foreign-policy bureaucracy, its standard operating procedures (SOPs) and routines, bureaucratic infighting, and so forth constrain foreign-policy change. Even in the societal cluster of inputs, constraint on change is the rule rather than the exception. Though public opinion may change, a relatively stable opinion vis-à-vis the Soviet menace and America's containment policy dominated the period from 1947 through the 1990s: the Cold War consensus. Hence the authors *explicitly* argue continuity in U.S. foreign policy as their principal thesis. Similarly, an excellent book that makes at least an *implicit* argument for continuity, is Leslie Gelb and Richard Betts' *The Irony of Vietnam: The System Worked*. Among other things, the authors construct a well-reasoned argument that the Cold War consensus that was created in the crucible of the Turkey and Greece "crises" of 1946–1947 and subsequent events, eventually resulted in the Vietnam War, involving several presidential administrations. Indeed, they argue that Vietnam was effectively the inevitable product of said consensus.[3] Implicitly, the authors make the case for continuity in U.S. foreign-policy output.

Which argument—continuity or change (discontinuity)—is accurate? How is one to teach one's students about foreign policy and international politics if such a seemingly simple issue cannot be resolved? While no comprehensive attempt to answer the question will be examined here, it is worth considering. The fact is this: The answer to whether U.S. foreign policy is best described as continuous or discontinuous comes down to how one defines foreign policy.

FOREIGN POLICY: A CONCEPTUAL DEFINITION

In using Melanson's *American Foreign Policy since the Vietnam War* as one of multiple texts to teach U.S. foreign policy, this author has intentionally juxtaposed various texts whose theses argue discontinuity in U.S. foreign policy (i.e., frequent change, either implicitly or explicitly) as a counterargument to Kegley and Wittkopf's continuity argument. In attempting this pedagogical strategy, this author has typically begun each course of instruction with Kegley and Wittkopf, inasmuch as the authors begin with a clear, conceptual definition of U.S. foreign policy that proves quite useful. Kegley and Wittkopf define U.S. foreign policy as "the goals that the nation's officials seek to attain abroad, the values that give rise to those objectives, and the means or instruments used to pursue them" (Kegley and Wittkopf 1996, 7). Their definition has the benefit of defining foreign policy in terms of three relatively discrete and identifiable concepts: *goals* and/or *objectives*; *values* or *ethos*; and *instruments*.

Kegley and Wittkopf conceptualize U.S. foreign policy (Y) as an output using a funnel as a metaphor. Each cluster of inputs (independent or X-variables) goes into the funnel resulting in U.S. foreign policy. Quite cleverly, the authors do not attempt to specify which variables are more influential than others generally; instead, throughout the remainder of the text they examine each cluster of independent variables, then discuss their relative effect by discussing an intervening variable they introduce: process. Process proves the messy part of U.S. foreign policy. The relative weight of each cluster of independent variables depends on issue area, crisis versus routine situation, and so forth. For example, one would properly expect former President George H. W. Bush to influence U.S.-Sino relations more than U.S.-Nigeria relations given Bush's experience as U.S. liaison to China (c. 1970s) prior to his tenure as president. Thus, in said issue area, one would expect the individual cluster to exert more influence. Similarly, during a foreign-policy crisis—defined in Chapter 2—the individual and role clusters might reasonably be expected to exert more relative causal influence than, say, societal and governmental inputs, by virtue of defining characteristics of crises. (See Figure 1.2.)

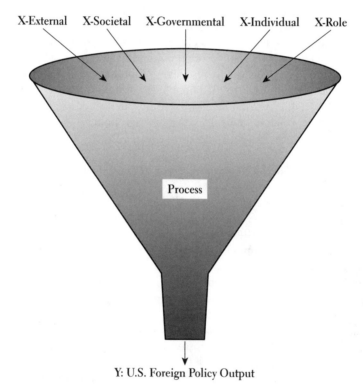

Y: U.S. Foreign Policy Output

FIGURE 1.2   FUNNEL OF CAUSALITY

This funnel illustrates exogenous (X) inputs and endogenous (Y) output (Rosenau's framework) *viz.* U.S. foreign policy.

Source: From Wittkopf, Kegley, and Scott, *American Foreign Policy, Sixth Edition.* © 2003. Reprinted with permission of Wadsworth, a division of Thomson Learning: www.thomsonrights.com. Fax 800-730-2215.

Using a similar, albeit more earthy metaphor, one might think of U.S. foreign-policy process as making sausage. *It is messy.* Various ingredients—inputs, or independent variables—go into the sausage-grinding machine; not all of those ingredients are necessarily visually pleasing. Ultimately, what comes out in the sausage casing is U.S. foreign policy, the dependent (Y) variable. The messy grinding up of the various inputs is, accordingly, process. One who frequently enjoys eating sausage may find it altogether more reassuring *not* to focus too closely on process. By contrast, one who wishes to understand U.S. foreign policy *must* consider process carefully. Kegley and Wittkopf argue that the output—the sausage, continuing the metaphor—has remained relatively stable over time; beginning in 1946–1947, and continuing through the end of the century, U.S. foreign policy has changed only incrementally from year to year, administration to administration, Congress to Congress. For the sake of brevity, U.S. goals and objectives have been simplified here to: internationalism (versus America's historical isolationism); anti-Communism; containment of Communist expansion; interventionism; and the operationalization of containment in the form of nuclear deterrence.

Indeed, if one considers putatively different administrations, say Jimmy Carter's versus Ronald Reagan's, Kegley's and Wittkopf's argument appears to survive scrutiny. Carter may have begun his administration with a human rights–centric agenda and a somewhat naive view of the Soviet Union, but the second half of his tenure was strongly characterized by containing the Soviets and using Nixon-like geopolitical machinations to accomplish it. Similarly, Ronald Reagan may have been elected espousing strategies of rolling back Communism, building civil defense and even entertaining the notion that the United States could fight and win a nuclear war with the "evil empire," but by the end of his tenure, he reached one of the most far-reaching arms control agreements to date as a principal tool to contain the Soviets. In other words, despite potentially different agendas, two seemingly very different presidents ultimately were constrained to conform to America's long-term objective of containing Communism. Differences in tactics, rhetoric, and personalities notwithstanding, the sausage in its casing remained remarkably stable. Thus, it becomes critical to specify the indicators of one's dependent and independent variables. Kegley and Wittkopf clearly focus on generalizable trends as indicative of their dependent (Y) variable. In contrast, Melanson for example, examines "grand design" (relatively generalizable), "strategic objectives," "tactics," and "rhetoric" (what Melanson assesses as part of an administration's efforts to legitimate its policies). It is hardly surprising, then, that the respective authors reach contrasting conclusions with respect to the issue of continuity in U.S. foreign policy.

In what follows, we wish to observe U.S. foreign policy with a view toward understanding whether and, if so, how, 9/11 changed U.S. foreign policy goals and/or objectives. In answering this principal research question we will necessarily consider whether a foreign-policy event such as 9/11 permits changes in U.S. foreign-policy output. If one accepts the "continuity" argument, the research question may be framed thusly: Did the attacks of September 11, 2001, affect U.S. foreign policy continuity causing demonstrable and long-lasting change in its general directions?

If so, why? Since continuity is the rule, what made 9/11 the exception? That which we wish to observe—U.S. foreign-policy output—is the dependent variable (Y). In this context continuity means that the objective observer viewing U.S. foreign policy would conclude that it is generally stable. Insofar as changes occur, they occur only incrementally. If one accepts the discontinuity argument, 9/11 may simply constitute another factor leading to an already frequently changing U.S. foreign-policy output. Kegley and Wittkopf contend that U.S. policy of "containing" the Soviets only changed incrementally from Truman to Bush. While different approaches to containment may have been announced with rhetorical flourish by various administrations, U.S. policy remained that of containing the Soviets. The authors use the analogy of the stock market over time: On a day-to-day basis one sees fluctuation; over time, however, one sees a general upward trend (say from the 1950s to 1999). By contrast, the discontinuity argument may be framed as follows: Given the complex interaction of inputs—the personalities and life experiences of various presidents and their top advisors—U.S. foreign policy changes from administration to administration if not more frequently; consequently, it is hardly surprising that 9/11 would represent such a change. Important indicators of U.S. foreign policy are whether the president is a Republican or Democrat as well as the particular president's life experiences—and indeed, the same for all top U.S. foreign-policy officials. In short, the discontinuity argument holds that U.S. foreign policy has been demonstrably different during various administrations. Accordingly, that 9/11 occurred is simply another example of frequently changing output.

Having summarized two contrasting views of U.S. foreign policy, it is appropriate to make clear this author's own bias. This text takes for granted that U.S. foreign-policy output changes only incrementally over time. Vastly different administrations tend to follow the patterns of their predecessors. In other words, the bias here is that of accepting Kegley and Wittkopf's continuity argument: U.S. foreign policy is best characterized as a relatively stable output or generalizable trends that change only incrementally. Given said bias, let us now pose this text's principal research question directly. Did the events of September 11, 2001, mark a demonstrable change of direction—as did the onset of the Cold War—in U.S. foreign policy? Implicit in an affirmative answer to the research question is that any change caused by 9/11 will endure over time—at least over multiple presidential administrations, if not multiple generations, much like the Cold War consensus.

THESIS

In what follows, we shall assess U.S. foreign policy following the dramatic events of 9/11. We shall attempt to answer the research question by examining indicators in each of the clusters of independent variables; this text essentially employs the same analytic construct used by Kegley and Wittkopf. In using the Rosenau-Kegley-Wittkopf framework, we shall necessarily specify indicators of the concepts and variables: goals, values, and instruments. More specifically, the basic thesis is that following

9/11, the instruments and values of U.S. foreign policy changed relatively little. Instruments may be conceived of as a toolbox; all presidents use virtually every tool in the box eventually. Values are fairly stable by their nature. By contrast, goals and objectives of U.S. foreign policy have changed demonstrably. After a decade of casting about for foreign-policy direction during the 1990s—and in the interim simply continuing Cold War foreign policy—the events of 9/11 provided a unique impetus for change in U.S. foreign policy!

In particular, U.S. foreign policy has apparently become even more—much more—internationalist (versus isolationist), and the campaign against global terrorism has supplanted anti-Communism and containment of the former Soviet Union; even deterrence has apparently changed in response to 9/11. President George W. Bush has become, perhaps unwittingly, the Harry Truman of the twenty-first century. As was the case with Truman, events have overtaken the presidency of President Bush. September 11 in fact was a foreign-policy crisis, as will be demonstrated. After stumbling a bit initially, President George W. Bush seized the unique opportunity afforded him and in so doing, altered the course of U.S. foreign policy, something no other president since Truman has successfully accomplished. Finally, and as was the case in 1946–1947, the new trajectory of U.S. foreign policy will remain stable and change only incrementally over the next generation or more. Before turning to the evidence, however, some general observations about all of the independent variables are in order.

MULTICAUSAL FOREIGN-POLICY FRAMEWORK

Recall Figure 1.2 (on page 6), which was used to illustrate various foreign-policy inputs. The funnel construct is illustrative of two main points. First, it is not limited to analyzing U.S. foreign policy. Indeed, when Rosenau devised the framework, his purpose was to attempt theory building for the discipline known as comparative foreign-policy analysis (in Rosenau's case, across a large sample size—spatially). Kegley and Wittkopf have employed Rosenau's framework to assess U.S. foreign policy over a discrete time period, the late 1940s through the 1990s (i.e., temporally). Though inputs (clusters of X variables) presumably differ in terms of relative influence for each nation, each nation's foreign policy originates from the same set of inputs. Second, by its very nature, the framework depicts foreign policy as a multicausal process. Foreign policy for a given nation is the product of a complex interaction—process, as shall be seen—of the five clusters of inputs. Let us consider, briefly, the multicausal nature of U.S. foreign policy.

EXTERNAL-SYSTEMIC

The reader will note that four of the five U.S. foreign policy inputs shown in Figure 1.2 (on page 6) are domestic in nature. Indeed, only external-systemic inputs represent the relatively intuitive notion of international politics known as *realism* (a.k.a.

realpolitik), arguably the most enduring of theories of state behavior in international politics. Put simply, the theory suggests that state behavior is a product of self-help given the anarchical structure and/or nature of the international system. To use an analogy, states are billiard balls and the billiard table is the international system. Having no recognized arbiter above the state (billiard balls) to adjudicate disputes, the balls collide and behave in predictable and similar ways. Determinants of the collision are the mass and/or size of the balls and the momentum with which one ball hits another. What is inside the ball matters little. Balls of similar mass, size, and momentum will behave similarly.

The external-systemic cluster of variables represents events that occur internationally, external to the United States, creating a set of stimuli to which U.S. decision-makers respond. Another way to conceptualize political realism is using the stimulus-response model represented in Figure 1.1 (on page 3). Nation-states respond to external stimuli: threats and/or opportunities. Thus, U.S. foreign policy essentially responds to external stimuli. Some stimuli are seen as threats by the United States and its decision-makers: Iraq's invasion of Kuwait in 1990, former Yugoslavia's disintegration during the 1990s, India's and Pakistan's respective explosions of nuclear bombs (late 1990s). Other external stimuli are seen as opportunities: Anwar Sadat's unilateral recognition of Israel, which eventually led to the Camp David Accords; Gorbachev's *perestroika* and *glasnost*, which led to the eventual end of the Soviet Union as America's primary national-security threat; and the economic and political changes external to the United States, which fostered the conditions for NAFTA's eventuality.

The remaining four independent-variable clusters are domestic—and perhaps less intuitive at first glance. Consider the time-honored aphorism about foreign policy that "politics stops at the water's edge." In other words, when it comes to foreign policy, the stakes are so high—state survival—that domestic political considerations do not apply. Such arguments contend that state survival necessarily trumps domestic political considerations. Contrary to the aphorism, however, the remaining four clusters of exogenous variables posit that politics neither stops at the water's edge nor anywhere else. Domestic politics is a constant influence on U.S. foreign policy, a reality seldom appreciated by political realists.

SOCIETAL

Societal inputs are comprised of a cluster that includes the following: public opinion, the influence on policy exerted by the media, electoral politics, political-action groups, other special-interest groups, and so forth. The so-called CNN effect (note that the phenomenon now includes other cable networks) is a good example of a confluence of societal inputs. For example, when CNN's cameras focused attention on Somalia in the early 1990s, U.S. foreign policy followed. The CNN effect is illustrative of both public opinion and the media affecting U.S. foreign policy.

Consider another timely example, the issue of "gays" in the military. Were it true that only national-security interests dictate policy, the issue for policymakers would simply be whether or not gays in the military degrade U.S. military capabilities. The politics of gays in the military would be irrelevant. Having watched the Clinton administration grapple with the issue, one would be hard pressed to argue that only national-security interests led the Clinton Administration to its "revised" policy—a nominal policy revision at most—of "don't ask, don't tell." The reality is much more complex and political.

Indeed, the reality is that a plethora of special-interest groups exist that affect U.S. foreign policy. An example of such groups' influence is the business interests that lobbied Washington to normalize relations with Vietnam in the 1990s. Conversely, POW groups—influential lobbyists in their own right—lobbied against normalization.[4] Each group lobbied based on its own best interests: *viz.*, on its domestic concerns, its fund-raising practices, and so forth.

Another societal input is the U.S. election cycle, the four-year presidential election cycle as well as the midterm election cycle every two years. To suggest that a president makes foreign-policy decisions based solely on how well the policy will bear on elections is far too simplistic. Nonetheless, such political considerations work their way into the mix in various ways. An example might be Clinton's embrace of the Helms-Burton law. In other words, the administration's desire to assuage the Cuban émigré community in Florida (a large electoral-college state), one could argue, affected foreign policy during the Clinton administration. Indeed, CNN discussed how Attorney General Janet Reno's handling of the Elián Gonzalez case may have cost Gore the presidential election.[5]

Most persons take the media for granted as a source of influence. The old bromide that the nation's media outlets are liberal and that they influence public opinion in favor of liberal causes and candidates is a commonly held view, accepted, as this author has found anecdotally, by a majority of college undergraduates. However, others have made precisely the opposite argument. In Eric Alterman's book *Sound and Fury*, the author argues that a self-anointed elite (the "punditocracy"), comprised mostly of conservatives, sways public opinion toward conservative causes. Noam Chomsky, similarly, has argued in any number of books and lectures that the media is conservatively biased, quite the contrary of the commonly held liberal-bias view.[6] Societal inputs comprise a collection of societal influences that frequently combine to affect U.S. foreign policy in complex ways.

GOVERNMENTAL

This cluster of exogenous variables involves the large and Byzantine national-security apparatus that was created at the beginning of the Cold War. President Truman watched with growing anxiety the Soviet Union and its behavior following World War II. In fairly short order, Truman watched a chronology of aggression unfold. In 1946–1947, the Turkey-Greece crisis occurred, eventually causing the United

States to take military and political moves that resulted in the United States insinuating itself into what had previously been the British sphere of influence. In 1948, the Berlin blockade followed swiftly. In 1949, the People's Republic of China (PRC) arose from the ashes of the civil war between the nationalist KMT, which the United States supported, and the Chinese Communist Party, supported by the Soviets. In 1950, the North Korean regime, with *at least* tacit support from both the Soviets and the Chinese Communists, invaded South Korea in a daring and reckless *blitzkrieg* across the 38th parallel.

Each of these events was an external-systemic input. Events in Turkey and Greece as well events in Berlin collectively resulted in President Truman promulgating the Truman Doctrine, which in turn provided the context for what followed: America's Soviet containment policy; the creation of a new, large, and permanent national-security bureaucracy for the first time in U.S. history. To quote the Truman Doctrine briefly, it reads:

> I believe that it must be the policy of the United States to support peoples who are resisting attempted subjugation by armed minorities or by outside pressure.
>
> I believe that we must assist free peoples to work out their own destinies in their own ways.[7]

By declaring U.S. support for peoples who were being subjugated, by both internal (national-liberation movements) and external (read, Communism directed from the Soviet Union) stimuli, President Truman set the course of U.S. foreign policy for nearly the next fifty years. Even after the Soviet Union imploded in 1991, U.S. foreign policy continued to be containment—albeit containment whose object jumped from "ism" to "ism." That is, there appeared at times to be various contestants whom the United States contained: fundamentalism, nationalism, international drug trafficking (drug-lordism), or any number of additional national-security threats needing to be contained by U.S. forces for America's security. The national-security, U.S. foreign-policy bureaucracy created in 1947, whose origins and budgets were directly linked to containing Communism, produced bureaucratic momentum that continued to contain Communism well after the Soviet Union ceased to exist.

In 1947, Congress passed the National Security Act (NSA 1947). The statute attempted to formalize Truman's containment policy and, moreover, give the executive branch the tools to accomplish that policy. It and its 1949 amendment created the Central Intelligence Agency (CIA), the Department of Defense (previously the War Department), the joint command in the military, and the National Security Council with what would become known as the national security advisor (originally an executive secretary).[8] Thus, one may see how external inputs—in this case Soviet expansionism—provided a stimulus that interacted with domestic inputs resulting in roughly two generations of U.S. foreign policy. In the text that follows we will consider such interactions and, in particular, those interactions since 9/11 as process.

ROLE-INDIVIDUAL

Both James Rosenau and Kegley and Wittkopf differentiate role from individual inputs to U.S. foreign policy. Indeed, they are effectively opposite sides of the same coin. Individual inputs include the personalities, beliefs, and life experiences of key decision-makers. One could easily hypothesize, for instance, that one of President George H. W. Bush's defining life experiences included World War II. Accordingly, his beliefs might easily have been shaped by the "lessons of appeasement," a common view held by those of his generation. President George W. Bush's beliefs, by contrast, may well have been affected more by the "lessons of Vietnam" than by events in Europe before his birth or while he was a young child.

Role theory is the basis of role inputs. Role theory posits that the office one holds shapes the person more than the person shapes the office. Thus no matter who might hold the office of the presidency, specific and somewhat predictable role expectations constrain individuality and cause the president to behave in certain ways that conform to said expectations. The expectations might be self-imposed—that is, the person holding the office constrains himself or herself, or they might be expectations of other influential persons in the administration, or they may be expectations held by society at large. To cite a simple example, recall when President Clinton was queried on whether he wore boxer shorts or fitted underwear. On the face of it, the question was harmless. That the president of the United States would be asked such a question, let alone that he would answer it, caused a maelstrom of incredulity among many in the public and the media. The "role" of the presidency precluded the possibility of such trivialization of the office.

Role theory, it should be stressed, applies to others in the administration as well. Key foreign-policy decision-makers including the president's chief of staff, his secretaries of state and defense, his national security advisor and so on are all subject to expected behaviors that are thought to constrain their behavior in various ways. As will be seen later, for practical purposes it is often difficult to differentiate whether a particular action or decision is a result of role or individual beliefs. In this text role and individual inputs are considered in one chapter. Where a plausible case may be made that decisions and/or actions are clearly the result of one or the other, an attempt to do so is made.

SUMMARY

Having summarized the independent-variable clusters (inputs) that produce specific U.S. foreign policy and international politics, let us now consider each cluster of independent variables separately in detail as they have produced U.S. foreign policy since 9/11. after examining each we shall then turn to the interactions between independent inputs, namely process, and assess whether and to what extent these inputs have affected U.S. foreign policy and international politics since the trauma of 9/11.

NOTES

1. John Lewis Gaddis, *Strategies of Containment* (Oxford: Oxford University Press, 1982). Richard A. Melanson, *American Foreign Policy since the Vietnam War*, 2nd ed. (New York: M. E. Sharpe, 1996).
2. Charles W. Kegley, Jr., and Eugene R. Wittkopf, *American Foreign Policy: Pattern and Process*, 5th ed. (New York: St. Martin's Press, 1996); James N. Rosenau, "Pre-Theories and Theories of Foreign Policy," in *Approaches to Comparative and International Politics*, ed. R. Barry Farrell (Evanston, IL: Northwestern University Press, 1966), pp. 27–92. Also James N. Rosenau, *The Scientific Study of Foreign Policy* (New York: Nichols, 1980).
3. Leslie H. Gelb and Richard K. Betts, *The Irony of Vietnam, The System Worked* (Washington, D.C.: Brookings Institution, 1979).
4. M. Kent Bolton, "Vietnam Crucible," in *Third World–United States Relations in the New World Order*, ed. A. Grammy and Kaye Bragg (New York: NOVA Science Publishers, 1996).
5. CNN, *Inside Politics*, March 20, 2002.
6. Eric Alterman, *Sound and Fury* (New York: HarperPerennial, 1998). Please note that for present purposes Alterman's argument is being simplified. Alterman takes on the media's "objectivity" and corporate ownership of the nation's media outlets, among other issues. For Noam Chomsky's views on the media's influence on U.S. foreign policy, see Noam Chomsky, *The Fateful Triangle: The United States, Israel, and the Palestinians* (Boston: South End Press, 1983). Also see Chomsky and Edward S. Herman, *Manufacturing Consent: The Political Economy of the Mass Media* (New York: Pantheon, 2002).
7. *Congressional Record*, vol. 93, March 12, 1947.
8. John Prados, *Keeper of the Keys* (New York: Morrow, 1991).

EXTERNAL-SYSTEMIC INPUTS
TO U.S. FOREIGN POLICY

The first major innovation [of President Bush's National Security Strategy] is Bush's equation of terrorists with tyrants as sources of danger, an obvious outgrowth of September 11.

—John Lewis Gaddis, "A Grand Strategy,"
Foreign Policy, November–December 2002.

On a clear Tuesday morning, September 11, 2001, a hijacked Boeing 767 en route from Boston to Los Angeles, smashed into the North Tower of the World Trade Center at 8:45 A.M. (EDT). Eighteen minutes later at 9:03 A.M., a second hijacked 767 smashed into the south tower. At 9:41 A.M. a third hijacked plane, this one a Boeing 757, crashed into the west side of the Pentagon, exploding in a holocaust that would continue to burn for days.

At 9:50 A.M. the South Tower collapsed, as much of a horrified nation watched it on television. Meanwhile, a fourth plane, thought to be directed at another Washington, D.C. target (possibly the Capitol), nose-dived into the ground in rural Pennsylvania at 10:06 A.M. creating a thirty-five-feet-deep crater, so pulverizing the plane that no debris larger than a phone book could be found. At 10:28 A.M. the North Tower collapsed.[1] Thus occurred the 9/11 terrorist attacks, surpassing even Pearl Harbor in terms of deaths (some 3,000). Distinguishing it further from Pearl Harbor was that the victims of 9/11 were civilians not combatants.

President Bush would later characterize said events thusly: "On Tuesday, our country was attacked with deliberate and massive cruelty." Continuing, he identified what he saw as America's responsibility in reaction to these events. "Just three days removed from these events, Americans do not yet have the distance of history. But our responsibility to history is already clear: to answer these attacks and rid the world of evil."[2]

In a subsequent "Address to a Joint Session of Congress and the American People," some eight days later, President Bush placed the events of September 11 into historical context:

> On September 11, enemies of freedom committed an act of war against our country. Americans have known wars—but for the past 136 years, they have been wars on foreign soil . . . Americans have known casualties of war—but not at the center of a great city on a peaceful morning. Americans have known surprise attacks—but never before on thousands of civilians. All of this was brought upon us in a single day—*and night fell on a different world, a world where freedom itself is under attack.* (italics added)[3]

For present purposes, we are particularly interested in President Bush's assertion that "night fell on a different world." How different? Had the world changed enough to affect fifty-plus years of U.S. foreign policy direction and momentum? Have any of the three major U.S. foreign-policy objectives—internationalism (versus the previous 200 years of isolationism), anti-Communism, and Communist containment—changed as a result of September 11? These questions will be answered in subsequent chapters.

EXTERNAL-SYSTEMIC INPUTS IN RESPONSE TO 9/11

We begin with the external-systemic cluster of inputs not because this category is more weighty in affecting foreign policy on a day-to-day basis but, rather, because the initial planning and funding of what would become the 9/11 attacks appropriately fit in the external cluster. The attacks themselves were clearly precipitated by an international conspiracy. The cabal's planning resulted in 9/11 but began abroad. The attacks had their origins in such disparate locales as Canada, Europe, South Asia, and even in Southeast Asia, that is, external to the United States.

The characteristics of the 9/11 attack themselves deserve special consideration. Notably, for the first days following the attacks, the attacks were properly characterized as a "foreign-policy crisis." A foreign-policy crisis has been precisely defined as a decision-making setting that

> (1) threatens the high-priority goals of the [decision-makers], (2) restricts the amount of time available for response before the decision is transformed, and (3) surprises the [decision-makers] by its occurrence. . . .[4]

Clearly, the president and his foreign-policy advisors perceived the attack as a threat to America's very existence, at least on September 11. Anyone who watched the president's early remarks could see that he looked like the proverbial deer in the headlights. Neither the president nor his advisors—nor anybody else for that matter—knew what if anything else might be coming or what the dimensions of the attack would eventually be. The threat to the United States was perceived as serious enough for the president to take extraordinary measures during the first several hours. These measures included effectively closing down air travel in the United States (9:50 A.M. EDT), placing the U.S. military on maximum alert (about 1:00 P.M. EDT), and dispatching Navy missile destroyers to New York (around 2:50 P.M. EDT). Indeed, the national-security chain of command's uncertainty about what more might be under way caused the Secret Service to spirit the president out of Florida, and to fly him around the country from place to place, returning to Washington only at 7:00 P.M. Tuesday evening. Hence, the high-threat criterion of a foreign-policy crisis was clearly met for the first few days (discussed later).

It is also clear that decision-makers perceived the situation as one to which they had to respond instantly. Not knowing what additional attacks might be in the offing, decision-makers had very little time to linger over making crucial decisions to forestall further threats and attacks. Recall that throughout the day, Tuesday, there were continuous updates on cable news about additional attacks (e.g., the State Department) though these reports proved apocryphal. Nonetheless, the administration's decision-makers properly mobilized, making decisions quickly and decisively in response to newly perceived threats. The short-time criterion was clearly met.

Finally, there has not been any credible report that administration decision-makers anticipated the attacks. It was widely believed among foreign-policy elites and pundits that, generally speaking, the United States would become a target of terrorism in the near future. (The United States had already become a victim of international terrorism in the first World Trade Center attack. But those perpetrators had seemed somewhat amateurish.) Most experts anticipated terrorists attempting to perpetrate a biological or chemical attack on America. There had been reports that the CIA and/or FBI *should* have anticipated the attacks. But "should have anticipated" and actually anticipating 9/11 are two very different things. Clearly, the administration's foreign-policy decision-makers and, for that matter, the American public, were clearly taken by surprise. Thus, the surprise or failure to anticipate criterion was met.

Demonstrating that 9/11 met the definition of a foreign-policy crisis is more than a mere academic exercise. The significance of a foreign-policy crisis is that during such events, the typical foreign-policy processes are largely circumvented. During a foreign-policy crisis, individuals—the president, his national security advisor, the secretaries of defense and state, and others—have far more opportunity to put their personal *imprimatur* on foreign policy. Put differently, the societal and governmental inputs are greatly diminished, for the length of the crisis, and are overshadowed by individual and perhaps role input. The foreign-policy decision-making dynamic is thus atypical over the short term; eventually the normal dynamic returns, as we shall discover in the narrative that follows.

EFFECTS OF EXTERNAL-SYSTEMIC INPUTS TO U.S. FOREIGN POLICY SINCE 9/11

Let us now consider some of the relevant external-systemic inputs since 9/11 and their effects on U.S. foreign policy. It would be nearly impossible to present each and every external input to U.S. foreign policy, given time and space constraints, even if every input could be determined. Doubtless, events have happened since 9/11 that have affected U.S. foreign policy in some way but that have not been made public knowledge. But we can attempt to be as comprehensive as possible while focusing on the most important of these inputs.

On the day after the attacks, NATO took the historic and unusual step of invoking Article V of the Washington Treaty, which declares that an attack against one NATO member is an attack against all its members (i.e., collective security). It is unclear precisely how U.S. foreign policy responded to that specific action. Minimally it gave the administration some sense of confidence that it was not in this new war alone, perhaps bolstering the president's resolve. (By analogy, Margaret Thatcher was said to have had a personal discussion with Bush senior within days of Saddam's invasion of Kuwait, which reportedly stiffened Bush senior's resolve.) Similarly, on September 14, several European nations observed three minutes of silence to demonstrate solidarity with America. Similar to NATO's action on September 12, the Organization of American States (OAS), again showing remarkable and somewhat surprising solidarity, declared "reciprocal assistance" under the Rio Treaty on September 21. These actions permitted flexibility to the administration's subsequent efforts at coalition building.

On September 15, erstwhile pariah state Pakistan offered to support the United States and grant U.S. jets overflight permission in Pakistan's airspace. After years of a pro-Pakistan foreign-policy tilt in the India-Pakistan conflict, U.S.-Pakistan relations had deteriorated in the 1990s. Recall, moreover, that Pakistan had been on a U.S. diplomatic black list for exploding nuclear weapons a few years earlier. Consequently, the United States had sought to isolate Pakistan, embargoing certain items (like dual-use technologies). The United States had also refused to send F-16 jets to Pakistan even though Pakistan had already paid for them, though the reasons for this refusal were somewhat complex; nor had the United States returned the money the Pakistanis had paid. India too had been subjected to some of the same actions, though relations with India seemed to have been improving, relatively speaking, during the same time period.

Prior to 9/11, only three nations had diplomatic ties with the Taliban regime in Afghanistan: Saudi Arabia, the United Arab Emirates (UAE), and Pakistan. On September 22, the UAE severed diplomatic ties with the Taliban. On September 25, Saudi Arabia followed suit. The situation was more complicated for Pakistan. Pakistan and Afghanistan both share large Pashtun ethnic groups. Furthermore, Pakistan's equivalent of the CIA and FBI combined, the ISI, had largely created the Taliban regime.[5] Though it took more time, Pakistan's leader, Pervez Musharraf eventually ended diplomatic relations as well. With the Taliban regime completely isolated and with newly found diplomatic goodwill, the administration was permitted unusual flexibility in formulating foreign policy for what would soon become the "war on global terrorism."

The Security Council of the United Nations soon invoked Chapter VII of the UN Charter, the collective-security clause. Additionally it adopted a wide-ranging anti-terrorism resolution, an action the United States had been seeking. Indeed, the administration began the diplomatic *pas de deux* almost instantly following the attacks. It appears that Secretary Powell's and others' efforts were paying dividends in the UN. Another example—both an external input and an indicator that the administration's efforts were successful—was seen on October 4. That was the day that Prime Minister Tony Blair (who had been exceptionally friendly with President Clinton and was rumored to think somewhat less of President Bush) publicly linked the September 11 attacks to Osama bin Laden, saying that there was "absolutely no doubt that bin Laden and his network are responsible" for the attacks. The same day, Pakistan's President Musharraf announced that U.S. evidence, as presented to him, "provides sufficient basis for indictment" of bin Laden "in a court of law."

President Bush had already identified bin Laden and his al Qaeda organization as the perpetrators. Bush and his team had been taking some flack as a result. It had become clear that among the instruments of U.S. foreign policy the administration would employ, some type of military response would be included. Obviously, since the Taliban regime had given bin Laden sanctuary for years, whatever military response the administration chose would initially focus on Afghanistan. Some Gulf states and a few others had been trying to forestall a U.S. military response for their own reasons and had been requesting to see what evidence the Bush administration had. (This same ploy would recur when war with Iraq loomed in 2003.) The administration declined on the grounds that doing so could compromise intelligence sources, which of course was seen by those who requested the evidence as proof that the Bush team had no such evidence. Thus when Blair announced there was "absolutely no doubt" and Musharraf claimed a "sufficient basis," both announcements gave the administration limited political coverage. One might argue that Britain's support of the U.S. position was practically a foregone conclusion, hence, the limited political coverage. When Musharraf made the same sort of announcement after receiving U.S. intelligence, it was even more important to specific international constituencies (e.g., countries with large Muslim populations). (Note: Since the military campaign *Operation Enduring Freedom* began on October 7, 2001, these announcements proved fortuitous.)

October 4 was a particularly busy day. In addition to the announcements just noted, a Russian airplane, flying from Tel Aviv, Israel, to Novosibirsk, Russia, exploded over the Black Sea. Initially, many in an already jumpy nation feared that it was another terrorist attack. It turned out to be an errant Ukraine missile launched during a military exercise and probably had little if any effect on U.S. foreign policy. Though not an external input per se, October 4 was also the day that the anthrax scare began. An editor at the *Sun* tabloid in Florida was diagnosed with anthrax and subsequently died. With the nation already on edge, combined with the Russian plane, it initially appeared that a new wave of terrorism might be commencing. Thus external events combined with an internal event that was perceived as originating externally; Americans were becoming more certain that the United States did indeed live in a "new world" as Bush had declared. This provides a clear example of how the various inputs interact to shape foreign policy. In this case it led to a public who increasingly supported their president thus permitting Bush wide latitude, as we shall see.

What happens in the global economy may often constitute an external input to which U.S. foreign policy ultimately responds. On October 6, as the economic ramifications of the 9/11 attacks on America's economy were becoming clear, the G-7 finance ministers (the Group of Western Industrialized nations) and central banks issued a communiqué vowing "to monitor exchange markets closely and co-operate as appropriate" in order to forestall a global recession. Clearly a global re-cession combined with America's own recession would have greatly constrained what the Bush administration would have been able to do in its war on terrorism over the medium-to-long term. As we know, the Bush administration has repeatedly vowed to be patient and take as long as it takes to defeat global terrorism, whether years or decades.

MILITARY ACTION BEGINS

On October 7, 2001, U.S. and British troops launched military operations against the Taliban regime in Afghanistan. The battle had been joined. Though there were protests in some corners (e.g., Pakistan), there were far fewer than pundits had pre-dicted. For present purposes, it demonstrates how seemingly marginally important external inputs can shape U.S. foreign policy. This is not to suggest that the war began on October 7 as a direct result of the previous enumerated inputs. On the contrary, military-contingency plans likely dictated the timing much more direct-ly (i.e., governmental inputs). Rather, it is to suggest that, though difficult to quan-tify, such external inputs interact with other inputs and shape foreign-policy output.

On the day the military campaign began, bin Laden released a statement over *Al Jazeera* lauding the 9/11 attacks as well as declaring: "Neither America nor the people who live in it will dream of security before we live it in Palestine, and not before all the infidel armies leave the land of Muhammad." Two days later, on Oc-tober 9, al Qaeda spokesman, Sulaiman Abu Ghaith, issued a statement calling for a holy war against the United States.

October 10 proved interesting in terms of external inputs to U.S. foreign pol-icy. Recall that the administration had announced freezing terrorists' assets as one of its foreign-policy instruments. America's putative ally, Saudi Arabia, refused to freeze assets of organizations linked to bin Laden, effectively refusing to cooper-ate fully with the United States. This set off a maelstrom of political commentary in the United States criticizing the Saudi regime, another example of the various inputs' interaction. The U.S. foreign-policy result was that the administration was forced to issue numerous statements suggesting the Saudis *were* cooperating with the United States in numerous other ways. On the same day Italy's prime minis-ter, Silvio Berlusconi, announced broad political support for the U.S. efforts against terrorism.

A few days later on October 13, Pakistani police fired into a crowd of anti-American protesters. It was not the first day of such protests. The Musharraf gov-ernment had watched several days of anti-U.S. protests limited principally to

Islamabad, Karachi, and other cities in the mostly Pashtun areas of the Northwest Frontier Provinces. It is unclear whether the United States pressured Musharraf to act or whether his own growing sense of alarm caused it. Though there would be subsequent protests, they never gained the momentum once predicted. It did lead to an additional improvement in Pakistani–U.S. relations that ultimately proved useful to the Bush team.

On October 15, the Saudi Interior Minister condemned the air strikes in Afghanistan. According to the Saudi Press Agency, the Minister said: "We are not at all happy with the situation . . . [but] this in no way means we are not willing to confront terrorism." That same day, Washington, D.C. became consumed with bioterrorism as a letter to Senator Tom Daschle tested positive for anthrax.

On October 17, President Bush departed for Shanghai, China—announcing that "the main thing that will be on my mind is . . . to rally the world against terrorists"— while Secretary Powell met with India's Minister of External Affairs. As noted earlier, both India and Pakistan had been on a diplomatic black list since exploding nuclear weapons a few years earlier. However, in the case of India, Washington had been gradually moving toward a *rapprochement* going back to the Clinton administration. Thus Powell's visit to India was somewhat less surprising than the relationship that was building with Pakistan. In any event, the result of the meeting was Powell's declaration that "the United States and India stand united against terrorism and that includes terrorism directed against India as well." Perhaps to assuage Pakistan's possible alarm with Secretary Powell's visit to India, President Bush released $50 million in aid to Pakistan (actually a second installment of $50 million) the same day, another foreign policy instrument. On the same day, both Australia and Canada made gestures of solidarity to the United States. Australia's prime minister announced that Australia would be sending 1,500 troops as well as naval vessels and aircraft to support U.S. military action in Afghanistan. Canada's prime minister, Chretien, dispatched Canadian ships to the Arabian Sea.

On October 19, Pakistan made it known that it would allow U.S. and coalition forces to use the Dalbandin airbase in western Pakistan, arguably demonstrating what $100 million will buy in that part of the world. This was operationally significant for the U.S. military, which had been flying all its sorties off ships. President Bush's pledge to "rally the world against terrorists" as he departed for the Far East was evidently paying dividends. At the Asia Pacific Economic Cooperation (APEC) summit, China's then president Jiang Zemin and President Bush met privately. One result of their meeting was President Jiang's pledge of "firm support and cooperation in support of the war against terrorism."

Over the next several days the following external-systemic events occurred. The British announced that Britain would send additional ships, aircraft, and troops to bolster the war effort. Pakistan's General Musharraf announced new governmental measures to check the anti-American rallies in Pakistan. And in a token but symbolically important move, Turkey announced that it would be sending ninety troops to northern Afghanistan to train troops of the Northern Alliance, the group the United States had been supporting.

On November 3, *Al Jazeera* released another bin Laden videotape in which he condemned Saudi Arabia. Unlike previous tapes, however, bin Laden's tirade focused on other Arab leaders who had associated their nations with the United Nations. His condemnation was, apparently, predicated on a revelation to Mohammed. Egypt's Foreign Minister responded the following day by announcing that the war in Afghanistan was a war between bin Laden and the world rather than Christianity and Islam, a message the United States had been trying to get out among the Islamic world.

A day after Egypt's announcement, Saudi Arabia, perhaps feeling heat from both bin Laden and countless Saudi doubters in the United States, announced that the Saudi regime signed the 1999 accord that it had hitherto declined to sign. The international accord called for governments to choke off money to international terrorist organizations. The following day, November 6, the Northern Alliance captured three critical districts in Afghanistan, near the strategic northern city of Mazar-e-Sharif (sometimes spelled Mazar-i-Sharif). One day later, making good on Prime Minister Berlusconi's earlier commitments, Italy's Parliament voted to deploy 2,700 troops to Afghanistan.

Over the next several days, the Taliban regime collapsed surprisingly quickly. Mazar-e-Sharif fell and, like a domino, began a series of other cities falling in rapid succession. During this period—early to mid-November—bin Laden met with a Pakistani journalist and told him that al Qaeda possessed both nuclear and chemical weapons. Japan deployed three Naval ships to the Indian Ocean (November 9). And as a sign that the Taliban regime was actually overthrown, if not completely vanquished, on November 19, a television station in Kabul signed on for the first time since the Taliban had taken power five years earlier.

While Indonesia's leader Megawati Sukarnoputri had visited Bush in Washington in the first few days after 9/11, little support had been forthcoming from Southeast Asia. Normally, U.S. foreign policy is relatively unhindered by countries like Indonesia and Malaysia. However, in President Bush's war on terror, such countries may prove quite pivotal. Indonesia, for instance, is the nation with the largest Muslim population in the world. Thus it was quite important when, on November 19, both Indonesia and Malaysia announced that they would be willing to send troops to Afghanistan, provided that the United Nations established a peacekeeping presence. Together, Malaysia and Indonesia constitute some 20 percent of the world's Muslim population. Thus, like Egypt's earlier declaration that the war against bin Laden and terrorism was not a war between Christianity and Islam, this announcement provided some additional political coverage for the Bush administration.

On November 27 an important gathering of Afghans took place in Bonn, Germany. The UN sponsored the meeting at which representatives from the Northern Alliance, followers of former King Zahir Shah, and Pashtuns with alliances to either Pakistan or Iran met to discuss the future of Afghanistan. Ultimately (on December 3), the principal result was the formation of what became known as the interim government with Hamid Karzai as its temporary head. Just three days later, the Russians and Chinese concluded high-level talks they were holding and pledged that they would cooperate with each other to fight terrorism irrespective of where it originates. Both countries had their own reasons for allying themselves with the United States: Both have indigenous "Muslim problems" associated with separatist movements.

In the early part of December, the battle of Tora Bora, in Eastern Afghanistan near the Pakistan border, took place. For about two weeks there were daily reports about the success, then the failure, of the campaign. At one point, cable news programs and newspaper articles claimed that the United States had bin Laden cornered. By the end of the campaign it would turn out that most of al Qaeda's top officials, as well as a good number of its soldiers, had escaped—apparently into the porous borders of Pakistan.

Several important external-systemic inputs occurred in quick succession in mid-to-late December. On December 20, interim leader Hamid Karzai arrived in Kabul with a contingency of British peacekeeping troops. Two days later, the new government was sworn in. The same day, on a flight from Paris to Miami, alleged "shoe bomber" Richard Reid was prevented, by the airplane's passengers, from detonating a bomb over the Atlantic Ocean. Intelligence developed later would show an association between Reid and elements in Pakistan suggesting, perhaps, an association with al Qaeda itself. On December 26, Karzai pledged his government to the war on terrorism saying that "there is no way . . . that we can allow Afghanistan to be made the home of terrorism" again. And in videotape that shook the world and certainly the American public, on December 27 *Al Jazeera* broadcast another bin Laden tape in which bin Laden bragged of the planning of the 9/11 attacks and labeled it a "blessed terror."[6]

Prior to January, rumors existed that that al Qaeda had cells in Southeast Asia— specifically Malaysia, Indonesia, and the Philippines. On January 10, Singapore's Defense Minister announced that Singapore had uncovered and prevented several planned attacks by arresting fifteen suspects allegedly associated with al Qaeda.[7] More information would soon be forthcoming in the media regarding Singapore and terrorist cells elsewhere in Southeast Asia. In Indonesia, for instance, it was reported that al Qaeda was "lurking." "Since the 9/11 attacks on New York and the Pentagon, signs of al Qaeda activity in Indonesia had multiplied. U.S. and Indonesian intelligence officials announced they believed hundreds of foreigners who may be linked to al Qaeda and coming from as far away as Europe visited a secret training camp" in the jungles of Indonesia. Over several decades at least and as recently as the late 1990s, groups of Muslims had variously attacked and/or fought with ethnic Chinese and Indonesian Christians—in some cases resulting in actual pogroms. Consequently, U.S. officials as well as others following the war on terror began asking just how extensive were al Qaeda's connections in Southeast Asia? How well coordinated were the groups in the Philippines, Singapore, Indonesia, and elsewhere in Southeast Asia? As it would soon turn out, these were appropriate questions to be asking.

The *Los Angeles Times* reported on January 12 the broad dimensions of the al Qaeda presence in Singapore. Singapore clearly was assisting the United States since the arrests instantly provided new information that could be used by the U.S.

government. Reportedly, this new evidence illustrated "the most comprehensive look yet at an alleged al Qaeda plot in the region." Largely home-grown members of a coalition partner of al Qaeda—known in Singapore as *Jemaah Islamiah* (hereafter JI)—were divided into cells that had different tasks and apparently different contacts to further compartmentalize the cells' plots. The cells included one whose task was to direct attacks on American service members on transit busses. Another cell, which had been active since at least 1997, was to survey U.S. institutions and buildings used by the U.S. government for eventual targets. A third cell was tasked with targeting American military aircraft stationed or harbored at Singapore's Paya Lebar air base.[8]

There were several disturbing issues associated with the presence of these al Qaeda–linked cells. One issue was that while the cells were comprised largely of locals, their common leader was an Indonesian cleric—Hambali—implicitly suggesting a larger organizational structure linking Singapore, Indonesia, and the Philippines. In fact, an article published the following month confirmed the Indonesia connection to Southeast Asia's far-flung al Qaeda affiliates.

> The Bush Administration, frustrated that the Indonesian government has failed to crack down against the threat of terrorism, has urged officials here to begin a search of an Indonesian cleric believed to be the point man for al Qaeda in Southeast Asia . . . .
> The officials contrast the help in fighting terrorism that they are receiving from Singapore, Malaysia and the Philippines with what they characterize as a lack of energetic cooperation from Indonesia, the world's most populous Muslim country. The C.I.A. said last week that Indonesia was a likely place for al Qaeda, Osama bin Laden's organization, to base further operations.

Reportedly, the CIA's risk assessments indicated that Indonesia was "potentially a big threat"[9]

A second issue was that such cells could exist at all—in some cases for some four or five years—in an authoritarian state like Singapore. Singapore, it should be stressed, is the same government that has rules and punishments for any number of "crimes" that would seem laughable in the West—leaving urinals and toilets unflushed, graffiti, and so forth. The point is not to make a value judgment—none is intended. Rather, Singapore is a very tightly run state with very proficient police and intelligence agencies, and it is therefore surprising that al Qaeda cells could go undetected for so long. A third concern involved is the proportion of Singapore's Muslims. Singapore is comprised of an approximately 15 percent Muslim population. Therefore, some 85 percent of the population—with whom, incidentally, relations have not always been harmonious—had neither noticed nor been especially suspicious of the Islamic extremists living among them (ibid.). In fact, that they were discovered was due, in part, to a tape found in a cave in Afghanistan, not Singaporean informants.

Once news began breaking regarding al Qaeda in Singapore, the floodgates of terrorism evidence opened. On January 11, the *Washington Post* ran a story entitled "Al Qaeda Feared to Be Lurking in Indonesia." The article quoted intelligence agents to the effect that they had uncovered a presumed terrorist plot the previous August that was directed against the U.S. diplomatic compound. The author attributed the plot to bin Laden. Moreover, "officials" told the *Post* of their growing alarm about the terrorist network in Indonesia and "sleeper cells" presumed to be operating there. Indonesian officials told the *Post* of "several hundred people" from Europe, Pakistan, and the Middle East who had entered Indonesia over the past year "posing as aid workers" but actually meeting up with al Qaeda operatives.[10]

While intelligence was exposing al Qaeda operatives in Southeast Asia, the U.S. government was busy announcing that, henceforth, foreign-policy threats were likely to be of the terrorist variety, specifically, biological, chemical, and/or other weapons of mass destruction (WMD). This was significant given that the Bush administration (specifically Secretary of Defense Donald Rumsfeld and the president) had campaigned to cancel the 1970s ABM treaty and implement a missile defense. The article cited an unclassified National Intelligence Estimate to the effect that "for the first time [the United States] is 'more likely to be attacked with [weapons of mass destruction] using *non-missile means*' than conventional weapons systems" (italics added).[11]

Around the same time a flurry of activities regarding Iraq became public. Pundits on cable news programs began discussing the "unfinished business" left at the conclusion of the Gulf War, some ten years earlier. The Arab League secretary-general was reported to be in Baghdad warning Saddam Hussein to take no action that could be construed as provocative from the U.S. viewpoint. In another interesting turn of events, the United States announced that it would not destroy nuclear warheads—previously agreed to be destroyed by the United States—but, rather, that the "Pentagon disclosed in a major report on nuclear forces . . . that it wants to hold on to the weapons as a hedge against new threats to U.S. security," particularly "in light of the world's uncertainties and dangers,"[12] that is, a continuation of deterrence.

Approximately one week later, U.S. intelligence sources reported an intelligence windfall resulting from operations in Afghanistan. Apparently, U.S. troops found, at the home of top al Qaeda lieutenant Mohammed Atef, videotapes connecting bin Laden to the hijackers. The man seen laughing on the videotape was to have been one of the 9/11 hijackers, but was denied entry to the United States on a couple of occasions. It later became evident that the man, Ramzi Binalshibh, wired some $14,000 to Zacarias Moussaoui, a man currently in jail and the only person thus far indicted for the 9/11 attacks.[13] (Binalshibh, incidentally, is currently in U.S. custody in an "undisclosed" location.) As is well known, the Justice Department believed Moussaoui was the "twentieth hijacker" who would have been on one of the planes had not the authorities picked him up in August.

While the breadth of terrorist networks was being exposed across Southeast Asia, the United States made a somewhat controversial move. It sent troops—a foreign-policy instrument—to the Philippines to help "train" Filipino troops fighting both *Abu Sayyaf* and other separatist movements in that nation. We have seen that apparent links between al Qaeda and *Abu Sayyaf* exist. The move was controversial in the Philippines due to their Constitutional restrictions. It was controversial in the

United States as it represented "Washington's biggest expansion of the war against terrorism since Afghanistan."[14] Furthermore, *Abu Sayyaf* has been described by some as more mercenary than terrorist. The group had abducted Westerners and had held them for ransom rather than religious, philosophical, or ideological reasons. Nonetheless, some six hundred American troops were sent in for a six-month deployment. (Some U.S. troop presence remains there as of this writing, 2003.)

President Bush and Secretary Powell had put extraordinary efforts into the building of coalitions—what they had taken to calling "overlapping coalitions." Among their Herculean efforts was bringing Pakistan's President Musharraf on board the U.S. effort to fight terrorism. In so doing, the administration had managed to balance the particularly thorny relations between Pakistan and India. Thus it was particularly unfortunate when, in mid-January, relations between the two longtime enemies threatened to erupt in war.[15] Beyond the obvious threat that two nuclear powers could go to war, the fracture also hurt U.S. efforts in Afghanistan. While the Indo-Pakistan conflict escalated, the United States was mopping up the Tora Bora mission and was involved in a similar mission elsewhere in eastern Afghanistan. As with Tora Bora, a number of al Qaeda remnants were believed to be in the mountains, which the United States was bombing. The United States had reportedly "learned" lessons from Tora Bora, namely, that a blocking action was needed to prevent al Qaeda from escaping across the Afghanistan-Pakistan border. Alas, the lessons had not been properly learned, for the public would soon discover that senior al Qaeda leadership escaped over the border yet again.

To complicate matters even more, as Pakistan and India relations were threatening to explode, the administration's anti-terror efforts were deteriorating in the Middle East. Demonstrations against America had been relatively muted in the Islamic world as already noted. To be sure, there had been limited demonstrations in Pakistan, Indonesia, and elsewhere. Consequently, several Bush administration officials (including the president) had repeatedly declared that America's war on terror was not a war on Islam. In fact, after those initial demonstrations, the United States seemed to be winning the public relations campaign. Just when the administration seemed to have a handle on it, Israel intercepted a shipment of armaments from Iran to Palestine. Some fifty tons of weapons were interdicted on the *Karine A*, providing at least circumstantial evidence to Israel's claim of a terrorist axis between the Palestinian Authority, Hizbullah, and Shia Muslim elements within Iran.[16] According to administration sources, Hizbullah was second only to al Qaeda in terms of terrorist activities and was on the State Department's "terrorist list."

The same day, the American public learned of additional evidence of al Qaeda activities in Southeast Asia. The *Washington Post* reported that the FBI had been busy in Singapore and elsewhere since 9/11. The piece reported that "intelligence officials say that 'the next face of this is not going to be an Arab face, but possibly Indonesian, Filipino, a Malaysian face, or even African.'" It was becoming ever clearer to Americans that the global-terrorist hydra was not simply an Afghanistan problem but rather worldwide. On the heels of the alert regarding Malaysia and Singapore—and as noted previously, Indonesia—an article in the *Los Angeles Times* noted that al Qaeda was active in the Philippines as well.[17] *Abu Sayyaf* may have been mercenary, but it was more: At a minimum, the group was helping al Qaeda by giving it sanctuary.

Concomitantly, America's putative ally, Saudi Arabia, began a public discussion about whether and how long it would allow the United States to keep troops stationed in that nation. The publicity surrounding the Saudi position, not surprisingly, caused some consternation in the American public as well as within the administration. For months the administration had been claiming the Saudis were being exceptionally forthcoming with help in the U.S. war on terror. Now some of the royals were undercutting the administration's efforts. The evolving Saudi position threatened to "complicate the Saudi-American relationship, which was put under great strain since the events of September 11."[18] The publicity surrounding the Saudi consideration of telling the United States it had "overstayed its welcome" set off a public discussion — in both the print and electronic media — that will be discussed in Chapter 3 under societal inputs. It is worth noting it here however as an external input.

Clearly, the administration's attempt to cobble together overlapping coalitions in response to September 11 needed attention. The Bush administration had, to its credit, put considerable effort into building European, Arabic, and Islamic coalitions to prevent the war on terror from resembling a war on Islam. The president had put his considerable prestige on the line in the process. Saudi discontent threatened both. Nor was it only the Saudis who were expressing misgivings. As noted, one of the principal foreign-policy instruments used by the administration was to freeze the assets of al Qaeda. The day after the Saudis' misgivings were exposed, the *Los Angeles Times* noted that another supposed ally, the UAE, were, to put it charitably, acquiescing in the transference of money from UAE sources to al Qaeda to the tune of $120,000.[19] The same story reported that chemicals — presumably to be used by al Qaeda for chemical weapons — were also shipped from the UAE to Afghanistan.

While relations with presumed allies may have been undergoing tough times, the Bush administration was working hard to develop new coalition partners. Prior to 9/11, relations were on the mend with Yemen. Indeed, it was the attack on the *USS Cole* that had been refueling in a Yemen port that put terrorism on the radar screen for many Americans. By mid-January (2002) Americans learned that the United States was renewing and even strengthening ties with the Yemeni government.[20]

The Saudis apparently underestimated the backlash their public discussion would cause. As a result of it, they reacted rather oddly, clearly reflecting the rifts within the House of Saud. Criticizing what the Saudis believed was a too pro-Israeli stance by the United States, Crown Prince Abdullah nonetheless reaffirmed the Saudi–U.S. relationship. Most of the 9/11 hijackers came from Saudi Arabia, causing some discomfort in Saudi Arabia and a good deal of scrutiny by Western media. Thus while Abdullah criticized the "indefensible" position the United States held on the Israeli–Palestinian conflict, the Prince also confirmed that bin Laden and al Qaeda had actively sought to "drive a wedge" between the United States and the Saudis. Crown Prince Abdullah suggested that bin Laden had "picked young Saudis, and he was able to brainwash" these youth as a means of effecting 9/11.[21]

So just as the Bush administration's efforts to build coalitions were seemingly coming unraveled, the Saudis seemed to be making an effort, however ineffective, to rebuild their relations with the United States. Additionally — in a somewhat surprising move, given the deterioration of relations over the April 2001 "spy plane" incident — the Chinese government began cooperating with the United States. "Now China is quietly sharing intelligence with the CIA on Chinese Muslims in Afghanistan and is cooperating with the U.S. efforts to freeze terror-linked financial accounts in Hong Kong."[22]

As effectively as the Bush administration had been in putting together anti-terror coalitions and keeping them together while under duress, the administration's efforts nearly came to naught late in January. Trouble had been bubbling just below the surface since 9/11. In January, as so many feared, Pakistan and India escalated their hostilities. An attack in Calcutta was blamed by the Indian government on terrorists with alleged links to Pakistan's intelligence services. As the *Los Angeles Times* put it: "The Indian allegation about the Calcutta attack further complicated efforts to defuse a volatile military standoff between the two nuclear-armed neighbors." On the same day the U.S. coalition with Pakistan and India threatened to unravel, new reports of al Qaeda's activities in Southeast Asia were published. On January 23, both the *New York Times* and the *Christian Science Monitor* published such articles. The *New York Times*, for instance, reported on al Qaeda operatives in Indonesia causing troubles while the *Monitor* cited the breadth of activities throughout Southeast Asia, from Singapore to the Philippines.[23]

Within a matter of days, reports of growing radicalism in some of America's staunchest allies in the Middle East appeared in the media.[24] Nearly simultaneously, the *Los Angeles Times* published an incredible exposé on Mohamed Atta, the alleged ringleader of the 9/11 hijackers. Similarly, the *Monitor* published an article detailing the alienation of young Arabs and the links such alienation has to terrorism, something that many in the West were having difficulty comprehending.[25] While understanding the motivation of terrorists was finding an unsympathetic audience in the United States, new evidence of the extent of al Qaeda's plans for America was being unearthed. U.S. troops were finding a wealth of information in Afghanistan, left behind in former al Qaeda redoubts and caves. The documents showed that al Qaeda had an interest in U.S. nuclear power plants, historical landmarks, and water-treatment plants.[26] Clearly most attentive Americans (the so-called attentive public) could comprehend how serious a threat al Qaeda represented and were becoming increasingly alarmed about it. As if Americans needed another reminder, Secretary of Defense Rumsfeld told the National Defense University that the United States "must prepare now for potential surprise attacks 'vastly more deadly' than" those experienced on 9/11.[27] Just days after Secretary Rumsfeld warned of future surprise attacks, FBI Director Robert Mueller announced that "preventing terrorist attacks is now the FBI's primary mission."[28] Not to be outdone by the FBI, DCI (Director of Central Intelligence) George Tenet, in his first public testimony since the attacks, warned Congress that while al Qaeda had been harmed, it still posed the biggest threat to the United States.[29] If for no other reason, this was a significant admission, given Bush's and Rumsfeld's insistence during the previous year that rogue nations with missiles were America's biggest threat. Rhetoric aside, these bureaucratic maneuvers implicitly focused on the efficacy of Bush's campaign commitment to missile defense. (Potential bureaucratic machinations will be considered in more detail in governmental inputs.)

Thus the dimensions of the terrorist threat were becoming clear to the American government and public. While most Americans supported their government's response to the threat as appropriate, governments elsewhere were beginning to express some apprehension. The *Far Eastern Economic Review* noted that several governments in Southeast Asia were feeling discomfort as America finished up in Afghanistan and broadened its efforts to include the region. The article went so far as comparing America's actions to its earlier actions leading to Vietnam. "Into this arena [Southeast Asia] step the Americans, viewing Southeast Asia much as they did in the 1950s and 1960s in the lead-up to their involvement in Vietnam as a problem."[30]

As it turned out, the United States was not nearly done in Afghanistan. The Afghanistan "model," namely using opposition forces in situ, was running into difficulties. America's allies, the so-called Northern Alliance were a disparate group of different ethnicities with sometimes competing interests. "This intense fighting is the first between rival Afghan warlords since the Taliban were defeated two months ago. And it portends grave difficulties for the fragile government of Mr. Karzai, as well as for American special forces on the ground. . . ."[31]

As noted, overlapping alliances were one of the administration's principal tools in fighting terrorism. However, keeping the various actors happy was not always simple. As some Southeast Asia leaders were expressing apprehension and just as tribal infighting was being reported in the Northern Alliance, the Bush administration got positive confirmation that another one of its coalitions was in relatively better shape. Sino–U.S. relations were continuing their remarkable and rapid *rapprochement*. The Chinese government was coming to the conclusion that 9/11 linked the United States and China in a common interest.[32] By contrast, the next day Russia peremptorily announced that America ought not to expand its war on terror to include Iraq,[33] evidently fearing, correctly, that Iraq would be America's next target. Just as Russia was offering its unsolicited advice, a U.S. delegation to an international security conference (held in Europe), was lectured by several European leaders about America's unilateralist tendencies. The problem, it seemed, was that only when the United States needed European help did the Americans consult with its NATO partners. Many in Europe felt the United States needed to consult its partners more frequently; that is what partners are supposed to do.[34]

Immediately following the 9/11 attacks President Bush had personalized them by characterizing bin Laden as an "evildoer" who must be brought to justice. During the battle of Tora Bora, government officials noted that they had heard bin Laden's voice over field radios. Later, there were several reports that bin Laden was likely lying in the bottom of a cave, dead. Thus it was particularly problematic when reports surfaced that bin Laden, as well as dozens of al Qaeda's soldiers, had escaped. Perhaps more troubling was the allegation that Iran had allowed bin Laden safe passage.[35] The United States had been engaging in a complex Kabuki dance with President Khatami who supposedly represented reform in Iran. This suggested one of two scenarios, neither desirable. One, Khatami was not the reformer the United States had hoped. Two, the clerics from the 1979 revolution still held more power than Khatami. Either way, the development suggested that a U.S–Iran *rapprochement* was not in the foreseeable future.

AMERICA BROADENS ITS ANTI-TERRORISM FOCUS

If al Qaeda posed the biggest threat according to the CIA and FBI, President Bush's "axis of evil" speech made it clear that terrorism was not limited to bin Laden and al Qaeda. Though we shall consider the politics later in government inputs, it is worth noting here that articles about threats posed by both Hizbullah and North Korea were published in early February. One could cynically argue that administration officials were becoming concerned about the future of the missile defense program since the ubiquitous unnamed government official provided some of the details for the articles.[36] North Korea was known to have relatively long-range missiles and thought to have an ambitious program to build a new generation of missiles with even longer ranges.

From the beginning of the war—in early October—through January, scarcely a negative story had appeared in the major media. Public support was heavily in favor of the administration's war on the global-terrorist hydra. The first mainstream-media critiques of the war appeared in February. The first article reported a botched raid by Filipino troops with American advisors going after *Abu Sayyaf*. Rumsfeld had previously assured the public that American troops would not be involved in actual fighting there, only training. The following day another critical story appeared. In December, an aerial attack in Paktia Province had been characterized by Secretary Rumsfeld as a great success. The *New York Times* reported that the group may well have been loyalists to the new interim government instead.[37] Virtually every war since Vietnam has been compared at some time to that war. In shades of the Phoenix program during Vietnam, the *New York Times* article reported that American target selectors had apparently been duped by Afghanis with their own agendas, reminiscent of Phoenix.

Adding insult to the administration's injury, the rift that had been developing between the Bush administration and its Saudi ally resurfaced. The *Washington Post* reported that the Saudi anger with the administration "came as a shock" to Bush and his top advisors and that the administration "went to extraordinary lengths to try to repair" the relationship. So concerned was Bush that he sent a personal letter to Crown Prince Abdullah. The Saudis had not exactly been forthcoming with intelligence; now they were threatening to end all cooperation.[38]

In mid-February, an anonymous "American official," leaked a story about one of bin Laden's top lieutenants, Abu Zubaydah, now thought to be third in command.

The article noted that even while the war continued in Afghanistan, Abu Zubay-dah was actively planning to hatch new attacks on American and European tar-gets. Both the British and the Germans were reported to have broken up plots since 9/11. It was therefore disturbing to read of Zubaydah's efforts to activate "sleeper cells" in the United States.[39] (Note: Zubaydah would be apprehended in early April in what would be hailed as an intelligence coup; he remains in U.S. custody in an "undisclosed" location.)

Thus while things were seemingly breaking America's way in South Asia, the president began to broaden his anti-terror focus geographically as well as to assert America's presumed leadership role. In mid-February President Bush set off Sat-urday (February 16) for a three day tour of Asia, during which he would strength-en the anti-terror coalition as well as return to the issues "he initially intended to make a cornerstone of his administration's foreign policy." The trip was "designed to signal that the war on terrorism has not diverted U.S. attention from either its broader agenda or the rest of the world." Prior to his departure, the president used his regular Saturday radio address to highlight U.S. foreign-policy goals: "a better world beyond terror—a world of greater opportunity and more open trade, stronger security and more individual freedom." He also reiterated his axis-of-evil speech by noting that "Washington will not allow the North [Koreans] to 'threaten freedom with weapons of mass destruction.'"[40]

So much for the good news and the revival of U.S. values and goals. No soon-er had the president prepared to fly off for Asia than one of the Ministers in Karzai's interim government was assassinated. As the *Los Angeles Times* reported, "A slain Cabinet minister was buried on a muddy hillside here Saturday, the fog that shrouded his simple wooden casket echoing the cloud of suspicion and intrigue that surrounds his death and threatens to envelop Afghanistan's fragile peace and struggling government." As if the assassination of one of the U.S.-fostered gov-ernment's ministers was not bad enough, speculation circulated that "many oth-ers" were busy planning coups.[41]

The weekend of February 16 (Saturday) and 17 (Sunday) turned out to be a very busy weekend. One could imagine President Bush in the middle of a three-ring circus. On the one hand, mostly good (albeit with a bit of bad) news out of Afghanistan was one ring. The second ring was the president's determi-nation to go on the road espousing U.S. values and objectives in Asia. The third ring seemed to come out of the blue. Thomas Friedman published an op-ed piece in the *New York Times* regarding a new Saudi vision on ending violence in the Palestinian–Israeli conflict and eventually normalizing relations with Is-rael. Following an interview with Crown Prince Abdullah, Friedman revealed that Abdullah had a "plan" on his desk that amounted to UN Resolution 242 — i.e., land for peace—and linked a Palestinian state to the Arab world normaliz-ing relations with Israel.[42]

Intriguing as it may have been, it had a long distance to travel from Crown Prince Abdullah's desk to the forthcoming Arab Summit (scheduled for late Feb-ruary). Moreover, Bush was on the road and was trying to focus on coalition building, imbuing Asia with U.S. values, and likely left scratching his head about the Saudis. Regrettably, the president's balancing act would become more problematic. He was met at his arrival in South Korea with anti-American protests. Apparently many Koreans, particularly college students, took umbrage with the president's characterization of North Korea as one of the axes of evil; it seems it flew in the face of South Korea's own, highly celebrated, policy, of normalizing with North Korea: the so-called sunshine policy.[43]

As President Bush continued his Asia tour de force, his axis-of-evil speech may have been affecting politics in Iran. Somewhat surprisingly, Iran's President Khatami had issued a statement of condolences after the 9/11 attacks. In fact, some in the administration—mostly from the State Department—were hoping for improved relations with Iran's reformers. Khatami was a two-time elected president of Iran, and was thought to have been slowly gaining ground against the theocracy that had led Iran in the 1980s and most of the 1990s. One cannot be certain how much effect Bush's public declaration of Iran as "evil" had on Iran's politics, but it would appear that the "hard-line clerics" used his speech as an opportunity to reverse some of the reformers' gains. A *Washington Post* reporter thought the link was obvious. "The confusion was evident in the bitter quarrels between reformers and conservatives over improving ties with the United States, and in the fallout from President Bush's State of the Union address." The same article continued: "Bush had called Iran part of an 'axis of evil' that supports terrorism and seeks to acquire weapons of mass destruction—a comment many analysts said damaged the reform movement and strengthened conservatives."[44]

It is difficult to ascertain accurately the calculation that went into the axis-of-evil speech: Was it Bush's real thinking? Had neo-conservatives in the administration (e.g., Rumsfeld, Wolfowitz, Carl Rove, and others) seized the speech-writing apparatus and managed to have the line inserted? Was Bush simply placating a specific constituency in his Republican Party? Were enemies of the moderates (e.g., enemies of Powell, Rice, and others) making political moves to win Bush to their side? Who can say? What one can say is the speech caused no small degree of consternation internationally and played out on programs like CNN's *Crossfire*, MSNBC's *Hardball*, and others for weeks. Whatever the genesis of the "axis-of-evil" line, Secretary of State Powell was left to pick up the pieces as the president's Asia road show moved from place to place. In Japan, for instance, after Prime Minister Koizumi pooh-poohed Bush's harsh language, Powell quickly gathered the media—pool reporters following the president as well as foreign journalists—hastening to "tell reporters . . . that America's allies should not fear 'a state of war tomorrow'" and warning those gathered: "Let's not swoon."[45] Others suggested that Powell's job was actually to assuage European concerns.

> Secretary of State Colin L. Powell, who joined Bush here, [in Japan] responded to some European critics of Bush's aggressive posture, saying some of them "have perhaps gone a little far" with their objections. . . . "We'll be in contact with you. We'll be in discussion with you. We will share with you our ideas and our vision.[46]

Whoever Powell's audience was, the entire affair seemed to hint of camps or factions within the administration. Less clear was which group was in control and when. It appeared at times that whoever last spoke to Bush was the faction in ascendancy.

Near the end of the president's Asia junket, he doubtless was looking for some positive news for a change. Right on cue, President-cum-General Musharraf announced a move the United States had been agitating for, almost since 9/11. Namely, Musharraf announced the "crackdown" on militants, arresting some 2,000. In so doing, the general was effectively curtailing the power of his own intelligence services.[47] Recall that Pakistan's intelligence services had largely created the Taliban regime and supported them over time. As we shall see later, Musharraf's "crackdown" turned out to be a stop-gap expedient as he later released many of the 2,000. Nonetheless, it was surely welcome news at the time.

On the final leg of the president's sojourn, he stopped over in China, where he met with then President Jiang Zemin and his heir apparent, Vice President Hu Jintao. Given the previous years' tense relations — Taiwan Straits, the spy plane debacle — taken with China's decision to cooperate in the war on terror, on balance the trip turned out to be relatively successful. Minimally, Bush met the man who was slated to take over for the aging Jiang (fall 2002), thereby establishing a continuity of relations. Moreover, Jiang and Bush agreed to work cooperatively vis-à-vis North Korea, a nation over which China has unusual influence and, as we have seen, one of Bush's axes of evil. Finally, Bush got a commitment from Jiang for a reciprocal trip to the United States.[48]

Nearly overshadowing all the foreign-policy news was the kidnapping and killing of *Wall Street Journal* journalist Daniel Pearl. His death, the eventual recovery of his body, and still later a videotape of the brutal murder were all covered ad infinitum resulting in additional external inputs. In Pakistan, however, his murder became a major issue for Musharraf. President Musharraf used Pearl's death as a pretext to crack down further on radical Islamic extremists. The United States, in turn, used Musharraf's crackdown as a pretext to rally around Musharraf as a true U.S. ally in the war on terror. Ironically, however, the coverage of the Pearl story also exposed either Pakistan government duplicity or factionalism in Pakistani politics. "Investigators believe . . . that some of the kidnappers may have been involved in the December 1999 hijacking of an Indian Airlines jet to Kandahar, Afghanistan. During that incident, Indian authorities released Saeed [reported ringleader of the kidnappers] and two other Islamic militants in exchange for the 155 passengers and crew. Saeed had been jailed in India in 1994 for kidnapping Western tourists."[49] Apparently Musharraf's crackdown had been inconsistent, at best, suggesting Musharraf's incompetence, malfeasance, and/or governmental factionalism.

In fairness to Musharraf, the political pressures on him from all sides were extreme. Pakistan's intelligence services were thought to be rife with pro-Taliban elements. The ethnic Pashtuns in Afghanistan have family members across the border in Pakistan. When the United States initially began the military campaign in Afghanistan in early October (2001) anti-U.S. rallies occurred in some Pakistani cities. Further, frequently when Musharraf has cracked down on "militants" and/or "extremists" in Pakistan, his actions elicited terrorist counterattacks in Pakistan. Hence, Musharraf could be seen, figuratively, as walking a tightrope between U.S. and fundamentalist Islamic demands. Additionally, as Musharraf sought to gain control over his own intelligence services, he was potentially creating powerful new political enemies. It should be recalled that Musharraf came to power in a coup fostered, in part, by the ISI (his intelligence services). It was not, therefore, terribly surprising to find that as Musharraf met U.S. interests, bomb plots—and even Pearl's abduction and murder—were direct responses to his pro-U.S. leanings. As a "senior military source" told Scott Baldauf, "The biggest problem we have here are the rogue elements in the intelligence agencies, especially those who at some time became involved with the CIA."[50]

Around the same time some good news came out of Europe. Since 9/11, most Americans had become aware that al Qaeda's far-flung cells were entrenched in Europe, notably in Germany, Britain, and Italy. In late February the press reported that a key al Qaeda ringleader was convicted in Italy. "Police believe Ben Khemais was sent from Afghanistan to supervise bin Laden's terrorist operations in Europe." No small fry was Ben Khemais apparently.[51] The news was quickly followed by another report out of Italy in which it was reported that four Tunisian immigrants in Milan were convicted on conspiracy charges having conspired to aid and abet terrorist activities.[52] The same article revealed that the much-discussed Hamburg cell as well as other cells in Germany, Spain, France, Britain, and Belgium were similarly encountering legal problems, presumably, helping to put them out of business.

After several weeks of negative stories coming out of Afghanistan—bombing mistakes, general chaos in the interim government, assassinations, Pakistani backlashes, and so forth—the administration could take solace in positive actions against al Qaeda in Europe. It was therefore curious that the administration announced the broadening of the war on terrorism to South America, an action that could alienate some of America's coalition partners. The previous administration had been giving billions of dollars in aid to Colombia to fight insurgents. As a product of continuity, the Bush administration continued and increased American actions in Colombia. It is unclear whether the administration was attempting, therefore, to prepare the public for a broader war or whether there were underlying political calculations in their announcement. In either case, it was reported that, according to administration officials, "Some senior officials are also pushing for the administration to assert, for the first time, that Colombian rebels are a specific target of the worldwide U.S. war on terrorism."[53]

An "expert" on Colombia at the Inter-American Dialogue research organization in Washington, D.C., characterized the proposed move as "a radical departure" for the administration. Clearly it is not unusual for critics to critique administration foreign policy—the reader need only read coverage of Clinton's foreign policy over his eight-year tenure. More interesting still was the implication in the article that a political brouhaha was underway between the neo-conservatives and moderates in the administration (discussed infra in governmental inputs in Chapter 4) (ibid.).

The reader will recall that President Bush had immediately personalized the war on terror in two villains: Taliban leader Mullah Omar and Osama bin Laden. This happens to be a common device in U.S. foreign policy—indeed, other nations do the same thing. President Clinton vilified Serbia's Milosevic when it suited his purposes; former President Bush vilified Saddam Hussein. It is not particularly surprising therefore that this President Bush would act similarly. The problem with associating the war on terror with the personification of "evildoers" is that the public came to expect the evildoers' demise. In mid-February, reports continued to appear asserting that both men had escaped the intense U.S. efforts to bomb them in their caves or hunt them down "dead or alive," as Bush put it.[54] As previously discussed, other reports had al Qaeda members slipping across the border into Iran.[55] The implication, for anyone who had followed the Omar/bin Laden stories, was obvious: Omar and bin Laden may well have escaped Afghanistan unscathed. (Interestingly, the alleged source of the press story on Iran's complicity in helping al Qaeda was a Pentagon official, perhaps one associated with the neo-conservatives in the administration. It is interesting to note that Interim President Karzai has no choice but to have good relations with Iran— they share a large border and there exists a large ethnic Iranian population in Afghanistan—so the Pentagon official was actually undermining his shop's mission in Afghanistan by leaking.[56])

There had previously been rumors and a few pundits discussing al Qaeda's activities in Somalia. In a special feature for the *Los Angeles Times*, the authors reported on the pervasiveness of such activities. The article also publicized the links between al Qaeda and the Somalis who had shot down the American helicopter in the early 1990s—the so-called Black Hawk Down incident.[57] Finally, by the end of February, three additional bits of evidence appeared indicating that the war on terrorism was neither going to be a short-term commitment nor an easy feat, as the president had, to his credit, warned the public. First, the foreboding that had begun over chaos and ethnic fighting within Afghanistan was exacerbated by what one article called a "growing sense of urgency." Second was the discovery of a plan of al Qaeda-linked plots to bomb or poison—or use any other number of nefarious ways of causing harm—the U.S. Embassy in Rome. Finally, news of al Qaeda activities in far-flung locales such as the Caucasus and Mali appeared.[58]

SUCCESSES AND FAILURES IN THE WAR ON TERROR

March, too, turned out to be a very busy month for the administration's war on terror. Bombing campaigns in Khost and Gardez, relearning lessons thought to have been learned from earlier campaigns, India and Pakistan seemingly heading toward war—a war that the public were repeatedly reminded could conceivably go nuclear—and reports of al Qaeda activities in new geographic areas were among the media reports of external inputs to U.S. foreign policy. March had barely begun when news of al Qaeda-linked terrorist cells in hitherto unmentioned Bosnia was published. Worse still was a report in the media that these cells had been plotting against American interests in the region. "Following a two-week surveillance operation, police in Macedonia today shot and killed seven men described by the Macedonian government as members of a terrorist cell that was planning to attack the U.S., German, and British embassies in Skopje, the capital."[59]

A spate of stories appeared characterizing a new U.S. bombing campaign in eastern Afghanistan. Indeed, one would be hard-pressed to know what was actually happening, given the number of print-media pieces and the sometimes conflicting ways newspapers variously described the war day by day. Initially, for instance, the *Los Angeles Times* simply reported that the United States was pounding al Qaeda members. On the same day in the same paper another story reported that "[i]n planning the current air and ground assault in the eastern Afghan mountains near Gardez, U.S. military strategists drew on the lessons of last year's disappointing campaign in Tora Bora. . . ." Subsequently, the *Monitor* characterized the campaign as necessarily having to shift strategies in midcampaign—the implication being the original strategy was flawed. The *New York Times* reported that the fighting was fierce and a victory was not going to be easy. The reader may recall that the first night of this particular military action witnessed a tragedy involving noncombatants. The full story trickled out over several days as military authorities in Washington, D.C. gathered information in the fog of war.[60]

Despite the relentless bombing campaign, alas, al Qaeda was reportedly still able to regroup elsewhere. The *New York Times* reported that "[n]ewly detected Internet traffic among al Qaeda followers, including intercepted e-mail messages, indicates that elements of the terror network may be trying to regroup in remote sanctuaries in Pakistan near the Afghan border, government officials say." Thus the question had to be asked whether the United States had actually learned earlier lessons. Curiously, on the same day, another reporter suggested that the United States was gaining an edge in the battle. Within a couple of days other reporters had the Afghan government rushing to the front to assist U.S. troops.[61] It was difficult for one to figure out just what was happening. What one can say is this: U.S. troops pulled out and headed back to their base by March 11. Hinting that the lessons "learned" from Tora Bora were less than successfully implemented, the *Los Angeles Times* reported that the U.S. military—back at its base camp—began pointing fingers at their Afghan compatriots for failures at Gardez."[62]

Beyond the daily vagaries of the bombing campaign and whether or not the United States was fighting a successful war, a couple of additional incidents occurred externally that affected U.S. foreign policy. First, relations between India and Pakistan took a turn for the worse again. After a number of incidents, violence flared between the two nuclear powers. Both India and Pakistan mobilized troops to their respective borders. Concomitantly, trouble seemed to be brewing in Iraq; minimally, the administration was attempting to float trial balloons on an eventual war with Iraq. In an unusual move, "U.S. officials Wednesday gave diplomats here [the UN] a high-tech slide show of satellite photos . . ." that the United States contended demonstrated Iraqi malfeasance of one sort or another.[63]

If the administration had intended its slide show as a trial balloon, it was quickly popped. One of America's staunchest allies in the region, Jordan's King Abdullah, publicly warned Vice President Cheney, who was on a Middle East junket to explain U.S. policy vis-à-vis terror as well as Iraq, that "U.S. military action against Iraq could undermine stability in the entire region."[64] The king mused publicly that it was difficult for him to understand what sort of calculus Washington could possibly be using that would have the United States attacking Iraq while the Israeli–Palestinian conflict threatened to engulf the entire region. It turned out to be a harbinger of the Vice President's remaining stops with Cheney receiving a similar lecture from Hosni Mubarak of Egypt—another staunch U.S. ally in the region.

On the other hand, there was some good news regarding the war on terrorism, generally, about the same time. After Bush announced the Bush Doctrine—either you are with us in the war against terrorism or you are with the terrorists—the Yemeni government almost immediately made it clear it wished to be in the former category. Spring saw a continuation of the improvement in relations. These developments were more than merely symbolic. First, Osama bin Laden's family came from Yemen. Though generations had lived in Saudi Arabia, the family originated from and bin Laden had family and roots in Yemen. Second, elements of al Qaeda and other elements friendly to bin Laden remained in Yemen. Thus it was an important development when Vice President Cheney, on the aforementioned junket, visited Yemen and secured a commitment to aid the United States in its campaign.[65] Sudan demonstrated remarkable flexibility in aiding the U.S. cause as well.

A strange development occurred in mid-March: the revelation that the United States had likely suffered an earlier terror attack—with a Boeing 767, no less—without realizing it. Recall that in October 1999, EgyptAir Flight 990 crashed inexplicably. The final report was released in mid-March (2002) concluding that one of the pilots had deliberately crashed the jumbo jet killing all its passengers—an ominous omen of things to come.[66] Indeed, over the months since the 9/11 attacks, information trickled out piecemeal suggesting several indicators that terrorists would use jumbo jets against the United States (and/or others). Unfortunately, neither the Clinton nor Bush administrations picked up on the cues.

Since the beginning of America's war on terror, the violence in the Middle East threatened to intensify, resulting in problems for U.S. foreign policy vis-à-vis Arab and Muslim nation-states. The so-called second *intifada* (Palestinian Uprising) had been simmering for well over a year. By mid-March 2002, the violence had escalated to such an extent that it threatened to erupt in a terrible holocaust. Such a result threatened America's war on terror in several ways. First, politically the Bush administration found itself attempting to balance political forces at home in the form of various special-interest groups (societal inputs) and factions of Congress (governmental inputs). Second, the United States has real strategic interests in the region and another Israeli–Arab war (à la the Six Day War or the Yom Kippur War) put said interests at tremendous risk. Third, Arab—and more broadly, Muslim—support for the war on terror was predicated on the United States brokering peace between the Palestinian Authority and Israel. It could not have been good news for the administration, therefore, as the Israelis pushed forward with their own "war on terror" in mid-March.[67]

About the same time, activities were reportedly picking up in Iraq. As noted, the administration had likely floated a trial balloon vis-à-vis Iraq. The balloon had been popped repeatedly by the closest of U.S. allies in the region, *viz.*, both Egypt and Jordan had made it clear to the United States that any action in Iraq would perforce be subordinate to the Israeli-Palestinian crisis. One had to wonder, then, about an article published on March 15 concerning Iraq. According to reports, an al Qaeda–linked group was reported to be operating in northern Iraq—i.e., in the Kurdish regions presumed to be an area associated with U.S. efforts to topple Saddam. Accordingly, "[a] radical Islamist group—with possible links to Osama bin Laden and Saddam Hussein—[was] growing and threatening the stability of the Kurdish region of northern Iraq." The original source of the information was apparently Kurdish resistance groups.[68]

In better news, U.S. activities in Afghanistan were paying unexpected dividends. One article, talking about documents found in postaction military searches, began by discussing an oath from a presumed al Qaeda fighter to "kill infidels" for the remaining days of his life. Importantly, these searches were turning up information that could be used to prosecute the war on terror. "The oath, found in a house in Kabul used by a Pakistani Islamist group, was part of an extensive paper record that fleeing Taliban and al Qaeda fighters left behind last fall at sites across Afghanistan."

If discovering the documents was a positive development, some of the information contained within them was disturbing. The authors claimed, "Reporters for the *New York Times* collected over 5,000 pages of documents from abandoned safe houses and training camps destroyed by bombs." Among the spate of documents was an indication that some 20,000 "recruits" had passed through the Afghani training camps since 1996, coming from more than twenty countries, including Britain, Somalia, Malaysia, and Iraq. Documents also noted that the scope of al Qaeda's objectives "was the re-establishment of a Caliphate, the era of Islam's establishment in the eight century. The Caliphate 'is the only and best solution to the predicaments and problems from which Muslims suffer today and indubitable cure to the turbulence and internal struggles that plague them. . . .'" Similar documents were discovered by U.S. troops in cave-to-cave searches following the Gardez campaign. The breadth and depth of the terrorist training was truly disturbing in its substance as well as its comprehensiveness.[69]

At least military actions were paying tactical dividends in the form of vital military intelligence gathering. Diplomacy was a thornier matter. As noted earlier, Dick Cheney had already been warned against any sort of military attack on Iraq by two of America's staunchest Arab allies. The vice president landed in Saudi Arabia and quickly learned the Saudis held similar views. In what amounted to a lecture, Crown Prince Abdullah said: "I do not believe it is in the U.S. interest, or the interest of the region, or the world's interest" for the United States to get involved in Iraq. As the vice president continued his Middle East tour, he continued to hear a chorus of voices from America's "friends" in the region that the administration's focus ought to be the Israeli-Palestinian conflict. News was not all bad, however. The Saudi Crown Prince did accept an invitation to visit President Bush at his Texas ranch.[70] Cheney's road show may not have impressed America's Arab allies but it was reported to be causing a siege mentality in Baghdad and to have Saddam "extremely worried"[71] — in retrospect, perhaps the administration's actual rationale for Cheney's trip.

As important as the vice president's trip may have been, there existed numerous other problems with which President Bush needed to concern himself. The vice president was on his own, as it were, as activities in Pakistan overtook coverage of Cheney's trip. Extremists in Islamabad targeted a Protestant Church. Among those killed and/or injured were a U.S. embassy worker and her daughter.[72] Truly, President Musharraf's job balancing his alliance with the United States against his own political factions was dicey. Musharraf's own words clearly showed that he was up against long odds. A couple of months prior to the grenade attack on the church, he publicly chastised the extremism being taught in his nation's religious schools, called *madrassas*.

> "Mosques are being misused for propagating and inciting hatred against each other's sect and beliefs and against the government too," Musharraf warned in a speech in January. "Do we want Pakistan to become a theocratic state? Do we believe that religious education alone is enough for governance, or do we want Pakistan to emerge as a progressive and dynamic Islamic welfare state? The verdict of the masses is in favor of a progressive Islamic state."[73]

The problem was, and continues to be, the documents found in caves, safe houses and training camps indicated that al Qaeda and the Taliban—and by extension, those loyal to one or both groups, of whom there were many in Pakistan—wanted precisely the former.

As noted, it was difficult for the neutral observer to discern how well the campaign was going in the battles in eastern Afghanistan—whether at Tora Bora, Gardez or elsewhere. On the one hand, General Tommy Franks, the man in charge of the war, called the battle to "clear" the Shah-i-Kot valley (part of Operation Anaconda in Paktia province, and the Gardez cave complexes) an "unqualified success." On the other hand, a day or two later, the general commanding troops in Paktia province and eastern Afghanistan (General Franklin "Buster" Hagenbeck) noted that the enemy was "regrouping" and going to great lengths to prepare counteroffensives. At the same time, the British announced that they would be increasing the number of their troops in Afghanistan in response to "*a call for help from the Pentagon*" (italics added), further adding to the confusion.[74]

What was not confusing was the seriousness with which al Qaeda and its recruits took their task of reestablishing a caliphate. The *New York Times* reported that the United States had "discovered a laboratory under construction near Kandahar, Afghanistan, where American officials believe al Qaeda planned to develop biological agents." The same day, the Associated Press filed an article that reported: "Al-Qaida [*sic*] terrorists planned a devastating attack on Americans in Sarajevo after meeting in Bulgaria to identify European targets."[75] Clearly there existed no confusion regarding al Qaeda's goals and views of its enemies.

Recall that Russia quickly embraced America's war on terror. Though it clearly was a calculated decision based on self-interest (*viz.*, Russia's own "Muslim problem"), President Putin was nonetheless one of the first world leaders to call President Bush with his condolences following 9/11. Similarly, Putin was an early visitor to Washington to show Russia's solidarity. In late March, Russia's "Muslim problem" came into high relief. "Some reports say U.S. forces may now be squaring off against the same deadly foe in Afghanistan—hundreds of Chechen fighters who have embraced al Qaeda's global jihad."[76]

Additional bin Laden "sightings" occurred near the end of March. Throughout the U.S. military involvement in Afghanistan, reports have appeared from time to time that a tall Arab was sighted with an entourage of protectors. Some reports would sight bin Laden with his principal advisor, Dr. Ayman al Zawahiri, an Egyptian who had linked up with bin Laden years earlier. (In fact, Zawahiri is frequently characterized as the intellectual foundation for al Qaeda's well-planned operations.) Other sightings had bin Laden with a small group of guards crossing a border—typically the Afghani border with Pakistan but sometimes Afghanistan's border with Iran—spiriting himself back and forth. While still others had him in Iran. Defense Secretary Rumsfeld and other Pentagon officials had begun downplaying bin Laden sightings months earlier. Nonetheless such sightings continued to be reported.[77]

An alert, which caused some consternation in the Italian tourism industry, also was released at the end of March. American citizens could be targeted by extremist groups in four Italian cities on Easter Sunday, according to U.S. officials. The four cities identified were Venice, Florence, Milan—where, as noted previously, al Qaeda linked cells had been discovered earlier—and Verona.[78] Tourism had understandably plummeted since 9/11. Hence Italian concerns with such announcements were easy to understand. The U.S. government, on the other hand, has an obligation to make warnings public when such information becomes available. The two allies' actions demonstrate an interesting phenomenon: A domestic action caused another country (an ally in this case) to behave in some fashion (an external input) to which U.S. foreign policy eventually had to respond: diplomatic hand-holding to smooth things over between the United States and Italy.

On the same day the warning about threats to Americans in Italy was released, Crown Prince Abdullah again made news. The *Washington Post* reported that some Arab nations were balking at Abdullah's initiative. Thus it was important when, the following day, the *Los Angeles Times* published an article that reported: "The Arab world today for the first time collectively offered Israel recognition, security and 'normal relations' in exchange for full withdrawal from Arab land held since 1967 and a 'just solution' for Palestinian refugees." Though understood by all the principals to be only a beginning point of any subsequent negotiations, the White

House welcomed the announcement. Though hardly surprising, bin Laden's apparent denouncement of the Saudi plan did add to the accretion of evidence that he had survived America's massive bombings of eastern Afghanistan.[79]

Just as things were looking up for the administration, what with the news of unanimous consensus on normalization of Arab-Israeli relations, events took a negative turn yet again in Israel. Another suicide bomber destroyed himself, injuring twenty-nine Israelis, in a Tel Aviv Café. The Israeli response was to surround Arafat's compound, destroying much of the compound and surrounding environs. The Israeli siege of Arafat lasted several days beginning another escalation in tensions in the regions as well making things more difficult for the Bush administration's foreign policy. These events occurred just when Secretary Powell—and the United States more generally—was accumulating overtime attempting to ratchet down tensions.[80]

If Vice President Cheney's trip to rally support for U.S. policy vis-à-vis Iraq had received less than spectacular reviews, Bush suffered similarly poor results. As tensions were escalating in the Middle East, President Bush received a diplomatic rebuff from Crown Prince Abdullah of Saudi Arabia. Saddam Hussein announced, apparently attempting to preempt the Bush administration diplomatic efforts to build an anti-Saddam coalition, that he would respect Kuwait's borders henceforth. Previously, Saddam had stubbornly clung to the position that Kuwait was a province of Iraq. But according to Prince Abdullah Saddam was shifting his position. "Abdullah said today that he accepted the Iraqi promise on face value," and, moreover, that "Iraq agreed to accept inspectors as part of the cease-fire agreement that ended the war [in 1991]."[81]

As we have seen, good news follows bad news and vice versa. Accordingly, the following day, the Pakistani government captured a top lieutenant in the al Qaeda organization. In the few months following the 9/11 attacks, Americans had been repeatedly told that the hierarchy, to the extent that one existed in al Qaeda, was as follows. Osama bin Laden was the symbolic leader. His second in command—and many argued the intellectual behind al Qaeda, was Dr. Ayman al Zawahiri, the head of the Egyptian affiliate of al Qaeda, *Islamic Jihad*. And his third-in-command was Muhammud Atef. Atef, however, died in the Tora Bora campaign. Moving into third place with Atef's death was Abu Zubaydah. The Pakistani government, evidently working with American elements (FBI), captured Zubaydah at the end of March. Zubaydah, a 30-year old Palestinian, was known to have taken over as chief of operations for al Qaeda after Muhammud Atef was killed in November.[82] Recall that in February, Zubaydah was reportedly activating sleeper cells across Europe, one of the few concrete indicators that al Qaeda still functioned, if only in a diminished capacity. (As it turned out, Zubaydah would become a recurring "source" of information for various government threat warnings through spring and summer 2002.) Though initially Zubaydah was seen as an unlikely candidate for Musharraf to turn over to the United States—it was thought that such a move would result in street protests—the general released him to American custody within days.[83]

More positive still, North Korea announced that it would resume talks with the United States. Recall that President Bush identified North Korea as one of the three axes of evil in his state-of-the-union speech. Thus, however one wished to interpret the wisdom of the president's axis-of-evil hyperbole, a relatively positive reaction was coming out of North Korea. Taken together with the Saudi vision for Middle East Peace and Arab consensus on it, these clearly were positive developments from the administration's perspective. On the other hand, Arab leaders were arguing that Palestinian violence against Israeli targets was distinguishable from "terrorism" as it involved a people being "occupied." The president's foreign-policy team was experiencing simultaneous successes and setbacks. Perhaps under the circumstances, that is as much as could be expected.[84]

Foreign policy, in fact, is notoriously fickle: It is always the situation that a mix of positive and negative outcomes and developments exist at a given time. To cite an example, recall one of President Reagan's foreign-policy "victories": saving the American medical students in Grenada. Just one week earlier, some 280 U.S. Marines had lost their lives in a tragic foreign-policy fiasco in Lebanon. President Bush was finding out the same truism: Positive news on one front typically accompanies negative on another. It therefore came as no surprise that with all the activities and chaos in the Middle East, the administration made the decision to hold off on its plans to introduce evidence of Iraq's malfeasance at the UN.[85] The Bush team had earlier made public their intention to present evidence to the Security Council that would prove Saddam had active weapons-of-mass-destruction programs underway.

As the administration struggled to keep Saddam Hussein in its sights despite Arab resistance, Saddam launched another preemptive action. The Bush administration had recently cited the "Afghanistan" model as a possibility for Iraq, *viz.,* U.S. aid to existing insurgents in situ. In Iraq, these insurgents consisted principally of Kurds in the north and Shia Muslims in the south. "An assassination attempt against a leading pro-Kurdish leader in northern Iraq underscores the risk that the United States and its allies are taking *as they weigh options to topple . . . Saddam Hussein*" (italics added). The entire affair was eerily reminiscent of some of bin Laden's men, posing as journalists, assassinating a key leader of the Northern Alliance in Afghanistan. Interestingly, the story in the *Monitor* quoted William Safire, a long-time Saddam baiter and a *New York Times* columnist: "One surviving attacker, now in Kurdish custody, according to . . . William Safire . . . said a cadre of '60 Islamic terrorists, trained in Afghanistan by Osama bin Laden were assigned to infiltrate northern Iraq and kill.'"[86] Links between al Qaeda and Saddam, as noted, were being made in the media and by the administration.

Multiple threats and various government warnings had become de rigeur since 9/11 and in particular since the Homeland Security Director had released his color-coded schemata. Among the warnings, Americans had come to worry about bridges in California, nuclear power plants nation wide, dust-crop airplanes, and any number of biological, chemical and other nuclear threats. In mid-April a new threat was identified: the so-called dirty bomb (that is, a conventional bomb packed with radiological materials). Such a device was presumed to be far simpler to obtain and fabricate than a true nuclear device and, therefore, more realistically within the means of al Qaeda and like-minded organizations.[87] Regrettably, this was only the beginning of many such threats over ensuing months.

Just days after this new threat became common parlance in the U.S. vocabulary, Americans began to learn of problems with their alliance partners in Afghanistan. For example, one piece reported: "Fierce fighting erupted Friday just west of Kabul between two rival militias," said to be competing for territory around the capital of Afghanistan. Another reported "Afghan [Interim] Defense Minister Mohammed Fahim was nearly killed by an explosion in the Pashtun tribal area near Jalalabad earlier this week. . . ." The U.S.-sponsored coalition appeared to be fraying at the edges.[88]

Meanwhile, the personification of President Bush's "evildoers," namely bin Laden, released another video to *Al Jazeera* and other Arab media outlets with his number-two man, Dr. Ayman al Zawahiri, seeming to taunt the administration. While the Bush administration had been somewhat coy about whether bin Laden was alive or dead, once this video was released the administration publicly "concluded" that bin Laden had escaped the Tora Bora bombings.[89] On a more positive note, the symbolic leader of Afghanistan, King Zahir Shah, finally returned to his country after many false starts. The king had begun to return to Afghanistan several times but had been discouraged by the United States, due principally to the chaos on the ground.[90] The day after the king returned, an interesting and controversial poll was published suggesting that Europeans saw the United States as being at fault for most of the difficulties in the Middle East. "People in Europe, while sympathetic to recent American efforts in the Middle East, strongly feel that the United States has not done enough to bring about a peace settlement, according to coordinated polls in Britain, France, Germany, and Italy." Furthermore, a "key reason for the European unhappiness appears to be much greater sympathy for the Palestinians than found in the United States."[91]

Yasser Arafat was holed up in his Ramallah compound and — due partly to substantial pressure from Israel, the United States, and others — he finally made a speech in English and Arabic in which he denounced terrorism against Israeli noncombatants. In an Associated Press translation, Arafat was quoted as expressing "deep condemnation for all terrorists activities," by any group or state. Arafat's *al Aqsa* brigade had been implicated in several suicide attacks in Israeli cities. Thus Arafat managed to condemn his own group, other groups over which he may have had little control, and Israel. This language came in the first paragraph. In the third paragraph, Arafat condemned "all attacks targeting civilians from both sides. . . ." The remaining four paragraphs basically condemned Israel for its past behavior and asked for U.S. and international help in resolving the crisis.[92]

While his screed against Israel was suspect, Arafat's statement nonetheless was a condition that Israel and the United States had demanded for some time. The issue turned on Arafat's reported propensity for issuing statements in English denouncing terrorism, then making statements in Arabic in which he tacitly gave terrorism his blessing. In this case, making the statement in Arabic, unambiguously denouncing terrorism was therefore critical to lessening tensions in the region. The U.S. government proclaimed victory. However, one of its strongest Arab allies, Saudi Arabia, used the occasion to "warn" the administration of "grave consequences" if the United States did not soon rein in Israeli action, read occupation.[93]

Meanwhile, U.S. officials were congratulating themselves for getting Arafat's speech accomplished. The Saudis were both warning and reassuring the United States that Arafat was attempting to save his own skin as well as any semblance of a peace process. As the complex diplomatic dance occurred over Middle East politics, news broke of additional terrorist activities in Southeast Asia, hardly a positive development for the administration:

> Three Southeast Asian countries—Malaysia, the Philippines and Indonesia—yesterday stepped up the crackdown on militancy as part of ongoing sweeps against terrorism in the region.
>
> The biggest operation was in Malaysia, where 14 suspected members of the Jemaah Islamiah (JI) were arrested in separate raids, which also turned up a map of the country's largest port.[94]

As news in parts of Southeast Asia reminded the administration and the public that the global-terrorist hydra was ubiquitous indeed, a story appeared in the *Washington Post* that both indicated possible success in the war on terrorism while recalling Vietnam-era stories of what, in today's lexicon, has become known as "mission creep":

> Covert U.S. military units have been conducting reconnaissance operations in Pakistan in recent weeks and participated in attacks on suspected al Qaeda hideouts there, opening a new front in a shadowy war being waged by the United States along the mountainous Afghan–Pakistan border, according to military officials.

Reminiscent of Vietnam:

> "We have to get them to shoot at us," said one soldier. It is frustrating, one official said, because this tactic effectively means that al Qaeda "has the offensive." Also, the al Qaeda attacks are frequently from within larger groups of bystanders on the streets of villages and towns . . . making the decision to counterattack difficult, officials said. "The decision to shoot or not is one of the toughest decisions," said one source.
>
> The enemy fighters tend to have sophisticated communications equipment and "better survival gear than we have," said one knowledgeable source. Some of the fighters have carried U.S. equipment that apparently was captured in last month's battle in the Shahikot Valley.
>
> The al Qaeda members have impressed their American opponents with their military skills, most notably an ability to observe U.S. combat techniques and adjust accordingly.[95]

But this was not Vietnam; nor was it that era. That same day, a report came out of Egypt that young Egyptians were hearing and fulfilling the call of martyrdom. Young Egyptians were being "celebrated in Egypt as the first in a new line of Arab martyrs to the Palestinian cause."[96] No longer could Americans or Westerners take comfort in their beliefs that a few radical *Jihadists* comprised America's foreign-policy threats. Clearly, the problem was more widespread than many previously believed; rather, it was truly the global-terrorist hydra.

Simultaneously, more disturbing news originated in Tunisia, a former French colony and predominantly Muslim. Reports never clearly identified the attack as al Qaeda directed, but the implication was clear. As the *Monitor* reported, while "the terror attack on North Africa's oldest synagogue, which killed seventeen people earlier this month, has few of the markings of recent al Qaeda strikes," there was at least minimal indication of al Qaeda's complicity. "[I]t is the taking back of Arab homelands, an act that some extremists with al Qaeda leanings refer to as the 'purification of Islamic lands,' something Ayman al Zawahiri, leader of the Egyptian *Jihad* terror organization and Osama bin Laden's right hand man," has repeatedly cited as a goal.[97]

As discussed earlier, Southeast Asia was a region in which some al Qaeda–linked activities were increasingly appearing. In fact, some reports had al Qaeda fleeing to Southeast Asia to set up base camps in which to rest and regroup. In June, Deputy Defense Secretary Paul Wolfowitz made a whirlwind trip to the Philippines to shore up support for America's mission there; in fact, he reportedly mentioned that he favored expanding activities against al Qaeda–linked terrorists in the region. In a bit of a surprise, Nepal was similarly reported in early May as having an insurgency, whose members were "Maoists" according to Nepalese officials.[98] There was no indication that they were al Qaeda related, or even Islamic, but the timing added to the general apprehension that the war on terror was growing. It therefore provided some comfort when later in the month a report was published indicating that the United States would soon be leaving the Philippines.[99]

Around the same time, Russia formally joined in the U.S. anti-terror campaign. As reported, Russia had its own reasons—*viz.*, Muslim separatists in Chechnya—for joining America's war on terror. Late in May 2002, the *Monitor* reported a formal partnership.[100] Initially the relationship was hailed as an indication of the Bush foreign-policy team's deftness in coalition building and general political acumen. By June and July, Bush's presumed deftness would be more carefully scrutinized by various print media.

One question that arose in the spring was whether and to what extent the U.S. government had been successful in disrupting al Qaeda's operations. After all, very few additional attempts to attack the United States or its assets had occurred. FBI Director Robert Mueller and others had announced that some six or so attempts had been thwarted but gave few details about the nature of the alleged attempts. Richard C. Reid, the so-called shoe bomber, was well known and had been linked to al Qaeda but his attack seemed quite amateurish by comparison with the planning that went into the 1998 embassy bombings and/or the *Cole* attack and 9/11.

In June, however, another seemingly amateurish operation was "thwarted" by the federal government. Jose Padilla, supposedly an al Qaeda recruit, was arrested in Chicago in May. The *Washington Post* reported: "The American citizen suspected of plotting to detonate a *radioactive bomb* on U.S. soil met in late March with senior al Qaeda officials, who sent him to scout possible U.S. sites for attacks with 'dirty bombs' or conventional explosives" (italics added). Reportedly, information from Abu Zubaydah led U.S. authorities to monitor Padilla. Beyond the obviously troubling aspect of the case—*viz.*, plotting to explode a radiological bomb—was the fact that he was an American citizen. The implication was that al Qaeda was now finding ways around the post-9/11 tightened security, that is, using Americans with American passports. Padilla, known as Abdullah al Muhajir, once arrested was classified as an "enemy combatant," despite his American citizenship and eventually ended up in a military brig without access to a lawyer.[101] The Padilla affair lent credibility to the Reid–al Qaeda links given the amateurish nature of both operations. An optimist could plausibly argue that, taken together, al Qaeda was having to scrape the bottom of the barrel—that is, the administration's war on terrorism was succeeding. The same article discussed another apparent al Qaeda operation that had been prevented. Al Qaeda operatives were captured in Morocco. "In a separate development, officials in Morocco said yesterday that they have arrested three Saudi nationals who were planning attacks on U.S. and British warships in the Straits of Gibraltar" (ibid.). Subsequent reports noted that "interrogations of the three men, who appeared briefly in court in Morocco on Friday but have not made public statements, have created what officials describe as a fuller understanding of al Qaeda's strategy since its expulsion from Afghanistan, and provided clues about the organization's persistent, though impaired, vitality." Among other things, the report claimed "bin Laden's instructions were behind a string of recent attacks, including Friday's bombing at the U.S. Consulate in Karachi, Pakistan." It identified one Saudi national, Zuher Hilal Mohamed al Tbaiti, married to a Moroccan wife, whom authorities said "was in the first phase of a three-step operation aimed at launching suicide attacks on NATO ships in the strait."[102]

Another question circulating (discussed in societal inputs in Chapter 3) was just how good an ally Pakistan was proving. Some op-ed pieces questioned, effectively, whether getting in bed with Musharraf was a worthwhile endeavor. Musharraf was surely aware of the debates about him in America. On the positive side, Musharraf had cracked down on some of the more radical Islamic groups in Pakistan. He had also helped on the Pearl investigation and allowed the FBI to enter Pakistan to capture high-level al Qaeda operatives wanted by the United States. And in contrast to the punditocracy's predictions, he turned over Zubaydah to American officials. In mid-June his forces captured Americans who were associated with al Qaeda and allowed the United States to interrogate them. Pakistani officials said that "some of those detained appear[ed] to be Westerners who have been drawn to militant Islam." As it happened, some of the Americans had studied at the same *madrassa* at which John Walker Lindh—the "American Taliban"—had studied just prior to going to Afghanistan.[103] It is difficult to correlate these actions with debates in the United

States but it is not beyond the realm of plausibility that Musharraf took dramatic actions, at least partly, to dampen media criticisms in the United States. He was certainly aware of discussions in the West regarding his *bona fides*. In any event, the following day a car loaded with explosives was parked near the American consulate and detonated,[104] demonstrating again that Musharraf exercised limited control over what goes on in Pakistan. Just two weeks later, Musharraf would be accused of trying to grab power extraconstitutionally, making it exceptionally confusing to assess Musharraf's control and efficacy as an ally.[105]

Meanwhile, in Afghanistan things were looking better. The *loya jirga*—a grand council of elders from the various ethnic factions that had been promised when the interim government that had been cobbled together months earlier in Germany—finally came to fruition. Hamid Karzai, the interim leader, whom the United States had supported, was elected in an overwhelming fashion to be the "transitional head of state" for the next eighteen to twenty-four months. He received 1,295 out of 1,575 votes.

> Karzai's election by delegates from all over Afghanistan begins a new phase of the process that Afghans and foreign governments hope will bring representative government to a land beset by war and ruled by Soviet proxies and Islamic clerics for more than two decades.[106]

The *Washington Post* spoke in relatively glowing terms and asserted the *loya jirga* was clearly a positive development, though it would soon become clouded somewhat by controversy with allegations of representatives being pressured to vote for Karzai.[107]

If positive momentum was building in Afghanistan coupled with some positive developments in Pakistan, the mess in the Middle East continued to plague the U.S.-led war on terrorism. After months of an action-reaction dynamic between Palestinians and Israelis and of Arafat's reticence to make more than nominal positive announcements that might further the peace effort, he finally relented. "Yasser Arafat convened his new cabinet today, saying he will soon set a date for elections and calling for an end to violence so that peace can take hold." He also "reiterated his commitment to peacemaking, despite more than 20 months of bloodshed in a Palestinian uprising against Israeli occupation." It would be only twelve days later that he would defiantly suggest that the elections were a foregone conclusion and that he would remain the leader of the Palestinian people for the foreseeable future.[108]

A relatively disturbing piece was published in mid-June describing the regrouping of al Qaeda. The military campaign had indeed been successful insofar as it caught al Qaeda members who were unable to escape Afghanistan. However, several *had* escaped. "A group of midlevel operatives has assumed a more prominent role in al Qaeda and is working in tandem with Middle Eastern extremists across the Islamic world." The article linked the American Consulate bombing to their work. According to the authors, "Internet traffic among al Qaeda followers indicates that elements of the network have regrouped—some in remote sanctuaries in Pakistan, government officials said." It also cited a classified investigation—apparently leaked to the authors—in which the FBI and CIA concluded that the U.S.-led war had "failed to diminish the threat to the United States." Rather, it had dispersed what was already a loose coalition of groups over a larger geographic area, arguably making the war effort more difficult.[109]

As was the case with Musharraf, the Saudi royal family's commitment to the war on terror had been discussed, principally on the op-ed pages. It had been alleged, for instance, that the Saudis had been reluctant to share information with the United States that would allow the United States to freeze terrorists' assets. The Saudis had of course denied the accusations. On June 18, the *New York Times* reported: "Saudi Arabia, reversing months of denials that any members of al Qaeda might be lurking in the kingdom, announced today that it had arrested members of the terrorist network that it believes tried to shoot down a U.S. military aircraft with a shoulder-fired missile." Yet another report had Syria—which had been very quiet to date—reportedly interrogating a key player in the 9/11 attacks. Mysteriously, the man the Syrians had was an ethnic Syrian of German citizenship whom the German government thought America had been holding. It had caused a bit of a diplomatic row earlier in the month.[110]

Alas, just when it looked like the administration had momentum on its side again, the Middle East reignited. A twenty-two-year-old Palestinian from Nablus detonated himself on a Jerusalem bus killing nineteen Israelis. Israel's response was as swift as it was predictable. Israeli Defense Forces reseized specific Palestinian towns and villages, including Jenin, the town that had been the topic of much controversy and where it was alleged the Israelis had committed a massacre. The Palestinian suicide bomber and the Israeli reaction started another cycle of action-reaction bloodletting.[111]

Further confirmation appeared that bin Laden and his top lieutenant, Dr. Ayman al Zawahiri, had survived the various major bombing campaigns in which the United States had hoped it had killed one or both of them. The Arab news channel, *Al Jazeera*, aired an audiotape in which a "bin Laden spokesman," Abu Ghaith, announced that both were alive and well and planning new attacks on America. Ghaith noted that al Qaeda would "choose the right time, place and method" for the next series of attacks. Another report confirmed that bin Laden had been behind the Tunis blast where a synagogue had been essentially rammed with a tanker truck, killing seventeen persons.[112]

In mid-2002, a spate of new information regarding the global-terrorist hydra appeared. On June 26, 2002, the *Washington Post* published a story about "cyber" attacks by terrorists. The U.S. military found—some months earlier—a home in Afghanistan with documentation that informed U.S. analysts that al Qaeda had devoted resources to "hacking" into America's infrastructure that had become dependent upon the Internet. On the same day, CNN cited a government report that four suspects had been arrested at a U.S. naval base "taking pictures" of U.S. naval ships.[113] The reader may recall that late June 2002 was a controversial time from a domestic-policy standpoint: the use of "under God" in the pledge of allegiance, school vouchers, Western fires rampaging, Enron followed by WorldCom and Global Crossing crashing, and so forth. Additionally, a PEW Foundation poll was released showing continued high support for President Bush, though interestingly, less confidence in his ability to handle U.S. economic issues. Moreover, the *Arab Human Development Report 2002* warned that "[p]er capita income growth has shrunk in the last 20 years to a level just above that of sub-Saharan Africa. Productivity is declining. Research and development are weak or nonexistent. Science and technology are dormant." While the report did not correlate the "stagnation" to terrorism, the implication was clear: Some 280 million Arabs were feeling dispossessed and disaffected and there were millions of angry Arab youth out there with little for which to hope or live.[114] Further, said youth were presumably ripe for recruitment by al Qaeda and others.

NOTES

1. Times and descriptions for the following 9/11 narrative come from the *Los Angeles Times*, 12 September 2001, pp. A1–A28, *ad passim*, as well as the Brookings Institution, Foreign Policy Studies (hereafter Brookings Chronology): http://www.brook.edu/dybdocroot/fp/projects/terrorism/chronology.htm.
2. President George W. Bush, Remarks at National Day of Prayer and Remembrance, 14 September 2001. The National Cathedral, Washington, D.C.
3. President George W. Bush, Address to a Joint Session of Congress and the American People, 20 September 2001, United States Capitol, Washington, D.C.
4. Charles F. Hermann, "International Crisis as a Situational Variable," in *International Politics and Foreign Policy*, ed. James Rosenau (New York: Free Press, 1969), p. 414. Also Charles F. Hermann, *Crises in Foreign Policy* (New York: Bobbs-Merrill, 1969).
5. Ahmed Rashid, *Taliban: Military Islam, Oil and Fundamentalism in Central Asia* (New Haven, CT: Yale University Press, 2000).
6. Ibid.
7. Richard C. Paddock, "Singapore Says Terror Ring Planned Attacks on Americans," *Los Angeles Times*, 12 January 2001.
8. Ibid. Also see Bradley Graham, "Afghan Tape Helped Lead to Singapore Terror Cell," *Washington Post*, 12 January 2002, p. A-1.
9. Raymond Bonner and Jane Perlez, "Finding a Tepid Ally in the War on Terror, U.S. Presses Indonesia to Arrest 2 Clerics," *New York Times*, 17 February 2002. There is some confusion over the Indonesian cleric. In a subsequent story, the *Times* quoted Singaporean authorities identifying Abu Bakar Bashir, as the "ideological leader of *Jamaah Islamiah*." Richard C. Paddock, "Southeast Asian Terror Exhibits al Qaeda Traits," *Los Angeles Times*, 3 March 2002.
10. Paddock, "Singapore Says Terror Ring Planned Attacks on Americans"; Rajiv Chandrasekaran, "Al Qaeda Feared to Be Lurking in Indonesia," *Washington Post*, 11 January 2001, p. 1.
11. Bob Drogin, "Missiles Not Biggest Threat, Report Says," *Los Angeles Times*, 12 January 2002.
12. Paul Richter, "U.S. Shift Clouds Arms Deal," *Los Angeles Times*, 13 January 2002.
13. Eric Lichtblau and Josh Meyer, "U.S. Seeks Public's Help in Search for 5 from al Qaeda," *Los Angeles Times*, 18 January 2002.
14. Raju Gopalakrishnan, "Facing Criticism, Philippines Backtracks on U.S. Troops," Reuters, 18 January 2002.
15. Michael R. Gordon, "As Threat Eases, U.S. Still Sees Peril in India-Pakistan Buildup," *New York Times*, January 2002.
16. Nicholas Blanford, "Palestinian Ties to Iran, Hizbullah Look Firmer," *Christian Science Monitor*, 18 January 2002.
17. Eric Pianin and Bob Woodward, "Terror Concerns of U.S. Extend to Asia: Arrests in Singapore and Malaysia Cited," *Washington Post*, 18 January 2002, p. A-18. Also, "The Present Danger," *Washington Post*, 19 January 2002, p. A-26. Richard C. Paddock, "Asia Group Broken Up Last Month Had al Qaeda Training, Officials Allege." *Los Angeles Times*, 18 January 2002.

18. David B. Ottaway and Robert G. Kaiser, "Military Presence Seen as Political Liability in Arab World," *Washington Post*, 18 January 2002, p. A-1. Also see Colbert I. King, "Saudi Arabia's Apartheid," *Washington Post*, 19 January 2002, p. A-27.
19. Judy Pasternak and Stephen Braun, "Emirates Looked Other Way while al Qaeda Funds Flowed," *Los Angeles Times*, 20 January 2002.
20. Walter Pincus, "Al Qaeda Leader Talked of Plot against U.S. Embassy," *Washington Post*, 23 January 2002, p. A-9.
21. Philip Bennett and Steve Coll, "Prince Reaffirms Saudi–U.S. Alliance," *Washington Post*, 29 January 2002, p. A-1.
22. Richard C. Paddock and Bob Drogin, "A Terror Network Unraveled in Singapore," *Los Angeles Times*, 20 January 2002, Also see Henry Chu, "China Says Radicals Led Attacks and Colluded with Bin Laden," *Los Angeles Times*, 22 January 2002.
23. Paul Watson, "Deadly Shooting in Calcutta May Be Linked to al Qaeda," *Los Angeles Times*, 23 January 2002; Raymond Bonner and Jane Perlez, "Asian Terror: Al Qaeda Seeks Niche in Indonesia, Officials Fear," *New York Times*, 23 January 2002; and Dan Murphy, "'Activated' Asian Terror Web Busted," *Christian Science Monitor*, 23 January 2002, pp. 1, 4.
24. Paul Blustein, "Unrest a Chief Product of Arab Economics," *Washington Post*, 26 January 2002, p. A-1.
25. Terry McDermott, "A Perfect Soldier," *Los Angeles Times*, 27 January 2002, p. A-1; Michael Theodoulou, "Arab Press Finds Roots of Terrorism Closer to Home," *Christian Science Monitor*, 28 January 2002, p. 7.
26. Josh Meyer and Aaron Zitner, "Troops Uncovered Diagrams for Major U.S. Targets, Bush Says," *Los Angeles Times*, 30 January 2002.
27. Robert Burns, "Rumsfeld Warns of Deadlier Threats," *Los Angeles Times*, 31 January 2002.
28. Eric Lichtblau, "Terrorists Noted Flaws in Security, Report Says," *Los Angeles Times*, 1 February 2002.
29. John Lumpkin, "CIA: Al Qaeda Poses Largest Threat to U.S.," *Los Angles Times*, 6 February 2002. Also, David Stout, "C.I.A. Director Defends Agency and Warns of al Qaeda Threat," *New York Times*, 6 February 2002.
30. Barry Wain, "A Questionable Strategy," *Far Eastern Economic Review*, 31 January 2002.
31. Philip Smucker, "After the War, Fighting Begins," *Christian Science Monitor*, 1 February 2002, p. 6.
32. John Pomfret, "China Sees Interests Tied to U.S.," *Washington Post*, 2 February 2002, p. A-1.
33. Reuters, "War on Terror Should Not Include Iraq, Russia Tells U.S.," 3 February 2002.
34. Thomas E. Ricks, "European Security Leaders Alarmed by Bush's Stance," *Washington Post*, 3 February 2002, p. A-16.
35. James Risen and Judith Miller, "Bin Laden's Trail Is Lost, but Officials Suspect He Is Alive," *New York Times*, 4 February 2002; Esther Schrader, "Iran Helped al Qaeda and Taliban Flee, Rumsfeld Says," *Los Angeles Times*, 4 February 2002.
36. Barbara Demick, "Is N. Korean Threat Overstated?" *Los Angeles Times*, 6 February 2002; Nicolas Blanford, "Emboldened by U.S. Jibes, Hizbullah Prepares for War," *Christian Science Monitor*, 8 February 2002, p. 7.
37. Jane Perlez, "Botched Siege under Scrutiny in Philippines," *New York Times*, 9 February 2002; Barry Bearak, "Unknown Toll in the Fog of War," *New York Times*, 10 February 2002.
38. Robert G. Kaiser and David B. Ottaway, "Saudi Leader's Anger Revealed Shaky Ties," *Washington Post*, 10 February 2002, p. A-1.
39. Philip Shenon and James Risen, "Qaeda Deputy Reported to Plan New Attacks," *New York Times*, 14 February 2002.
40. Robin Wright, Mark Magnier, and Barbara Demick, "Bush Puts Asia Back at Top of Agenda," *Los Angeles Times*, 17 February 2002.
41. Valerie Reitman and David Zucchino, "Slaying of Afghan Minister Shakes Faith in Government, *Los Angeles Times*, 17 February 2002; Pamela Constable, "Karzai's Charges Raise Doubts," *Washington Post*, 17 February 2002, p. A-16.
42. Thomas Friedman, "An Intriguing Signal from the Saudi Crown Prince," *New York Times*, 17 February 2002.
43. Barbara Demick, "Visit Stirring up Anti-Americanism," *Los Angeles Times*, 18 February 2002.
44. John Ward Anderson, "Iranian Courts Target Reformist Legislators," *Washington Post*, 18 February 2002, p. A-19.

45. Robin Wright and Mark Magnier, "Bush Is Dogged by 'Axis of Evil' in Visit to Japan," *Los Angeles Times*, 19 February 2002.
46. Mike Allen and Clay Chandler, "Bush Says U.S. Will Pursue Campaign," *Washington Post*, 19 February 2002, p. A-1.
47. Douglas Jehl, "Pakistan Cutting Its Spy Unit's Ties to Some Militants," *New York Times*, 20 February 2002.
48. Edwin Chen and Henry Chu, "U.S. and China to Broaden Contacts," *Los Angeles Times*, 21 February 2002; Also, Elisabeth Bumiller, "Jiang Is to Visit the U.S. in October," *New York Times*, 21 February 2002.
49. Zahid Hussain, "Musharraf Wants Pearl Killers Caught," *Los Angeles Times*, 22 February 2002.
50. Scott Baldauf, "Musharraf Takes on Spy Agency," *Christian Science Monitor*, 22 February 2002; John Ward Anderson and Peter Baker, "Killers Likely Never Intended to Free Pearl," *Washington Post*, 23 February 2002, p. A-16.
51. Nicole Winfield, "Al Qaeda Leader Convicted in Italy," *Associated Press*, 22 February 2002.
52. Richard Bourdreaux, "Italy Convicts 4 Linked to al Qaeda," *Los Angeles Times*, 23 February 2002.
53. Paul Richter, "U.S. Debating Wider Assault on Columbian Rebels," *Los Angeles Times*, 23 February 2002.
54. *Canadian Press*, "Bin Laden and Mullah Omar Are Still Alive, Says Al-Qaida-Linked Organization," 19 February 2002.
55. John Diamond, "Al Qaeda Menace Believed Dispersing," *Chicago Tribune*, 20 February 2002.
56. Parisa Hafezi, "Karzai Pledges Good Relations with 'Brother' Iran," Reuters, 24 February 2002, http://reuters.co.uk/news_article.jtml?type=worldnews.&storyID=1223581.
57. Paul Watson and Sidhartha Barua, "Somalian Links Seen to al Qaeda," *Los Angeles Times*, 25 February 2002.
58. Alissa J. Rubin and David Zucchino, "Sense of Urgency Grows over Afghan Security," *Los Angeles Times*, 25 February 2002, Melinda Henneberger, "Rome Embassy May Have Been Bomb Target," *New York Times*, 24 February 2002; Nicolas Colomgant, "Mali's Muslims Steer Back to Spiritual Roots," *Christian Science Monitor*, 26 February 2002; Fred Weir, "A New Terror-War Front," *Christian Science Monitor*, 26 February 2002.
59. Peter Finn, "Macedonian Police Kill 7 Suspected Terror Cells," *Washington Post*, 3 March 2002, p. A-1.
60. Alissa J. Rubin, "U.S. Bombers Pound al Qaeda Mountain Lair," *Los Angeles Times*, 4 March 2002; John Hendren, "U.S. Took Time for This Afghan Raid," *Los Angeles Times*, 4 March 2002; Ann Scott Tyson, "U.S., Allies in a Riskier Kind of War," *Christian Science Monitor*, 5 March 2002; Michael R. Gordon, "No Easy Victory Is Seen in Fierce Strategy," *New York Times*, 5 March 2002; John Hendren and John Daniszewski, "Navy SEAL Was Captured and Killed," *Los Angeles Times*, 6 March 2002.
61. James Risen and David Johnston, "Intercepted al Qaeda E-Mail Is Said to Hint at Regrouping," *New York Times*, 6 March 2002; Bradley Graham and Vernon Loeb, "U.S. Forces Gain Edge in Afghan Attack," *Washington Post*, 6 March 2002, p. A-1. Also see Rone Tempest and Rone Daniszewski, "U.S. Forces Gain Ground in Afghan Mountain Battle," *Los Angeles Times*, 7 March 2002; Barry Bearak, "Kabul Rushes 1,000 More Men to Join G.I's on Battle's Sixth Day," *New York Times*, 8 March 2002.
62. Geoffrey Mohan and Esther Schrader, "Back at Base, U.S. Troops Say Afghans Failed Them," *Los Angeles Times*, 11 March 2002.
63. Reuters, "Violence Flares in India Kashmir," 5 March 2002. William Orme, "U.S. Alleges Iraq's Army Is Rebuilding," *Los Angeles Times*, 7 March 2002.
64. Alan Spires, "Jordan Advises U.S. against a Military Campaign in Iraq," *Washington Post*, 13 March 2002, p. A-24.
65. Alan Sipress, "Cheney Meets with Yemeni President," *Washington Post*, 14 March 2002.
66. Eric Malnic, William C. Rempel, and Ricardo Alonso-Zaldivar, "EgyptAir Co-Pilot Caused '99 Jet Crash, NTSB to Say," *Los Angeles Times*, 15 March 2002.
67. Mary Curtius, "Violence Unabated Amid U.S. Envoy's Mideast Visit Conflict," *Los Angeles Times*, 15 March 2002.
68. Catherine Taylor, "Taliban-Style Group Grows in Iraq," *Christian Science Monitor*, 15 March 2002.
69. David Rhode and C. J. Chivers, "Al Qaeda's Grocery List and Manuals of Killing," *New York Times*, 17 March 2002. Also see C. J. Chivers and David Rhode, "Afghan Camps Turn out Holy War Guerrillas and Terrorists," *New York Times*, 18 March 2002.

70. The quote is from Michael R. Gordon, "Saudis Warning against Attack by U.S. on Iraq," *New York Times*, 17 March 2002. Also see Alan Spires, "Saudis Rebuff U.S. Plan to Confront Iraq," *Washington Post*, 17 March 2002, p. A-22. James Gerstenzang, "Cheney Finds Israeli Issue Trumps Iraq," *Los Angeles Times*, 18 March 2002. The report of the Saudis accepting Bush's invitation comes from Reuters, "Saudi Prince Accepts Bush Invitation after Snub," 17 March 2002.

71. Scott Peterson, "An Uneasy Iraq Awaits U.S. Move," *Christian Science Monitor*, 25 March 2002.

72. Craig Pyes and Geoffrey Mohan, "Grenade Attack in Pakistan Kills Two Americans," *Los Angeles Times*, 18 March 2002.

73. Geoffrey Mohan, "Radical School Reform," *Los Angeles Times*, 23 March 2002.

74. General Tommy Franks quoted in Paul Haven, "As Operation Anaconda Winds Up, War Goes On," Associated Press, 18 March 2002. Also John Burns, "U.S. Commander Predicts End to Afghan Battle but Not to War," *New York Times*, 18 March 2002. The article in which the Pentagon was cited as asking for British help is T. R. Reid, "Britain Set to Bulk Up Its Afghan Deployment," *Washington Post*, 19 March 2002, p. A-16. General Hagenbeck's comments are in Associated Press, "U.S. General Says Enemy Is Regrouping," *Los Angeles Times*, 20 March 2002.

75. The anthrax lab was reported in Michael R. Gordon, "U.S. Says It Found al Qaeda Lab Being Built to Produce Anthrax," *New York Times*, 23 March 2002; Associated Press, "Al Qaeda Plot Revealed in Sarajevo," *New York Times*, 23 March 2002.

76. Fred Weir, "Chechnya's Warrior Tradition," *Christian Science Monitor*, 26 March 2002.

77. Ilene R. Prusher, "Local Afghan Commander Says Bin Laden and His No. 2 Have Been in the Khost Area," *Christian Science Monitor*, 26 March 2002.

78. Associated Press, "U.S. Citizens Warned of Threats in Italy," *Los Angeles Times*, 27 March 2002. The Italian government's response in Associated Press, "Italy Says Warnings Unfounded," *Los Angeles Times*, 29 March 2002.

79. Howard Schneider, "Abdullah Appeals for Broad Mideast Peace," *Washington Post*, 27 March 2002. The following day this story was filed: Sam F. Ghattas, "Arab Leaders Endorse Peace Plan," *Los Angeles Times*, 28 March 2002. Bin Laden's denouncement in "Purported bin Laden E-Mail Attacks Saudi Plan for Mideast," Reuters, 28 March 2002, in *Washington Post*, p. A-22.

80. Jason Keyser, "Bombing Injures 29 in Tel Aviv," *Los Angeles Times*, 30 March 2002, Israel's escalation found in Tracy Wilkinson, "Israel Attacks Arafat Compound," *Los Angeles Times*, 29 March 2002. Also Peter Grier, "Mideast Fractures Cause Global Stress," *Christian Science Monitor*, 29 March 2002.

81. Howard Schneider, "Saudi Puts Faith in Iraqi Pledge" *Washington Post*, 30 March 2002, p. A-12.

82. Michael R. Gordon, "A Top al Qaeda Commander Believed Seized in Pakistan," *New York Times*, 31 March 2002.

83. John J. Lumpkin, "Pakistan Hands over Senior al Qaeda," *Los Angeles Times*, 1 April 2002.

84. Soo-Jenong Lee, "N. Korea Resumes Talks with U.S.," *Los Angeles Times*, 8 April 2002; Howard Schneider, "Arab Ministers Urge Action against Israel," *Washington Post*, 7 April 2002, p. A-19.

85. Colum Lynch, "U.S. Postpones Plans to Reveal Findings on Iraq," *Washington Post*, 7 April 2002, p. A-22.

86. Scott Peterson, "U.S. vs. Iraq: Saddam May Have Fired the First Shot," *Christian Science Monitor*, 9 April 2002.

87. Abraham McLaughlin, "East Theft," *Christian Science Monitor*, 10 April 2002.

88. Respectively, Niko Price, "Rival Militias Battle outside Kabul," *Los Angeles Times*, 12 April 2002; Lutfullah Marshal and Philip Smucker, "An Assassination Attempt This Week Highlights a Divide between Pashtuns and the Northern Alliance," *Christian Science Monitor*, 12 April 2002.

89. Howard Schneider and Walter Pincus, "Bin Laden Video Includes Sept. 11 Praise," *Washington Post*, 16 April 2002, p. A-12. The administration's conclusion of bin Laden being alive is in Barton Gellman and Thomas E. Ricks, "U.S. Concludes Bin Laden Escaped at Tora Bora Fight," *Washington Post*, 17 April 2002, p. A-1.

90. Lutfullah Marshal and Philip Smucker, "The Afghan King Returned to Kabul Yesterday, while near Kandahar, An Errant Bomb Killed Four Canadian Troops," *Christian Science Monitor*, 19 April 2002.

91. Adam Clymer, "European Poll Faults U.S. for Its Policy in the Mideast," *New York Times*, 19 April 2002.

92. Associated Press, "Text of Arafat's Terrorism Statement," 13 April 2002.

93. James Gerstenzang, "Mideast," *Los Angeles Times*, 26 April 2002.

94. Brendan Pereira and Luz Baguiro, "Terror Sweep in Region Stepped up," *Strait Times Interactive*, 19 April 2002.

95. Dana Priest and Thomas E. Ricks, "U.S. Units Attacking al Qaeda in Pakistan," *Washington Post*, 25 April 2002, p. A-1.
96. Tim Goldern,"Young Egyptians Hearing Call of 'Martyrdom,'" *New York Times*, 26 April 2002.
97. Philip Smucker, "Blast May Mark Shift in Terror," *Christian Science Monitor*, 29 April 2002.
98. Reuters, "Nepal Kills 90 Maoist Rebels in Crackdown," *New York Times*, 3 May 2002.
99. Tyler Marshall and John Hendren, "U.S. to Leave Philippines Despite Hostage Situation," *Los Angeles Times*, 27 May 2002.
100. Peter Ford, "Cold War Won, Can NATO Fight Terror?" *Christian Science Monitor*, 28 May 2002.
101. Susan Schmidt and Walter Pincus, "Al Muhajir Alleged to Be Scouting Terror Sites," *Washington Post*, 12 June 2002, p. A-1.
102. Peter Finn, "Arrests Reveal al Qaeda Plans," *Washington Post*, 16 June 2002, p. A-1.
103. Dexter Filkins, "Pakistan Says It Seized Americans Tied to al Qaeda," *New York Times*, 13 June 2002.
104. Terrence Neilan, "8 Killed as Bomb Goes off Near U.S. Consulate in Pakistan," *New York Times*, 14 June 2002.
105. Karl Vick, "Pakistani Leader Accused of Trying to Grab Power," *Washington Post*, 28 June 2002, p. A-18.
106. Pamela Constable, "Afghan Assembly Elects Karzai," *Washington Post*, p. A-1.
107. Omar Zakhilwal, "Stifled in the Loya Jirga," *Washington Post*, 16 June 2002, p. B-7.
108. The quote comes from Mohammed Assadi, "Arafat Pledges Elections Soon," *Washington Post*, 14 June 2002, p. A-20. The subsequent announcement is in James Bennet, "Arafat Says Elections in January Will Decide His Leadership," *New York Times*, 26 June 2002.
109. David Johnston, Don Van Natta, Jr., and Judith Miller, "Al Qaeda's New Links Increase Threats from Global Sites," *New York Times*, 16 June 2002.
110. Neil MacFarquhar, "Saudi Arabia Arrests 13 Men Tied to Attack on a U.S. Base," *New York Times*, 19 June 2002; Peter Finn, "Syria Interrogating al Qaeda Recruiter," *Washington Post*, 19 June 2002, p. A-1; Steven Erlanger, "German Officials Deny Knowing Location of an Important Figure in Hamburg Plot," *New York Times*, 13 June 2002.
111. James Bennet, "Israel Acts to Seize Palestinian Land after 19 Die in Blast," *New York Times*, 19 June 2002; Molly Moore, "6 Die in Shootout at Settlement," *Washington Post*, 21 June 2002, p. A-1.
112. Sam F. Ghattas, "Al Qaeda," *Washington Post*, 23 June 2002, p. A-1; MacFarquhar, "Al Qaeda Says Bin Laden Is Well, and Was behind Tunis Blast," *New York Times*, 23 June 2002.
113. CNN, *Wolf Blitzer Reports*, June 27, 2002.
114. Barbara Crossette, "Study Warns of Stagnation in Arab Societies," *New York Times*, 2 July 2002.

SOCIETAL INPUTS TO U.S. FOREIGN POLICY

Some five months into the war on terrorism, the first stirrings of discontent are appearing in Washington over how far to expand the conflict and even over basic goals of the campaign.

—Gail Russell Chaddock, "Democrats Raise Doubts, Risking 'Unpatriotic' Label," *Christian Science Monitor*, 4 March 2002.

This latest round of a long-running policy debate also includes a new group of combatants: Christian conservatives.

Many in this pro-Israel camp see Biblical prophecy being played out in current events. They're rallying their members—and lobbying ideological allies inside the White House—to push the United States to stand squarely behind Israel. While they're hardly dictating U.S. policy, it's clear that these conservatives now have a strong voice in the debate.

—Abraham McLaughlin and Gail Russell Chaddock, "A Strong, New Pro-Israeli Voice Muscles into the Traditional Jewish-Arab Political Dynamic in Washington," *Christian Science Monitor*, 16 April 2002.

Therefore, a media corps that had just furiously denounced a "disinformation" scheme planned in the Pentagon demanded an immediate dose of disinformation from the White House. Dutifully, Condoleezza Rice disavowed the truth about the path to war and rebuked the spokesman who had uttered it, thereby mollifying the press, dovish partisans and Gaza terrorists.

What should Israel do to give Palestinians reasons to reorient their leader or replace him with a group that can control Hamas, end the carnage, and create a viable state? . . . [A]dvise [Arafat] that there will be no "Powell plan" rammed down Sharon's throat; instead, Arafat should aim for an interim agreement to be signed in a new Palestinian state's capital—which he should not expect to be Jerusalem.

—William Safire, "Ending the War Process," *New York Times*, 11 March 2002.

Recall Chapter 1, in which Kegley and Wittkopf, using Rosenau's comparative foreign-policy framework, characterized U.S. foreign policy as multicausal. It should surprise no one, therefore, that external-systemic inputs do not occur in a domestic-political vacuum, notwithstanding what the proponents of *realpolitik* might argue. Indeed, societal inputs are frequently quite influential in ultimately shaping U.S. foreign policy. Let us consider some of those societal inputs in some detail since 9/11.

INITIAL SOCIETAL INPUTS IN RESPONSE TO 9/11

Frequently when the United States goes to war, there is an initial rally-around-the-flag response in U.S. public opinion. It is therefore unsurprising that U.S. public opinion was very favorable—virtually unanimous—toward the administration and its policies soon after 9/11. The administration initially made several speeches suggesting a U.S. counterresponse would soon be forthcoming. Favorable public opinion continued months after the attacks and, in particular, once the war began in early October. The continued public support was likely due to the severity and proximity of the attacks. After all, the United States had never been attacked as it was on 9/11. The surprise attack at Pearl Harbor seemed relatively distant to many Americans. These attacks, in contrast, were directed at two of America's most famous cities, New York and Washington. Indeed, as of this writing (2003), the president's approval ratings remain surprisingly high.

Clearly, the sheer size and scope of the 9/11 attacks were shocking and led to a unique period of national unity, which was commented upon in numerous newspapers and cable news programs repeatedly. Furthermore, if Vietnam was the first "television" war and the Gulf War was the first instantaneous-television war, 9/11 represented the first war that would be covered instantaneously and simultaneously by multiple television outlets: twenty-four hour coverage for many months by CNN, MSNBC, and Fox News, to name the most popular ones. National unity, notwithstanding the constant bombardment of coverage as well as the daily news conferences (Mayor Giuliani, Departments of State, Defense, Justice, and the White House), led to a collective national anxiousness. It seemed as if the nation was waiting for the next shoe to drop, figuratively. The point is that the 9/11 attacks represented a unique experience and resulted in a unique public-government unity with the former extraordinarily supportive of the latter.

On October 4, the anthrax scare began. The public learned that an editor of the Florida tabloid the *Sun* became infected with inhalation anthrax. The man died just days later. Over the next few weeks, postal workers and media outlets became the targets of anthrax-laden letters. The scare eventually spread to the U.S. Congress, starting with the so-called Daschle letter. Amid the anthrax scare, the Senate passed an anti-terror bill, quickly followed by the House of Representatives (337–79). While the bill will be considered elsewhere, it is worth mentioning here since it was largely a response to public opinion.

By the end of October, Attorney General John Ashcroft issued his second warning in one month based on "credible evidence" of forthcoming additional domestic-terrorist attacks. His warning resulted in an amplification of unity of American public opinion not seen since the beginning of the Cold War. The reader may recall that days later, Governor Gray Davis (D-CA), apparently acting on intelligence from the U.S. government, warned Californians that bridges in San Diego, Los Angeles, and San Francisco were also likely targets of forthcoming terrorist attacks.

Illustrative of the public unity were public opinion numbers that were released in January, almost exactly four months after the attacks. The numbers reflected unity in public opinion in terms of activism and/or internationalism, the very tonic the president had been offering to heal America's 9/11 wounds. America was the world's only superpower; only its leadership could make things right. Public opinion is often thought to be fickle and capricious. The shear brazenness of 9/11, however, shocked the nation collectively and uniquely. At unique times—Pearl Harbor, the beginning of the Cold War, and 9/11—public opinion coalesces around America's foreign-policy decision-makers and the policies they espouse. President Bush had called the nation to war. Furthermore, it would be a war fought globally and over a sustained period requiring a global and sustained response. The *Christian Science Monitor* reported the following:

> In recent years, signs seemed to mount of America's isolationist tendencies. But in the wake of September 11, Americans' support for engagement in the world is surging. Favorable views of U.S. involvement in the world are hitting *levels not seen since World War II*. (italics added)

The article went on to note that Americans did not wish to send troops to every country in the world or to solve every problem.

> [M]any now believe the world's only superpower should help to resolve problems like the Mideast conflict, and should use its power to do things like promote democracy and reduce poverty worldwide—not just as military might.

The *Monitor* noted similar "blips" in public opinion had occurred previously, for example, after the Gulf War.

> But the percentages of Americans who support U.S. involvement in the world and efforts to forge a better view of the United States are all at new highs—in some cases even higher than President [George W.] Bush's ratings. People want a safer world— and they see making it a better place to live as one way to accomplish that.

Citing the Program on International Policy Attitudes and Pew studies, the article reported that some 81 percent of Americans prefer "a United States that takes an 'active part' in world affairs," with only 14 percent wishing the United States would take a less active role. "A comparison of results when similar questions have been asked in surveys since World War II shows the 81 percent marks a new high."[1]

President Bush's entire administration, by his own admission, was redefined by 9/11 and global terrorism. Tax cuts and budget surpluses were to be eclipsed, at least for the time being, by the war on terrorism.[2] In effect, Bush was proposing to pursue both guns and butter. And his popularity was soaring while he did so. As reported in the *Los Angeles Times*, "Several recent polls have found Bush opening huge leads over Democrats on issues demanding toughness, such as safeguarding national security and combating terrorism."[3]

INITIAL CRITIQUES OF THE WAR ON TERRORISM

Although the president was popular in the polls, some of the first criticism of his administration's strategy on terrorism began to appear in January (2002), on op-ed pages—albeit indirectly. Nicolas Kristof criticized the military's decision to classify POWs as illegal combatants and their warehousing in Cuba.[4] Kristof's critique was really about instruments of foreign policy. Moreover, they were directed at the Justice Department more than the Defense Department or the White House. (As will be seen, Kristof eventually set his sights on the latter institutions as well.)

Similar criticism of the Transportation Department's methods soon appeared. The newly created Transportation Security Administration (TSA) came in for particular scrutiny in February. Interestingly, the debate was not about its creation— i.e., a new bureaucracy that would normally raise the ire of conservatives—but, rather, its "transactional" and "behavioral" analysis software. It was from liberals, not conservatives. The *Washington Post* headline summed it up: "Intricate Screening of Fliers in Works: Database Raises Privacy Concerns."[5]

If partisan sniping was beginning—and to be accurate, it was very mild and very limited—it did not appear to affect the president's popularity, nor did it appear to affect his war on terrorism. In an intriguing article, Richard Morin and Dana Milbank reported the following:

> Bush's extraordinary level of popularity—higher and more protracted than any modern president—is all the more noteworthy because it comes at a time when the American public has significant doubts about the economy and other domestic matters.

The authors noted that while Bush's popularity was down from his October high of 92 percent, "eighty-three percent of the public approve of the job Bush is doing." Perhaps more importantly, the authors stated that "the president's enduring popularity has withstood doses of bad news because a *fundamental revision of voters' attitudes* following the September 11 terrorist attacks" (italics added).[6]

A "fundamental revision of voters' attitudes" apparently translated to mild critiques by the media that were relatively few and far between. Howard Kurtz, the well-known media critic, quoted liberal *Salon* editor David Talbot thusly: "America is not capable of using its unrivaled power for good—it must."[7] When "liberal" critiques become cheerleaders for a Republican president, something fundamental has changed! (Even as recently as early 2003, one could scarcely find substantive criticism of Bush's foreign policy.) One attitude that had not changed from the nation's inception is its attitude on viewing international events in terms of tyranny and thwarting it.[8] In the same article, Kurtz further quotes Talbot as noting that "America's power to reduce tyranny and terror to dust is actually what often makes civilization in today's world possible." Clearly, a new consensus against terrorism—read tyranny—inclusive of liberals and conservatives had emerged. The question, for our purposes, is as follows: How long will the consensus endure? Only if it lasts over a sustained period may we characterize it as the sort of fundamental change that accompanied the Cold War.

Indeed, indicative of a new public, antiterror consensus was the fact that Americans seemed willing to reconsider a new balance between security and civil liberties. The *Christian Science Monitor* noted the following:

> For the first time in a half-century, authorities are considering the legality and practicality of extreme measures, such as requiring the public to be tested for diseases or seizing property.
>
> As a result, the balance between public health and civil liberties, which in recent decades had been tilting more toward individual freedom, may be about to swing back. . . .[9]

Nor was it only "the masses" among whom a new consensus was emerging; similarly, a consensus appeared evident in elite opinion. An article on the Carlyle Group—an investment group whose board members include former Secretary of State James Baker, former Secretary of Defense Frank Carlucci, and former President George H. W. Bush, among others—reflected solidarity of elite opinion. The Carlyle Group, and its United Defense Industries, were aware that the post-9/11 consensus on Capitol Hill was "to open the funding spigot," making Carlyle especially bullish on the military-industrial complex. A United Defense prospectus declared: "The terrorist attacks of September 11, 2001, have generated strong Congressional support for increased defense spending." This, of course, was the same Congress that a matter of months earlier had leaders declaring that increased defense spending, when coupled with the Bush tax cuts, was "fiscal mismanagement, big time."[10]

Even the normally slow-to-change Pentagon was becoming unusually fleet-of-foot in terms of new strategizing. The Pentagon's new focus, one that was only taking shape glacially some eleven years after the Cold War's demise, reflected the impact of 9/11: "to transform the U.S. armed forces into a slim, trim, fighting force that can move halfway around the globe in a matter of hours and fight in conditions like the Afghan campaign."[11]

Further, a consensus against the global-terrorist hydra seemed to be holding globally. In the first few days following the 9/11 attacks, President Bush received visitors as disparate as Britain's Prime Minister Tony Blair, France's Jacques Chirac, and Indonesia's Ms. Megawati Sukarnoputri, reflecting global solidarity. Some four months later, Bosnia, a country with a large Muslim majority, handed over six suspected terrorists to the United States. Indeed, a Yale law professor, Ruth Wedgwood, approvingly commented on the unusual extradition as "appropriate" and as a "sheer wartime necessity."[12]

State governments were predictably an impetus behind the new consensus. First, there occurred a surge of patriotism in the states, reflected in citizens' representatives. Second, the new consensus potentially meant new funding from federal coffers. One reason—if not the principal reason—the defense industry, both the Pentagon and its contractors, was originally divided among virtually all fifty states was federal largesse. Jobs were linked to the rapidly growing national-security bureaucracy as the Cold War gained momentum. Thus, with defense-related jobs spread over almost every state in the union, each state's U.S. representatives could be counted on to vote for increased federal funding of the industrial-defense complex. (Witness the problems Congress has endured over the last twenty years each time the issue of closing obsolete bases has arisen.)

Since the end of the Cold War, many states have felt some pain due to the federal government's shrinking defense budgets despite the fact that the defense budget shrank very slowly in the late 1990s. States were eyeing federal coffers with new zeal: Perhaps the halcyon days of Cold War defense funding had returned. "The first installment in $1.1 billion bioterrorist preparedness funds was distributed to states and major cities [January 31], with nearly $20 million immediately going to California and Los Angeles County." Federal largesse's effects could be seen, to cite another example, in President Bush's signing some $2.9 billion in "bioterrorism funds" into law some three weeks previously. Health and Human Services Secretary, Tommy Thompson, was quoted as describing the appropriation as the "largest one-time investment in the nation's public health system ever";[13] and newly-created Homeland Security Director, Tom Ridge, characterized it as "Absolutely unprecedented."[14]

Clearly, societal inputs were affecting U.S. foreign policy: in mass public opinion, in the government's national-security bureaucracies, in state governments, and in elite opinion. Clearer still was the effect 9/11 was having on how the finite federal budget would be divided. Though discussed later in governmental inputs in Chapter 4, it is worth noting here that 9/11 directly affected defense spending. President Bush had already proposed an 11 percent increase in defense spending prior to 9/11. After 9/11, the president's defense proposal for 2003, by one estimate, was 14 percent higher than the Cold War average.[15]

It is true that partisanship had not completely disappeared in the months after 9/11. As we shall soon see, midterm-election criticism of President Bush's domestic policies grew in the spring as fall (2002) elections approached. It does appear, however, that the public, Congress, and media were prepared to give Bush wide berth. For example, in February, nearly five months post-9/11, Bruce Reed (president of the Democratic Leadership Council and former Clinton advisor) was quoted as saying that his party would fight the president in the months ahead when domestic politics were at stake. But when it came to the war on terrorism, specifically the president's newly created Homeland Security Department, the president would get all the support he asked for on the war and on homeland security.[16]

EFFECTS OF 9/11 ON PUBLIC OPINION

One indicator of whether 9/11 will have a lasting and fundamental effect on U.S. foreign policy has to do with how the nation's students are taught. Recall, a principal thesis of Kegley and Wittkopf's *American Foreign Policy* is as follows: U.S. foreign policy changed after 1946–1947 (the Cold War causing that change) by the emergence of a new consensus, which resulted in a foreign-policy output that could be seen changing only incrementally from the 1950s through the 1990s. In twenty years' time, will foreign-policy professors be using textbooks that argue essentially the same thing about 9/11, *viz.*, the attacks causing a similar turning point in U.S. foreign policy? Clearly we cannot be certain at this early juncture. What we can note is that the attacks have begun to have an effect on curricula. The *Washington Post* reported that the attacks and their aftermath "are taking front-and-center seat in the nation's classrooms, sparking a surge of student interest in topics from Arabic to crisis management and prompting educators in fields as disparate as Islamic studies and microbiology to revamp their courses."[17]

Another similarity to the post–Cold War period is the isolation of peoples based on their presumed ideology. Following the commencement of the Cold War, putative Communists and their "fellow travelers" were singled out in America. At its worst, during the McCarthy period, persons with suspect ideology were hounded out of the government and the entertainment industry. Islam per se is not an ideology. The global war on terrorism, however, views "radical Islam" or "fundamentalism" (*Jihadism*) as an ideology. Though it is too early to tell how enduring the current trend will be, Arabs, persons who "look like" Arabs, and, more generally, Muslims have been singled out and harassed. For instance, one reporter noted: "In those first five weeks, as the nation prepared to go to war, reports of violence against Muslims or those perceived to be Arab Americans captured headlines around the country."[18] Fortunately, by fall 2002, the harassment diminished. On the other hand, that Arabs and Muslims are singled out is clearly still the case: The FBI and other intelligence have singled them out for special questioning, and the TSA's and airport security's protestations to the contrary, several incidents have been reported in the media wherein Arabs and/or Muslims have been scrutinized more closely than others and even kept off flights.

Ironically enough, Muslims abroad hold views of one of America's societal inputs—the media—nearly diametrically opposed to the way most Americans view their media. The prize-winning reporter Thomas Friedman wrote an op-ed piece in which he reported a Saudi diplomat saying, "I hope you will not be insulted, but I have to ask you this question because it's around: Are Jews in the media behind the campaign to smear Saudi Arabia and Islam?" It is worth noting in response an interesting comment Friedman made regarding American ethos. In his attempt to explain the differences between Saudi and U.S. societies, Friedman wrote, "America is successful and wealthy because of its values, not despite them. It is prosperous because of the way it respects freedom, individualism and women's rights and the way it nurtures creativity and experimentation."[19]

EFFECTS OF PUBLIC OPINION ON U.S. FOREIGN POLICY

As noted in the previous discussion, there is evidence that mass public opinion changed as a result of 9/11; public opinion in turn affects U.S. foreign policy. Kegley and Wittkopf cite a three-fold division of public opinion: masses (some 88 percent), attentive public (some 10 percent), and elites (about 2 percent).[20] Among the latter group are decision-makers and opinion shapers. Clearly, members of the Supreme Court may be counted among said group. Thus it was interesting to read that 9/11 was "reverberating in the marbled halls of the U.S. Supreme Court"[21] the court of last appeal in the American system of jurisprudence and supposedly immune to public opinion. It seems that the new consensus was affecting even the Supremes.

About a week after the evidence regarding 9/11's effect on the Supreme Court was reported, evidence that the masses were giving their government tremendous latitude, reminiscent of the beginning of the Cold War, reappeared. Nary a voice was heard throughout 2002 as the government expanded its pervasiveness in society. "Anti-terrorist legislation enacted by Congress after September 11 expand[ed] the FBI's authority to eavesdrop and search e-mail and phone records." And here in California, Gov. Gray Davis was seeking similar powers.[22] What may be the most interesting aspect of all of this is the readiness with which Americans seem willing to accord their state and federal governments powers that, under normal conditions, precious few Americans would be willing to give them. The same article quoted a lawyer for the National Security Agency (NSA), the principal agency involved in intercepting electronic communications. The NSA is the agency, in fact, that was not even officially acknowledged until recent years. In Washington, D.C., an old bromide was that NSA stood for No Such Agency. In a telling reflection on post-9/11 American society, the former NSA official was quoted as saying "George Orwell underestimated our enthusiasm for surveillance. He correctly predicted that we'd have cameras everywhere. What he failed to imagine is that we'd want them so bad [sic] we'd pay for them" (ibid.).

Friedman has frequently been an impetus behind societal inputs, simply by virtue of his relevance to America's elite pundit class, that is, that small percentage of elite decision-makers in American foreign policy. In mid-February, he published an op-ed bombshell. Using his vast connections in the Middle East, Friedman published a piece in which he made public the Saudi crown prince's "vision" for Middle East peace. His vision, which would be ratified at the Arab Summit later that month, called for Arab recognition and normalization with Israel in exchange for a Palestinian state (effectively UN Resolution 242, which implied the 1967 borders.)[23]

MEDIA CRITICISM OF THE WAR ON TERRORISM

As noted, the media had (*has*) more or less given the administration a pass on the global war on terrorism. As months wore on, however, the pass did *not* include military SNAFUs. Howard Kurtz noted that the war coverage was turning negative for perhaps the first time. Several reports of Pentagon mistakes had appeared. By mid-February (2002) a more general sense of negative reporting appeared. "When U.S. soldiers conducted a raid north of Kandahar, Afghanistan, on January 24, it was initially reported as an American victory." More scrutiny revealed "a few reporters in Afghanistan began challenging official accounts. . . ." Kurtz admitted that the media were probably resenting the Pentagon's management of information rather than the mistakes themselves. Hitherto, the *Washington Post* reported that "Defense Secretary Donald H. Rumsfeld was hailed on magazine covers like a rock star." No longer. On Monday, the *Los Angles Times*, the *Washington Post* and the *New York Times* reported allegations by friendly Afghanis who reported mistreatment at the hands of the U.S. military. Additionally and, perhaps more importantly from a Pentagon-information standpoint, a "clash" between reporters in Afghanistan and military officials began to turn reporters from cheerleaders to scrutinizers—the media's role, after all. One reporter claimed to be threatened by U.S. soldiers when he sought to investigate a SNAFU. Leaked stories, it seemed—and leaks clearly coming from the Pentagon—began appearing. Simultaneously, Secretary Rumsfeld announced the Pentagon's intention "to prosecute anyone caught leaking classified information." Though focused on the person(s) in the Pentagon who leaked information, it was equally clear that Rumsfeld was upset with the media and its coverage. Understandable as Rumsfeld's announcement was, the irony was the Pentagon had been leaking positive reports for months, which had escaped Rumsfeld's ire.[24] Thus the more typical relationship between the U.S. government, in particular the Pentagon, and the mainstream media began to reestablish itself. For example, Jim Hoagland, another Washington syndicated columnist and pundit, published an article entitled "Assessing the War Honestly." Hoagland noted that wars produce temptations to pursue "objectives that are partisan, personal or bureaucratic," and that "[o]dds and history both suggest that somewhere in the Bush administration lurks the next J. Edgar Hoover or Oliver North waiting to ride the pendulum of emergency powers to extreme lengths."[25]

The media also began to criticize America's alliance with Pakistan. Doubtless, Daniel Pearl's case fueled criticism. Understandably, when one of their own was kidnapped and brutally killed, the media's attention focused more sharply on the goings-on in Pakistan. Consequently, Musharraf, America's newfound "ally," came in for a closer look. At one time Americans could at least feel confident that they had a partner they could count on, Pakistan; now all of that was about to change. Musharraf now faced the beginnings of a potentially ugly internal conflict, which some thought might cripple him or at least cripple his campaign against terrorism. Most Americans had little familiarity with the politics of Pakistan. Rather, they knew only that Musharraf had joined with the United States after 9/11. Now, however, regular Americans were learning that Musharraf's fight with the militants was serious indeed: Musharraf was up against a large constituency that disagreed with his alliance with America. Never mind that 100,000 unemployed Pakistani men, educated only in hatred and trained only for war, may pose a threat bigger than their slice of the electorate. "The power struggle, as the politicians [saw] it, [was] between them and Musharraf."[26] Of course, Musharraf was an important ally on whom U.S. strategy depended to some degree. Accordingly, the American public and the administration were counting on his being successful battling his own *Jihadists*.

Another issue cropped up in mid-February and proved controversial for the administration, though the controversy had a short shelf life. The controversy over government surveillance had scarcely been considered since 9/11: The public and the media wished to feel safe and if the government needed to use surveillance, so be it. When the government announced that it would place cameras around the nation's capital, it raised the ire of liberals, conservatives, and libertarians alike. For instance, William Safire, the well-known conservative columnist, reported that "Washington [D.C.] police opened the Joint Operation Command Center of the Synchronized Operations Command Complex," or S.O.C.C. in typical bureaucratese, to protect "vital national interest," to protect monuments in our nation's capital. Safire questioned whether protecting such monuments was a "vital national interest." "Is this the kind of world we want?" asked Safire.[27] Safire was effectively implying that the plan had the whiff of Orwell to it. Taken together with Hoagland, the criticisms demonstrated a broad ideological range of media beginning to become increasingly piqued by the government's actions in anticipation of possible future terrorist attacks.

Just as Safire fired off his missive on Big Brother, a *New York Times* colleague published an intriguing as well as informative assessment of the differences between U.S. foreign-policy goals and its European allies' vis-à-vis Iraq, not terrorism per se:

> However, while the man [Saddam Hussein] is dangerous and crazy, we do not know that he has weapons of mass destruction. He seems to have precious little connection to September 11. His army had been destroyed. . . . Europe learned a lesson in World War I: Slipping into conflict . . . became a basic fear. Europeans' great source of anxiety was the prospect of being caught in an uncontrollable military escalation.[28]

Additionally, elections were looming in both France (May 2002) and Germany (September 2002). Wars, at least those led by the United States, tend to damage pro-U.S. European politicians during elections. The possibility, therefore, that some Europeans might seek to create daylight on Iraq, if not terrorism generally, predictably existed. America's European allies, predictably, began dragging their collective feet on Iraq and suggesting the Americans ought to consider carefully any warlike proclivities vis-à-vis Iraq (ibid.).

If there were major differences between Europe's view and the U.S. view of the world, insofar as Iraq was concerned, there was also growing evidence that U.S. society was closing ranks: Where ethnic, racial, and other cleavages existed before 9/11, after the attacks something changed. The reader may recall the publicity surrounding the publication of "Bowling Alone" in 2000, by Robert Putman. The piece argued that American society had suffered a breakdown of civic engagement and a common sense of "we Americans." Putman further argued that short of a "galvanizing" crisis—like war—things were unlikely to change.

Then came 9/11. "To gauge how much September 11 has transformed our values and civic habits . . . we resurveyed some of the 30,000 Americans whose civic habits we observed in 2000." Among other things, the new study reported "a significant drop in cynicism, large gains in trust of government, and moderate gains in trust of police, neighbors, co-workers, shop clerks, people with whom they worship, and even strangers."[29] The question is, of course, whether and to what degree these changes are temporary or will persist over time.

There were, to be sure, exceptions in terms of cynicism and sense of civics. As we have seen, Kristof of the *New York Times* had demonstrated cynicisms, at least nominally, toward America's war on terror. In particular, Kristof had aimed considerable scrutiny at America's seeming expansion of the war with so little public debate. In mid-February, Kristof questioned the "confusing" U.S. deployment "of troops in the Philippines." "One clue," argued Kristof,

> that the American aim in the Philippines is a feel-good declaration of victory more than defeat of terrorism is that we have no plans to pursue anyone to Sulu [a Filipino island]. Likewise, we have no plans to mess with the Moro Islamic Liberation Front, which has much stronger ties to terrorism and to al Qaeda, but which has thousands of fighters and is thus more formidable.

Abu Sayyef had been reported to be evacuating to Sulu Island from its Basilan Island home. In effect, Kristof was arguing U.S. foreign policy in the Philippines was more dog-and-pony show than substance.[30] Kristof was not, however, criticizing Bush's war on the global-terrorist hydra.

A critique of Bush came shortly, this one published by William Schneider. Schneider published a lengthy piece in the *Los Angeles Times* in which he analyzed the issue of U.S.–European differences in America's war on terror and the precise dimensions of the same, in Iraq. He also obliquely referred to American ethos, or at least the Bush administration's ethos. Schneider's assessment compared Bush to Reagan's "cowboy diplomacy" of an earlier era. Among the president's recent quotes and, according to Schneider, interpreted by Europeans as indicative of America's penchant for unilateralism, were the following: first, President Bush's State of the Union Address (a.k.a. Bush's "axis-of-evil speech"), criticized as simplistic by France, Britain, and Russia; second, Bush's "wanted dead or alive" comments, spoken, as irony would have it, before the National Cattleman's Beef Association; third, Bush's "either you're with us or you're against us" remark, the basis of what would become the "Bush Doctrine." Perhaps more interesting in Schneider's article, however, were the observations he made regarding values, goals, and ethos more generally. In comparing Presidents Reagan, Clinton, and Bush, he wrote the following:

> Bush's policy is the same as Reagan's—tough talk and a huge military build-up. He does not share former President Bill Clinton's ambitions. Clinton wanted to be known as a peacemaker. Bush is a war leader, a self-described "crusader for justice" *against evil and tyranny*. "Our cause is just, our cause is noble, and we will defeat forces of terror," the president told the troops in Alaska. (italics added)[31]

Whether or not one accepts his comparisons, Schneider clearly found the same tendencies in American foreign policy noted earlier in discussing America's mythology and its resultant behavior in international politics. Like all nations, America has its own unique myths about its origins, its history, and how its history fits in the larger international context. War has played a unique role in U.S. mythology-ethos. America's early history was that of an isolationist country. Only in the twentieth century did America forsake its isolationism once and for all to become an internationalist power. War was integral to that transformation in American mythology. First, World War I found a reluctant America joining only belatedly. World War II saw America joining the war only after Pearl Harbor. Importantly, America's ethos argues that following World War II, the United States was the only nation with the material and moral wherewithal to take on the latest and, arguably, most threatening of tyrants: international Communism in the form of the Soviet Union. The research question here turns around whether the war on terror is a comparably critical turning point in U.S. foreign policy as was the commencement of the Cold War. Thus, the way America views itself, its purpose, and its behavior in the war on terror is a critical comparison. One may see, at least superficially, very similar views of U.S. foreign policy's mythology to the early–Cold War period: America again sees itself as being dragged into a war it did not want, it did little or nothing to precipitate, and which it is now forced to lead.

Unsurprisingly, the 9/11 attacks caused American society to examine itself—albeit limitedly—and to examine its relationship to the Muslim world. Americans began to examine their own Muslim population. In late February, the *Washington Post* examined "Muslim schools" in the United States. Unlike the *madrassas* in the Middle East, the *Post* noted that America's Muslim schools study physics, differential equations, U.S. history, and English. "Then they file into their Islamic studies classes, where the textbooks tell them the Day of Judgment can't come until Jesus Christ returns to Earth, breaks the cross and converts everyone to Islam, and until Muslims start attacking Jews." Few Americans, doubtless, had ever even considered Muslim schools—or other parochial schools for that matter—with such a critical eye. What may have surprised Americans even more was the funding behind many of these Muslim schools and their curricula: one of America's "staunchest" allies in the Middle East, Saudi Arabia.[32] The parallel to Americans looking inward for identifiable enemies may be seen in the search for Communists within the government and in America's entertainment industry at the onset of the Cold War and its current scrutiny of America's Muslim population.

These phenomena, American ethos and mythology and Americans looking inward for possible identifiable enemies, have clear parallels to the onset of the Cold War. With respect to the former, Americans and their leaders see the global war on terror as another instance of an international tyrant dragging America into war. American ethos simply does not permit America's foreign-policy leaders openly to be warmongers. In fact, one could easily argue that the reason the Bush administration's apparent eagerness to attack Iraq received criticism, is that it looked to some as if America was "itching" for a fight, a view that runs counter to American mythology. The global war on terror, by strict contrast, was provoked.

MEDIA ALTERNATES BETWEEN CRITICISM AND SUPPORT OF WAR ON TERRORISM

Increasing, if still relatively mute, criticism was beginning to appear in the media, and in particular on the op-ed pages as well as among a few television pundits. Late in February an article appeared questioning Saudi benefaction of America's Muslim schools. The same day an article critical of the efficacy of the Bush-Putin partnership in anti-terror was published in the same paper. As noted earlier, both Russia and China had their own reasons for supporting America's war on terror: Each had their own "Muslim" problems. Fred Hiatt began his critique: "President Bush speaks the truth to evil." Hiatt continued, "So you might expect his administration also to want to speak truth to Russia, which is waging a war of increasing cruelty and criminality against a beleaguered ethnic minority in the breakaway province of Chechnya." Hiatt suggested that a fuzzy foreign policy of mixed signals to Russia was the inevitable result. Kristof took a swing at Bush's policy vis-à-vis North Korea on the following day.[33] What continued to be somewhat surprising was just how muted the criticisms of U.S. foreign policy remained, more than a year after 9/11. The public seemed little affected by op-ed and other media criticisms: Apparently the public scarcely scans the op-ed pages to inform its views on foreign policy. It lends anecdotal support, at least, to the thesis that the media follow rather than lead the public.

One item that did cause a media dustup was the Pentagon's creation of an official propaganda unit, what the *Los Angeles Times* characterized as "a high-level office to influence public sentiment abroad. . . ."[34] After its announcement at a daily Pentagon briefing, the media jumped on the notion. In one sense, it is quite ironic given that the United States has used what it calls "public diplomacy" for decades. (Bags of donated grain with Uncle Sam's picture, books in libraries, Radio Marti and Radio Free Europe are primary examples.) Hence, the United States has attempted to shape public opinion abroad since at least early in the Cold War. Nonetheless, once the Pentagon announced it was to create an office tasked with said activity, the media became extraordinarily exercised. Consequently, Defense Secretary Rumsfeld was forced to utter an unusual mea culpa: "The office is done. What do you want, blood?" (ibid.). Tellingly, most Americans would not accept an overt office of propaganda, despite the reality that every nation, including the United States, uses propaganda for its own purposes. The Information Office thus met a quick end.[35] Rumsfeld was obdurate to the end, characterizing ". . . the media . . . [as] 'off the mark.'" He told reporters at the Pentagon, "the office has clearly been so damaged that it's . . . pretty clear to me that it could not function effectively, so it's being closed down."[36]

While the Pentagon was adjusting to the realities of American society, POWs or "illegal combatants" were being held at the U.S. base in Guantanamo, Cuba. Under normal circumstances, such a POW camp would not make much news in the United States. These prisoners were said to be the worst of the worst, however, and U.S. lawyers were lining up to represent their interests. Moreover, an incident occurred that caused the "combatants"—legal or otherwise—to protest their environment. Apparently, one prisoner was prevented from wearing a headdress during prayer, as a security precaution and, according to the prisoners, as an infringement of religious rights. Consequently, the prisoner began a hunger strike, quickly joined by other prisoners in a show of solidarity. Initially, the story caused a stir in the media, doubtless due to America's own view of religious-political freedoms, but quickly disappeared as an understanding was worked out between captives and captors.[37] It demonstrates how a seemingly unimportant incident may actually reverberate with aspects integral to issues of America's ethos, ultimately affecting policy. American ethos is fundamentally reliant on religious-political freedom. Thus this story resonated with many Americans more than one might otherwise expect.

While the hunger strike occurred in Cuba, another Pentagon publicity faux pas hit the nation's major newspapers. Namely, the issue of "evil doers" returned to haunt the administration. Recall that President Bush initially personified terrorism and doers of evil in the person of, *inter alia*, Osama bin Laden. This may have been a natural and understandable reaction for the president (see individual inputs in Chapter 5). Moreover, a common U.S. foreign-policy ploy is to demonize the target of U.S. foreign-policy attention: whether Saddam Hussein, Slobodan Milosevic, Fidel Castro, or others. Unintentionally, as the war on terror continued month after month and Osama sightings recurred, the president's vilification of bin Laden resulted in many Americans coming to expect bin Laden's capture or death. Therefore, as 2002 came and went, questions were repeatedly raised by the media at daily Defense Department and White House briefings regarding whether or not the war on terror could be a success without bringing bin Laden to justice. American public opinion continued to reflect the desire, even if it would cost American lives and treasure, to see bin Laden's demise. In fact, some 60 percent of U.S. public opinion persisted to demonstrate a willingness to sacrifice for that goal well through 2002. What originally helped to focus U.S. foreign policy began to cause the White House and Defense Department problems. For instance, the *Christian Science Monitor* published an article describing the frustration Defense Secretary Rumsfeld experienced as bin Laden sightings recurred. "Try as he may, Defense Secretary Donald Rumsfeld cannot seem to shake the dreaded 'OBL' [Osama bin Laden] question—even coming from his wife Joyce." A frustrated Rumsfeld told the media that Osama "could walk in here tomorrow and al Qaeda would go on function-ing." Bin Laden's continued existence caused one defense official, to change tacks. Now defense officials were forced to distance their department from "the dreaded OBL question." Thus one defense spokesman was ultimately forced to claim "Osama bin Laden is a poor measure of effectiveness."[38] Unfortunately for the De-fense Department and the administration, the public had begun to measure suc-cess in terms of whether the military got bin Laden and, the Defense Department's protests notwithstanding, now the media and the public were locked onto bin Laden's demise precisely as an effective measure of success.

Additional publicity problems appeared in the media during the spring. The issue of Iraq divided top officials in the administration through early 2003. Among the hawkish officials were Vice President Dick Cheney (whom the reader will re-call was secretary of defense during the Gulf War), Deputy Secretary Wolfowitz, and his boss Secretary Rumsfeld. They and their colleagues were said to be eager to topple the Hussein regime in Iraq, citing the regime as a major source of glob-al terrorism. At the other end of the continuum were Secretary of State Powell and National Security Advisor Condoleezza Rice as well as various Congression-al members raising questions about the efficacy of such a move. Confusing mat-ters even more were those in the past administration (notably, former secretary of state Madeleine Albright), some of whom had evidently made plans to overthrow Hussein but had suspended the plans for various reasons. The entire Iraq im-broglio arose again in America's print media in March. Leaks of various opera-tional plans from the Defense Department and elsewhere were planted in the *New York Times*, the *Washington Post*, and the *Los Angeles Times*, suggesting fac-tions within the Pentagon, some of which appeared very reluctant to attack Iraq at present. The *Christian Science Monitor* published an article citing some of the differences within the administration as well as former Secretary of State Made-line Albright's plan to get rid of Hussein. The article made clear that Albright had outlined a plan to topple Hussein that ultimately died on the vine. It continued to note that the Bush "administration officials have made clear that Iraq is deemed the next 'evildoer' requiring action." Yet the same article reported that Secretary Powell assured Congress that no action against Iraq was "imminent," just as Dick Cheney was preparing to travel to the Gulf region to generate support for an even-tual action.[39]

While internal administration differences were aired in the media, previous bi-partisan cracks began to reappear, albeit on a minor scale. Military tactics in Afghanistan, eerily reminiscent of "pacification" in Vietnam, were noted at the beginning of March.[40] Substantively similar to "winning the hearts and minds" of the Vietnamese peasant, the tactics even reflected the penchant of the military during Vietnam of fabricating creative initializations: the Coalition Joint Civil-Military Operations Task Force (CJCMOTF). Comparisons to Vietnam began to take their toll in Congress, where minor grumbling among Democrats, principal-ly, began to appear, despite Legislative–Executive unity with respect to the global war on terrorism.

Key members of both Houses questioned "whether the White House is examining the military efforts without a clear explanation of its aims." Criticisms by Senate Majority leader, Tom Daschle, and Senior Senator Robert Byrd, created a political maelstrom. Daschle was quoted as saying, while questioning the expansion of the war, "I don't think it would do anybody any good to second-guess what has been done to date." He continued, "I think it [the war] has been successful. I've said that on many occasions. But I think the jury's still out about the future," obliquely referring to Iraq. Though scarcely critical, the Republican leadership fired back quickly. Senator Trent Lott "promptly issued a statement rebuking Mr. Daschle, saying: 'How dare Senator Daschle criticize President Bush while we are fighting our war on terrorism, especially when we have troops in the field?'"[41]

As the Democrats were reduced to criticizing nonissues, the public's consideration and debate of substantive issues was being obscured. U.S. unilateralism and increasing interventionism, for instance, were scarcely discussed in public. A little-publicized article discussing the government's budget appeared in early March. In what would likely shock most Americans, the *New York Times* editorialized that President Bush's desired budget "would soon be spending more on defense than all of the countries combined." *Pax Americana* was identified as a possible new direction of U.S. foreign policy. "Military action is only part of the foreign policy equation," enthused the editorial page. It continued, "Stable world order must be built on a broad international consensus, not on American military action alone."[42] Society's desire for security was becoming a very costly project indeed. And while it may well have been a project whose costs were justified, it was a project whose costs had not been debated publicly. In other words, and very reminiscent of the beginning of the Cold War, U.S. society was acquiescing and counting on its federal government to do what was best without holding said government accountable for what it was doing—a dereliction of society's responsibility in a democratic polity.

As marginal criticism of the administration's war effort began to appear—and to be clear, it was on the op-ed pages and not among the American public, per se—the *Washington Post's* Jim Hoagland asked a critical question, a question that had gone unasked for months. The reader may recall the popularity of the debate on "exit strategies" in the past decade or more of U.S. foreign policy. Congress criticized President Clinton, for instance, for having no exit strategy in Haiti or Bosnia and Kosovo. Former President Bush had been criticized for exiting too quickly during the Gulf War. During the late 1980s and throughout the 1990s, pundits and critics seemed to obsess over the issue of exit strategies. Yet scarcely anyone had asked the question about exit strategies with regard to the global war on terror. Bush's rhetoric, regarding "evildoers" begged the question. When would evil objectively be vanquished? Even if one granted that *evildoer* represented a figure of speech intended to represent global terrorism, how could one objectively measure when global terrorism had been defeated? At best, only a very subjective sort of answer existed. Thus when Hoagland finally raised the issue it seemed that an important debate might finally commence. "What comes next in Afghanistan?" asked Hoagland. "The Bush administration has eagerly and correctly emphasized that it saved Afghans from evil." Nonetheless, he stated that such simplicity "is an exaggerated assessment. But it is also a sign of the uncertainty and anxiety that America's sharp focus on its own priorities is stirring abroad. It underlines the need for Washington and other capitals to think anew—and together—about military power in the global era."[43] Clearly, the war on terror was a new type of war with new types of questions about how one measures success and when one knows one's war is over. Though few "regular" Americans were asking for answers to such important questions, the media *were* finally beginning to raise the issues. Hoagland's op-ed piece may have been a harbinger of the some deterioration of bipartisanship. Some six months after the 9/11 attacks, chinks in bipartisanship were finally appearing. Senator Daschle again attempted to question the administration's lack of dialogue, perhaps demonstrating a degree of desperation among Democrats or at least Democrats who might have presidential aspirations. More significantly, the *Christian Science Monitor* noted that some "five months into the war on terrorism, the first stirrings of discontent are appearing in Washington over how far to expand the conflict and even over the basic goals of the campaign."[44]

For our purposes, the question is whether or not bipartisanship was disintegrating or merely undergoing a temporary setback. The *Monitor's* assessment broached the issue of just how vitriolic the debate was: "Some Democratic lawmakers on Capitol Hill have been taken aback by the expansion of U.S. military aid to Yemen, Georgia, the Philippines, and other far-flung countries." Additionally, "the revelation of a 'shadow government' . . . surprised many in Congress. . . ." "Yet even mild stirrings of discontent have been fiercely denounced by Republicans as something just short of unpatriotic." The article made some anecdotal comparisons to the previous administration: "[T]he questions seem tepid, especially compared with the fierce objections lawmakers raised early on to U.S. commitments in places like Bosnia and the Gulf [i.e., the previous two administrations]" (ibid.).

While nominal debates were beginning to be heard on Capitol Hill, pundit William Safire began—as he had previously done in 1990 (see Alterman, *op. cit.*)—to beat the war drums with respect to Iraq, effectively countering those who were questioning the administration's neoconservatives and their ideas regarding Iraq. "As predicted here, Saddam Hussein—faced with the certainty of a U.S.-led overthrow of his brutal regime—has restarted the business of postponing the attack until he can finish making weapons of mass destruction." Said maneuver, Safire reasoned "leaves Iraq the chance to find a little wiggle room on the alternative to 'or else.'" No average op-ed columnist was Safire, who went on to enumerate what he thought the Bush administration ought to do with respect to Iraq: firm up America's special relation with Britain and Tony Blair to preclude the latter from going wobbly; stiffen Kofi Annan's resolve as well as the Security Council's with respect to UN inspections; obviate "nail-nibbling Democrats" from being fooled by Saddam's trickery; and issue an ultimatum to Hussein.[45] Safire was clearly attempting to provide political cover for those in the administration whose proclivities ran toward the hawkish end of the political continuum.

Another columnist, Jessica Mathews, took a 180 degree tack. Rather than focus on Iraq as a principal target, Mathews suggested that Iraq was precisely the wrong target, at least in terms of direct military action. Instead, she stated, "rather than seeking to oust Saddam Hussein from power, the U.S. goal ought to be to thwart his continuing attempt to acquire these weapons."[46] She also suggested that any U.S. effort to oust Saddam would require Russia's support and that the administration ought to concentrate on such an effort. In focusing on the military option rather than the diplomatic option, the neoconservatives were missing the bigger picture and moving the United States toward a war that would be foolish if not disastrous for the United States and its relations with its allies.

As previously noted, at the beginning of the Cold War when the U.S. national-security bureaucracy was first evolving into the behemoth it would eventually become, the Pentagon and Congress cleverly decided to spread federal largesse over the widest possible geographic area. Briefly, the strategy was premised on giving each state a stake in the growing national-security bureaucracy. The societal impact, however, was clear. Namely, virtually every state gained an interest in perpetuating the ever-growing national-security complex. Interestingly, there appears to be a parallel in today's war on terror. On March 6, the *Christian Science Monitor* published an interesting look at the evolution of the new Homeland Security Department. For example, in a mock exercise of specially trained first responders, SWAT team members, and "terrorists," which Homeland Security Director Tom Ridge held in Nevada, Senator Harry Reid (D-NV) angled for his state's share of federal monies. Reid predictably attempted to get some $250 million of the nearly four-billion-dollar homeland security budget up for grabs. Senator Reid was not the only state official who attempted to get his state's nose in the homeland security trough. Glenville, Illinois, officials were present as well. Detroit Community College looked for their share; another Michigan institution, Oakland Community College hoped from some. West Virginia too was represented. It was reminiscent of the early days of the Cold War and the way federal largesse was handed out to ensure jobs and money and, by extension, votes from states and districts within states.[47]

As homeland security gained momentum, the aforementioned Saudi plan continued to be debated by political pundits. Charles Krauthammer—neoconservative, first-tier pundit—described the Saudi plan as "misdirection" and "a transparent attempt to take world attention away from the source of the violence," namely, Arafat and the Palestinian Authority. Krauthammer, a columnist for the *Washington Post* also took the opportunity to take a shot at the *New York Times*, which had tacitly endorsed the plan in the previous weekend's columns. His swipe: "The audacity of the maneuver is breathtaking. But, why not? It is working. The *New York Times* bought the Saudi peace plan (last Sunday alone, lavishing two feature stories and nearly a dozen photographs over five pages. . .)." The Europeans, Krauthammer claimed, bought it, too. And he fretted that the Bush administration might be fooled as well.[48]

Krauthammer only implied that there existed within the Bush administration "hare-brained moderates" who might lead President Bush down the primrose path toward buying into pro-Palestinian policies, in other words, that so-called moderates were misguided and threatened to pull Bush in the wrong direction. Safire featured fewer nuances in his critique. On March 11, Safire plainly accused Condoleezza Rice (national security advisor and putative "moderate") of "mollifying the press, dovish partisans and Gaza terrorists." Additionally, he attacked Secretary Powell for "ramm[ing] down Sharon's throat" a peace plan that was counter to Israel's interests.[49] Two of America's top pundits from two of America's top newspapers were clearly making the case on behalf of Israel and linking Israel's fate to America's global war on terrorism.

Another editorial on March 7 advised the administration to involve Congress in the administration's global war on terror. As we have seen, growing concern over the expansion of the war was beginning to appear, albeit some six months after 9/11. More important than the editorial itself were the figures the editorial cited. It cited the $38 billion Homeland Defense budget. (For comparative purposes, the readers should know that the entire annual U.S. Intelligence budget—including the CIA, the NSA, the National Reconnaissance Office (satellites), and so forth—is estimated to be around $30–$35 billion.) As for the defense budget, in the aggregate over the next decade: "The administration has asked for $4.7 trillion over the next ten years for the Pentagon, $600 *billion more* than was anticipated before September 11," or an additional U.S. $60 billion per year. The 2003 budget alone "is supposed to be $379 billion, an increase of $48 billion"[50] (italics added). The question is whether the increase in defense appropriations is comparable to the increase in defense appropriations resulting from the commencement of the Cold War? (Note: Defense data are addressed, *infra*.)

Just days after the *Los Angeles Times* published its editorial on Congress and the cost of the war, an important article was published weighing security and civil liberties—obviously a debate that was beginning to percolate among the attentive public, if not U.S. society generally. The issue was the Patriot Act, which had been passed nearly unanimously and with unusual alacrity just after 9/11.

> The USA Patriot Act, signed into law by President Bush on October 26, broadened the government's power to monitor private conversations and e-mail, allowed police to obtain a search warrant and enter someone's home without his knowledge, and made it easier to deport noncitizens suspected of activity that endangers national security.
>
> A separate change in immigration rules permits the attorney general to keep foreigners in detention even when an immigration judge has ordered them freed.[51]

Interestingly, similar debates occurred early in the Cold War, ultimately culminating in the extreme (McCarthyism). The article continued, noting that free speech was potentially jeopardized by the act. Yet another controversy that arose only in July 2002, was the provision of the act that requested a sort of neighborhood watch, under which postal workers, utility workers, and other civilians who found themselves in someone's house and who determined through their own unspecified criteria that something seemed untoward, should contact the authorities. (The Justice Department called the program TIPS.) The Patriot Act passed Congress and was signed by the president fewer than two months after 9/11. What is striking is that so few Americans even bothered to scrutinize the act or what its implications might mean for America's future—perhaps because, after all, it was called the Patriot Act. To question it, therefore, was implicitly unpatriotic. Under normal times, a segment of American society would vociferously criticize such a program. After 9/11, however, few Americans even bothered to concern themselves; simply put, security dominated public concerns.

THE EMPEROR HAS NO CLOTHES: BUSH'S EXTRAORDINARY POPULARITY AND SEEMING IMMUNITY TO CRITICISM

Despite the relatively muted scrutiny of Bush's global war on terrorism found in the media, even fewer critiques existed in society at large. It is, to be sure, understandable that most American citizens would support their government during times of war. Moreover, given the dimensions and sheer shock of 9/11, the axiom holds truer still. In a direct rebuke to the thesis that a liberal media shapes American public opinion, however, the president and his policies remained extraordinarily popular. Few Americans concerned themselves with details of the actions their government was taking, thereby failing to hold their government accountable—the basis of the social contract and democracy. A PEW study, published in the *Washington Post*, showed that in mid-March some nine in ten Americans continued to support the military action in Afghanistan, unchanged from November." Further, even six months after September 11, the survey suggested that the Bush administration continued to enjoy nearly as much support for *a broad war on terrorism* [read Iraq] as it did in the weeks immediately after the attacks on New York and the Pentagon" (italics added).[52]

If certain pundits (Krauthammer and Safire) were sniping at the moderates in the administration—presumably with a view toward affecting policy and boosting the influence of the neoconservatives—other pundits were coming to the moderates' defense. Jim Hoagland penned a column about Pakistan's efficacy as an ally in the war on terror in which he wrote in glowing language about Secretary Powell. Hoagland first set the predicate. Namely, that Musharraf had been less than a stellar ally; indeed, Hoagland noted "Musharraf's failure to match promises with sustained action. . . ." Further, argued Hoagland, Musharraf's failures undermined Bush's policies. Hoagland then turned to Bush's foreign-policy team, to wit: Powell. "Powell swiftly and aggressively moved to manage the relationship." In his first success as chief U.S. diplomat, "Powell harried the Pakistani general into making a forceful speech on January 12 condemning Islamic extremism."[53]

The Pentagon, or more precisely Donald Rumsfeld, was enmeshed in another controversy during the same timeframe. Discussed in more detail in governmental inputs in Chapter 4, it is worth mentioning here inasmuch as it was widely discussed and debated among the punditocracy. The issue involved what the U.S. military would do once the military operations in Afghanistan were concluded. Virtually everyone agreed that the coalition forces would need to remain in Afghanistan indefinitely to make certain that Afghanistan would not slip back into anarchy. The British had committed to and, in fact, had already sent a peacekeeping force for said purpose. Rumsfeld, by contrast, had publicly and repeatedly announced that the United States was not interested in participating in such a mission. His position was that the United States had already done most of the heavy lifting by vanquishing the Taliban and should therefore not be obligated to remain for peacekeeping purposes. In April, a number of op-ed pieces appeared arguing both sides of the issue, stirring a public debate that eventually caused Rumsfeld to back away from his reluctance to allow U.S. troops to participate in postwar stabilization.[54]

If the Pentagon was struggling with negative publicity, the Justice Department enjoyed a brief period of smooth sailing. Though it caused a stir for a couple of days, the Justice Department sought new authority to monitor "suspect" individuals in the United States whom it suspected might be related to terrorism. Among other things, the new authority would permit the Justice Department to obtain "roving" wiretaps—i.e., rather than a court order to tap a single phone, they would be able to tap a person and all the phones that person might use wherever that person might be—a clear expansion of its previous authority. More troubling, perhaps, was that the Justice Department would also be able to monitor e-mail and obtain a list of phone numbers a suspect might call, casting the net rather widely.[55]

Publicity problems soon became the least of the Pentagon's or, for that matter, Attorney General Ashcroft's worries. The Palestinian-Israeli imbroglio reignited again in March; alas, those troubles continue as of this writing (2003). Increasing numbers of suicide bombers continued to enter Israeli cities targeting Israeli citizens (i.e., non-combatants). And the Israelis continued to respond in earnest. For purposes of societal inputs what is important is the spate of op-ed pieces that resulted and what, if any, effect they had on U.S. foreign policy. Additionally, how did special-interest groups (SIGs), on either side of the dispute, mobilize in conjunction with the op-ed writers to affect U.S. foreign policy?

Thomas Friedman, for example, wrote "[a] terrible disaster is in the making in the Middle East. What Osama bin Laden failed to achieve on September 11 is now being unleashed by the Israeli–Palestinian war in the West Bank: a clash of civilizations." In advocating what both Arafat and Sharon needed to do in order to calm things down, he mentioned a couple of SIGs—at first blush, strange bedfellows— which also needed to change their behavior.

> The other people who have not wanted to face facts are *the feckless American Jewish Leaders, fundamentalist Christians* and *neoconservatives* who together have helped make it impossible for anyone in the U.S. administration to talk seriously about halting Israeli settlement-building without being accused of being anti-Israel. Their collaboration has helped prolong a colonial occupation that now threatens the entire Zionist enterprise. (italics added)

Friedman suggested that a NATO-U.S. force would ultimately need to be inserted for the foreseeable future while Israel gradually withdrew its settlements.[56] (Senator Richard Lugar [R-IN] effectively made the same argument in June 2003.) As a major pundit, Friedman's opinion began a new round of debates regarding U.S. foreign policy generally and the Palestinian-Israeli "problem" specifically. Over the following few weeks any number of op-ed pieces and pundits on television and radio debated what ought to happen in the Middle East. Two basic camps emerged. One was the neoconservatives, whom Friedman had associated with Jewish-American interest groups and evangelical Christians. The neoconservatives felt that Israel should follow the U.S. model of handling terrorism. Namely, use military force to dismantle the terrorist infrastructure in the occupied territories. The second group, who might be called the moderates, argued that Israel had to withdraw its forces and head back to negotiations. (As is discussed later, the administration itself was split over the debate.) As the debate raged in the media, the bureaucratic battles raged, mostly latently, within the Bush administration.[57]

Another well-known columnist in Washington, D.C., the *Washington Post's* David Broder, opened yet another debate. Since 9/11, the Democrats were falling over each other to show support for President Bush—as discussed elsewhere, an unusual phenomenon, as they represent the loyal opposition. But here it was some seven months later and scarcely a partisan criticism had been heard. More importantly, the opposition party had hardly asked any questions about the conduct of the war or what the endgame might be. The war had expanded to several other countries and neither party had scrutinized it. This was not surprising for Republicans, but the Democrats, during normal times, would have been asking what the president had in mind and when it might be finished. Broder claimed that the "Democrats punted" and consequently had lost their bearing and their right to be a party for future leadership.[58] If the Democrats had lost their voice in U.S. foreign policy, William Safire had not. In a repeat of his war cries in 1990, he continued to beat the drums of war against Iraq. He argued that sixty al Qaeda terrorists were holed up in Iraq. Safire asserted, furthermore, the proposition, which had largely been debunked weeks earlier, that Saddam was associated with 9/11. Interestingly, Safire took a swipe at the *former* Bush administration and, once more, at Colin Powell in particular. And finally, he argued that it was time for the United States to take decisive action, *viz.*, war with Iraq.[59] There were other pundits, to be sure, arguing in Powell's behalf, though they were, at least temporarily, overshadowed by Safire's stature.[60]

For those who find it hard to believe that debates within the punditocracy and on the op-ed pages of major papers affect foreign policy, the Bush administration began backing away from its hard line on "nation building" and peacekeeping. Recall that candidate Bush campaigned against "nation building" as too much like Clinton foreign policy. And Secretary Powell had been a lone voice in the administration in suggesting that the United States ought to be involved after military operations in Afghanistan. Moreover, Secretary Rumsfeld and the neoconservatives had been adamant that the British and others should perform such functions. As we have seen, the president and Rumsfeld had been mildly criticized for taking said positions. It was therefore telling when, in mid-April, the *New York Times* reported: "George W. Bush delivered a remarkable speech this week in which he vowed to lead an international effort to rebuild Afghanistan on the model of the Marshall Plan for Europe after World War II."[61] Clearly the White House, as is the case with all White Houses, was affected by debates that took place on the op-ed pages.

Michael Kinsley, a former Washington "insider"—one-time editor of the *New Republic*, former regular on CNN's *Crossfire*, and so forth—left the punditocracy several years back in order to start an on-line publication, *Slate*. Those who enjoyed his syndicated columns when he was still in the nation's capital could still read him on-line. Sadly for his fans, however, he had largely disappeared from the op-ed pages. It was therefore telling to see him publish, in the *Washington Post*, one of the few substantive criticisms of Bush's foreign policy. He wrote: "Honest administrations are all alike, but each dishonest administration is dishonest in its own way. Actually, there are no honest administrations." He then went on to criticize the administration's policies on several substantive counts.[62]

In late May a particularly interesting article was penned comparing Bush's foreign policy, and American society's response, to the days of the Cold War. Suffice it to say for now that it argued that the Bush administration was using the global war on terrorism for self-serving political reasons. Specifically, it argued that the executive branch and its various foreign-policy agencies were issuing the plethora of terrorist warnings to rally American society behind the administration—in effect, to keep the president popular. What is more, and not unlike the Truman Administration as the Cold War began, it argued that 9/11 gave a previously directionless Bush administration its *raison d'être:* "Everywhere, the national security establishment is humming with new missions, new funds, new offices with esoteric names. . . ." And similar to the once fiscally frugal Truman administration in the late 1940s, "The Bush Administration has unlocked the federal Treasury to combat global terrorism. . . ."[63]

In a strange twist of the *Washington Post's* editorial tradition, the usually critical editorial policy—since the days of Nixon, at least—reminiscent of the early days of the Cold War, editorialized in favor of Bush's "axis-of-evil" strategy: "[The president] offered a rhetorical outline that, if realized in practice, *would make him one of the most aggressive of internationalists among presidents*" (italics added). It continued, "Given the threat the country faces, such presidential determination is essential, and welcome." The editorial specifically addressed the president's determination to "call evil by its name," and commented favorably on the president's decision to "act preemptively against its terrorist enemies and regimes that back them." Finally, it raised the issue of European reluctance to go along with the Bush plan and urged the president "to keep making the argument" to them in order to get them onboard.[64]

While the *Post's* editorial was rallying behind Bush's "preemptive" policy, its major competitor was busy criticizing Attorney General Ashcroft. To be clear, it was not criticizing the Bush administration's global war on terrorism. Rather, the critique was squarely aimed at Ashcroft and his recently announced decision to change

Immigration and Naturalization Service's (INS) modus operandi. The *New York Times* suggested that Ashcroft's plan to fingerprint foreign visitors from Muslim countries "is a poorly conceived and inadequate substitute for the serious overhaul of the immigration system that should be among Washington's most urgent priorities." The editorial conceded that it "is important that the country police its borders and enforce its immigration laws in a way that is both fair and effective."

> The war on terrorism requires overhauling the visa and immigration system for everyone, not just Muslim or Arab visitors. As he goes about the necessary business of tightening border security, Mr. Ashcroft should address basic problems rather than settling for quick but ultimately ineffective solutions.[65]

As has been noted, the media in general has been quite positive and supportive of the administration's war on terrorism. Indeed, virtually all the critiques through 2002 were aimed at Justice Department policies and Attorney General Ashcroft specifically.

The following day the same paper scrutinized the president's plans to overhaul the government, reorienting it to fight terrorism, likely the biggest threat to the United States for the foreseeable future. It bordered on being downright obsequious, demonstrating yet again how the media often follow public opinion rather than direct it. The editorial suggested that after months of attempting to tweak various parts on the fly, "President Bush belatedly but wisely told the nation last night that an ambitious reorganization of the government was needed to get the job done." The editorial specifically compared Bush's task to Truman's. "But no one should underestimate the obstacles *to pulling off the biggest overhaul of federal machinery since Harry Truman* and Congress established the Defense Department, the Central Intelligence Agency, and the National Security Council in the late 1940s." Nonetheless, his "proposal to draw together more than a dozen federal agencies in a new Department of Homeland Security" made sense. Similarly, the *Christian Science Monitor* published a feature article making the same sorts of comparisons to the commencement of the Cold War and post-9/11 activities. "It now appears that Washington's reaction to the events of September 11 *may represent the most intense period of self-examination and reorganization since the existing national-security bureaucracy was created after World War II*" (italics added).[66]

While media attention had largely been supportive of the administration's war on terrorism and many of its initiatives, it was late May and into June (2002) that more-than nominal criticisms of Bush's foreign policy began to appear with some frequency. Focusing in on Ashcroft again, Howard Kurtz suggested the beltway crowd was buzzing about the so-called dirty bomb and the arrest of Jose Padilla "not about the grim prospect that people might have been killed, but about the announcement. It does appear that John Ashcroft hyped the circumstances surrounding Monday's arrest of Abdullah al Muhajir [Jose Padilla], who was not exactly on the verge of setting off a radioactive bomb." Recall that after Padilla's arrest and a couple of days of dramatic media coverage on cable television and elsewhere, it turned out that Padilla was simply on a scouting trip. No such device had been made nor had Padilla any of the ingredients necessary to make one, much less the technical know-how. When the White House Press corps raised the issue of Ashcroft's dramatic announcement—Ashcroft had interrupted a trip to make the announcement himself—spokesman Ari Fleischer "dismissed such naysayers as 'the most cynical among the most partisan,'" and suggested such persons ought not to be taken seriously.[67] It was a rather strange overreaction given the incredibly positive coverage the media had generally given the administration since 9/11.

There were critiques, to be sure, regarding the administration's foreign policy when it came to the Middle East. One should understand, however, that even during the early and most intense days of the Cold War, presidents had been criticized with respect to the Middle East, a particularly emotional foreign-policy issue in U.S. society. Truman and Eisenhower were both criticized, for instance, as have been most presidents since. For President Bush, most of the criticism focused on the reluctance the administration showed in taking a leadership role early on in its tenure. It was not until after the war on terror began that the administration involved itself substantively in the Middle East; by then, Palestinian–Israeli relations had deteriorated to an almost hopeless degree. The *Washington Post* editorialized that the administration's Middle East policy showed signs of "drift." But for every negative article on Bush and the Middle East, an article favoring Bush's position would appear suggesting the administration was finally showing the sort of "moral clarity" vis-à-vis the Middle East that it was in the war on terror.[68] Thus, even when the media began criticizing Bush's policies with respect to the Middle East, pundits who lauded the same policies largely insulated the administration.

It was late June when Bush finally made a hard turn on the administration's Middle East policy. As noted, special-interest groups as well as editorials and the larger puditocracy had been publicly debating whether the United States should continue to try to broker peace or dump Arafat. Israel already had publicly announced it would not deal with Arafat. The hard turn came when the president received intelligence from the Israelis satisfying Bush that Arafat had authorized a $20,000 payment to a group implicated in a mid-June suicide attack. The Bush administration began publicly to take the Israeli stance. The change in policy proved controversial in some corners. George Will quickly approved of the administration's decision, however, giving the policy the *imprimatur* of one of Washington's leading pundits.[69]

Thus the administration had no real need to worry about or pay attention to the relatively few critiques it received. Additionally, U.S. society has continued showing remarkable unity since 9/11. Even race relations, one study asserted, had improved since 9/11. According to a recent poll by the *New York Times* and CBS News, "a growing number of New Yorkers say they have seen a remarkable change in race relations since the September 11 terror attacks." Nor was it simply New Yorkers and Easterners who were unified. The entire country seemed to have come together. The significance of this post-9/11 unity was twofold: First, it provided the administration wide berth in formulating policies since a unified populace tends to rally around the president; second, it affected partisan politics in Congress where representatives take such unity as support for the president's policies. Feckless Congressional members rarely show the fortitude of conviction necessary to criticize a popular president. On the same day, supporting the previous observation, the same paper editorialized about the cooperation the administration was receiving from Congress.

> To the surprise of many Washington veterans, Congress has gotten off to a fast start meeting President Bush's goal of creating a new domestic security agency this year. The White House has even had to acknowledge sheepishly that while Mr. Bush was racing around the country urging lawmakers to act immediately, the administration has not yet finished drafting a bill for them to pass.

"Posturing aside," the piece continued, both parties seem to realize they cannot go empty-handed before anxious voters about terrorist attacks."[70]

One debate—one on the margins of both Bush and Clinton foreign policy—that had been bubbling below the surface for months was whether or not preventable intelligence failures led to 9/11. In a sense it was a sideshow inasmuch as it would be difficult to pin any such failures directly on Bush or his foreign-policy team. After all, DCI and head of the CIA, George Tenet, was a Clinton holdover. And Bush-appointed director of the FBI, Mueller, could scarcely be blamed as he had been appointed only a week prior to 9/11. Nonetheless, Congress was gearing up for hearings on potential intelligence failures and what was needed to ameliorate perceived failures. Senator Bob Graham (D-FL) and ranking member of the Senate Intelligence Committee (and presidential hopeful in 2003) had come to the view that "September 11 was theoretically preventable, saying in a recent interview 'It could have been avoided if you had gotten all the information that was available before the eyes of a single human being or a common group of human beings so they could have had the chance to see the pattern those pieces of information were beginning to form.'"[71]

The aforementioned heat Rumsfeld and Ashcroft had taken on the detainee issue—in this case the issue of detainees who happened to be American citizens—raised its head in a slightly different form in late June. In a *New York Times* article, the author stated that two Americans were being held in military custody without access to lawyers, and linking it to Bush himself for the first time suggested that it might be "an overly broad assertion of presidential authority."[72] It certainly was not the first time a president had used "overly broad" assertion of power during war. Lincoln, for instance, repeatedly suspended due process during the Civil War; Truman overstepped his powers when he seized steel mills in 1952 during the Korean War; and Nixon abused his powers nearly his entire tenure. Doubtless, these examples will not be the last. And the media has in the past and will continue in the future to play its role as the fourth estate in society: the watchdog. Furthermore, it is a necessary function, for it protects the Constitutionally guaranteed civil liberties of all Americans. The media, though often unpopular, are needed to keep government honest—all branches. In terms of the effect such criticisms had, muted though they were, on foreign policy, such effects occur over time. A case in point: The McCarthy tactics of the 1950s took a couple of years to run their course and to cause societal changes that only eventually affected U.S. foreign policy. To date there has been only tepid pressure from American society to change the Justice Department's policies or a reaction to Bush's alleged "overly broad" exercise of presidential powers. Indeed, the public has seemed indifferent if not satisfied with the policies insofar as the policies appear to make the public feel safer. It will take time to affect foreign policy. The lack of public reaction is indicative of a weakness in the argument that the "liberal media," carps on presidents, particularly conservative ones, and that Congress responds and limits presidential flexibility. More likely, the media follows public opinion to a much greater degree than is frequently thought. Perhaps, as suggested by others, the media instruct the public regarding what to think about but not what to think (Kegley and Wittkopf 1996).

Of more concern to the administration was the increasingly likely reality that they had neither captured nor killed bin Laden. After the 9/11 attacks Bush personalized bin Laden's capture on a couple of occasions. Now that it was becoming evident that bin Laden had escaped and was reportedly directing some of his network—albeit, in diminished fashion—some in the punditocracy began raising the issue as an embarrassment to the administration. Bin Laden had recently been implicated in the Tunisia synagogue attack and possibly both the shoe-bomber (Richard Reid) and Padilla fiascos. Once again, however, the debate (if it can properly be called a debate) remained limited to a few op-ed pieces and the television talking heads. The public wanted bin Laden brought to justice as several polls demonstrated. But they were also willing to give the president time. While the public wanted bin Laden captured or killed, they were not clamoring for its immediacy. Most Americans were willing to demonstrate the patience the president had requested.

In late June–early July two related events occurred that, at least for a short time, generated some interest. The FBI announced another warning, suggesting that al Qaeda might be planning a July 4 attack. The warnings had become somewhat controversial because of how often they were issued, coupled with the fact that Homeland Director Tom Ridge was reluctant to change the color-threat-warning category. (If there was reliable intelligence of a threat, one could reasonably assume that the threat assessment would move to a higher level. The numerous issuances of warnings notwithstanding, Ridge had maintained the United States, with one exception, at the same level since the inception of his color-coded schemata.) Some began to muse that the public might become fatigued with the warnings and fail to take one seriously in the future with potentially disastrous consequences. Kristof implied another reason the FBI issued the warning—actually more benefit than reason. Namely, he suggested that machinations within the FBI had more to do with the anthrax investigation or, rather, its lack of results. Kristof's sources told him the FBI had actually discovered who was behind the anthrax attacks but did not want it known publicly. The implication was that whoever the culprit was, its announcement would embarrass the government.[73]

Certainly the public was not buying the conspiracy. Nor did the FBI's warning deter public celebration of the national holiday. In fact, July 4 celebrations turned out to be the most patriotic in memory. Despite the FBI's concerns that an attack might focus on Washington, D.C.'s July 4 celebrations in the Mall, a huge crowd attended the show. Indeed, it was not limited to the nation's capital. Huge crowds met and celebrated the nation's independence in city after city across the country. One *New York Times* article specifically noted the renewed patriotism. "Around the country, people are treating this Independence Day differently, with reactions from a fervent flowering of patriotism to a sense of somber reflection. Everywhere cities and towns are trying to strike a balance between the strong need to commemorate July 4 and the equally strong need to guard against terrorists seeking to prey on the day."[74]

As late as fall 2002, despite Osama bin Laden and his top lieutenants still being on the loose and despite the domestic controversies in which the administration found itself (Enron, Haliburton, and so forth), the Bush administration remained incredibly popular, as demonstrated by November's midterm elections. Further, following the administration's war in Iraq and, as 2004 presidential elections loom (summer 2003), polling data continue to show the president as exceptionally popular. Clearly, a post-9/11 consensus, similar to the early Cold War consensus, persists. Let us next consider governmental inputs in U.S. foreign policy following 9/11.

NOTES

1. Howard LaFranchi, "Public Sees New Global Role for U.S.," *Christian Science Monitor*, 11 January 2002, p. 1.
2. Ronald Brownstein, "New Era Means Trimming Tax Cut," *Los Angeles Times*, 14 January 2002.
3. Ronald Brownstein, "Debating War's Sway over Voters," *Los Angeles Times*, 24 January 2002.
4. Nicolas D. Kristof, "Let Them Be P.O.W.'s," *New York Times*, 29 January 2002.
5. Robert O'Harrow, Jr., "Intricate Screening of Fliers in Works," *Washington Post*, 1 February 2002, p. A-1.
6. Richard Morin and Dana Milbank, "Bush and GOP Enjoy Record Popularity," *Washington Post*, January 29 2002, p. A01. (Italics added.)
7. Howard Kurtz, "Patriotism Comes under Attack," *Washington Post*, 4 January 2002.
8. Walter S. Jones, *The Logic of International Relations* (Wyoming: Longman, 1996).
9. Liz Marlantes, "Bioterror," *Christian Science Monitor*, 17 December 2002. See also Peter Grier "Fragile Freedoms," *Christian Science Monitor*, 13 December 2001.
10. Robert A. Rosenblatt and Warren Vieth, "White House Sees Shrinking Budget Surplus," *Los Angeles Times*, 23 August 2001. See also Johanna Neuman, "Flood of Wartime Spending Keeps Nation's Capital Flush with Capital," *Los Angeles Times*, 22 January 2002.
11. Mark Fineman, "Defense," *New York Times*, 10 January 2002.
12. Carol Williams, "U.S. Spirits 6 Terror Suspects out of Bosnia," *Los Angeles Times*, 19 January 2002.
13. Megan Garvey and Carl Ingram, "Terrorism Grants Go to States, Cities," *Los Angeles Times*, 1 February 2002.
14. *Washington Post*, "Bioterrorism Bonanza" 6 February 2002, p. A-18.
15. Theresa Hitchens, *Press Release* (Washington, D.C.: CDI, January 31, 2002). As we shall see, it was rather steeper.
16. Francine Kiefer, "Medicare, Social Security Reform, and His Energy Plan Face Tough Prospects," *Christian Science Monitor*, 1 February 2002.

17. Amy Argetsinger and Valerie Strauss, "Schools Translate Terror into Curricular Changes," *Washington Post*, 8 February 2002, p. A-1.
18. Eric Lichtblau, "Bias against U.S. Arabs Taking Subtler Forms," *Los Angeles Times*, 10 February 2002.
19. Thomas L. Friedman, "Blunt Question, Blunt Answer," *New York Times*, 10 February 2002.
20. Charles W. Kegley, Jr. and Eugene R. Wittkopf, *American Foreign Policy: Pattern and Process*, 5th ed. (New York: St. Martin's Press, 1996).
21. Warren Richey, "Terror Could Tilt High Court on State Rights,"*Christian Science Monitor*, 11 February 2002.
22. David Sreitfeld and Charles Piller, "A Changed America," *Los Angeles Times*, 19 January 2002.
23. Thomas Friedman, "An Intriguing Signal form the Saudi Crown Prince," *New York Times*, 17 February 2002.
24. Howard Kurtz, "War Coverage Takes a Negative Turn," *Washington Post*, 17 February 2002, p. A-14.
25. Jim Hoagland, "Assessing the War Honestly," *Washington Post*, 14 February 2002, p. A-33.
26. Jackson Diehl, "Pakistan's Thorny Transition," *Washington Post*, 18 February 2002, p. A-23.
27. William Safire, "The Great Unwatched," *New York Times*, 18 February 2002.
28. Michael Nauman, "Why Europe Is Wary of War with Iraq," *New York Times*, 18 February 2002. Also see, "Cross Talk among Allies," *Washington Post*, 20 February 2002, p. A-14. Also, David Ignatius, "France's Constructive Critic," *Washington Post*, 22 February 2002, p. A-25.
29. Thomas H. Sander and Robert D. Putman, "Walking the Civic Talk after Sept. 11," *Christian Science Monitor*, 19 February 2002. See also, Terence Monmaney, "Living with 9/11 State of Mind" *Los Angeles Times*, 26 February 2002.
30. Nicholas D. Kristof, "The Wrong War," *New York Times*, 19 February 2002.
31. William Schneider, "A Reagan Echo," *Los Angeles Times*, 24 February 2002.
32. Valerie Strauss and Emily Wax, "Where Two Worlds Collide," *Washington Post*, 25 February 2002, p. A-1.
33. Fred Hiatt, "A Flinch on Chechnya," *Washington Post*, 25 February 2002, p. A-23. Nicholas D. Kristof, "Devils and Evil Axes," *New York Times*, 26 February 2002.
34. Esther Schrader, "Pentagon Closes Besieged Strategy Office." *Los Angeles Times*, 27 February 2002.
35. Eric Schmitt and James Dao, "A 'Damaged' Information Office Is Declared Closed by Rumsfeld," *New York Times*, 27 February 2002. For a humorous assessment, see Howard Kurtz, "A Leaky Ship Goes Under," *Washington Post*, 27 February 2002.
36. Thomas E. Ricks, "Rumsfeld Kills Pentagon Propaganda Unit," *Washington Post*, 27 February 2002, p. A-21.
37. Richard A. Serrano, "Detainees in Cuba Refuse to Eat after Cell Incident," *Los Angeles Times*, 1 March 2002.
38. Ann Scott Tyson, "Does bin Laden Matter Anymore? In the Pentagon Corridors, the 'Evil-Doer' Is No Longer the Focus — Even if Most Americans Think He's Supposed to Be," *Christian Science Monitor*, 1 March 2002.
39. Howard LaFranchi, "U.S. Seeks Right Equation to Topple Saddam," *Christian Science Monitor*, 1 March 2002.
40. Scott Peterson, "Special Ops Tackle Aide Mission," *Christian Science Monitor*, 1 March 2002.
41. Todd Purdum, "Democrats Starting to Fault President on the War's Future," *New York Times*, 28 February 2002; cf. Helen Dewar, "Lott Calls Daschle Divisive," *Washington Post*, 1 March 2002, p. A-6. Also, Dan Balz and Helen Dewar, "Daschle Defends Challenge of Bush on War," *Washington Post*, 2 March 2002, p. A-13; *Washington Post*, "Debating the War," 3 March 2002, p. B-6.
42. *New York Times*, "The Uses of American Power," 3 March 2002.
43. Jim Hoagland, "No Easy Exit," *Washington Post*, 3 March 2002, p. B-7.
44. Gail Russell Chaddock, "Soft Debate Surfaces on Terror War," *Christian Science Monitor*, 4 March 2002.
45. William Safire, "The Inspection Ploy," *New York Times*, 4 March 2002.
46. Jessica Mathews, "The Wrong Target," *Washington Post*, 4 March 2002, p. A-19.
47. Abraham McLaughlin, "Homeland Security," *Christian Science Monitor*, 6 March 2002.
48. Charles Krauthammer, "Saudi Peace Sham," *Washington Post*, 6 March 2002, p. A-19.
49. William Safire, "Ending the War Process," *New York Times*, 11 March 2002.
50. Editorial, "A War without Congress," *Los Angeles Times*, 7 March 2002.

51. Henry Weinstein, Darin Briscoe, and Mitchell Landsberg, "A Changed America," *Los Angeles Times*, 10 March 2002.
52. Richard Morin and Claudia Deane, "Poll," *Washington Post*, 11 March 2002, p. A-1.
53. Jim Hoagland, "Pakistan," *Washington Post*, 28 March 2002, p. A-29.
54. For example, see Richard Holbrooke, "Rebuilding Nations," *Washington Post*, 1 April 2002, p. A-15. Also, Sebastian Mallaby, "And Their Armies," *Washington Post*, 1 April 2002, p. A-15.
55. Editorial "Annapolis Takes on Terrorism," *Washington Post*, 30 March 2002, p. A-16.
56. Thomas L. Friedman, "The Hard Truth," *New York Times*, 3 April 2002. Abraham McLaughlin and Gail Russell Chaddock, "Christian Right Steps in on Mideast," *Christian Science Monitor*, 16 April 2002.
57. See Dan Balz and Dana Milbank, "Bush Doctrine Begins to Blur," *Washington Post*, 3 April 2002, p. A-1; George Will, "War and Then a Wall," *Washington Post*, 3 April 2002, p. A-23; William Safire, "Sharon on Survival," *New York Times*, 4 April 2002; Shibley Telhami, "Why Suicide Terrorism Takes Root," *Los Angeles Times*, 4 April 2002, Ellen Goodman, "Deluded Bombers," *Washington Post*, 6 April 2002, p. A-21; Zbigniew Brezezinski, "Moral Duty, National Interest," *New York Times*, 7 April 2002.
58. David S. Broder, "The Democrats Punt," *Washington Post*, 7 April 2002, p. B-7.
59. William Safire, "Saddam's Offensive," *New York Times*, 8 April 2002.
60. Richard Cohen, "Flunking Foreign Affairs," *Washington Post*, 18 April 2002, p. A-21.
61. *New York Times*, editorial. "Afghanistan's Marshall Plan," 19 April 2002.
62. Michael Kinsley, "Lying in Style," *Washington Post*, 19 April 2002, p. A-25.
63. William M. Arkin, "A Policy in from the Cold," *Los Angeles Times*, 26 May 2002.
64. "Taking the Offensive," *Washington Post*, 4 June 2002, p. A-16.
65. "Handling Foreign Visitors," *New York Times*, 6 June 2002.
66. "Back to the Drawing Board," *New York Times*, 7 June 2002. Peter Grier, "Security Shuffle," *Christian Science Monitor*, 7 June 2002.
67. Howard Kurtz, "The Second-Guessing Syndrome," *Washington Post*, 13 June 2002.
68. "Signs of Drift," *Washington Post*, 16 June 2002, p. B-6; cf. George Will, "Dispensing with Arafat," *Washington Post*, 6 June 2002, p. A-25.
69. Glenn Kessler and Walter Pincus, "Bombing Link Swayed Bush," *Washington Post*, 26 June 2002, p. A-1. George F. Will, "Dispensing with Arafat," *Washington Post*, 26 June 2002, p. A-25.
70. Dean E. Murphy and David M. Halbfinger, "9/11 Bridged the Racial Divide, New Yorkers Say, Gingerly," *New York Times*, 16 June 2002; Murphy and Halbfinger, "The New Politics of Anti-Terrorism," *New York Times*, 16 June 2002.
71. Carl Hulse, "Terror Inquiry Shines Light on Senator Seeking Stage," *New York Times*, 21 June 2002.
72. Katharine Q. Seelye, "War on Terror Makes Odd Twists in Justice System," *New York Times*, 23 June 2002.
73. Nicolas D. Kristof, "Anthrax? The F.B.I. Yawns," *New York Times*, 2 July 2002.
74. Pam Belluck, "With Patriotism Renewed, July Hits a Deeper Chord," *New York Times*, 4 July 2002. Also see Richard, Cohen "Born on the Fourth of July," *Washington Post*, 4 July 2002.

GOVERNMENTAL INPUTS TO U.S. FOREIGN POLICY

The nation's intelligence agencies failed to heed serious warnings dating back to the mid-1990s that the al Qaeda terrorist network was increasingly focused on striking targets in the United States and using aircraft as weapons, according to a report issued by congressional investigators Wednesday [September 18, 2002].

— Greg Miller, "U.S. Overlooked Terrorism Signs Well before 9/11," *Los Angeles Times*, 19 September 2002.

The CIA failed repeatedly before September 11 to share key information with the FBI about two al Qaeda suspects who became hijackers in last year's attacks, even after learning the men held U.S. visas, were in the United States, and had links to the bombing of the destroyer *Cole*.

It provided new evidence of what lawmakers called bureaucratic barriers, shortsighted policies and repeated blunders at CIA and FBI.

— Greg Miller, "Blunders Numerous before 9/11," *Los Angeles Times*, 21 September 2002.

Seeking congressional support for a war President Bush says he has not yet decided to wage, Defense Secretary Donald H. Rumsfeld told lawmakers Wednesday that Iraq poses the greatest threat to global stability.

Rumsfeld's testimony provided the Bush administration's strongest statement since Iraq offered Monday [September 16, 2002], to allow in international weapons inspectors . . . the United States wants much more from Hussein's regime.

— Maggie Farley and John Hendren, "Rumsfeld Makes Case for War," *Los Angeles Times*, 19 September 2002.

. . . Secretary of State Colin L. Powell is interested in how America is perceived abroad because he understands the importance of international public opinion in forming the coalitions and partnerships that the United States seeks on Iraq and other issues.

— Sonni Efron, "Slick Ads Won't Sell the U.S. Message to Arabs, Report Warns," *Los Angeles Times*, 19 September 2002.

Southern California's defense industry — the nerve center for advanced weapons and surveillance technology for the U.S. military — is quietly gearing up for a potential attack against Iraq.

— Peter Pae, "Southland Defense Industry Quietly Heeds War's Drumbeat," *Los Angeles Times*, 27 September 2002.

The governmental cluster of foreign-policy inputs involves the enormous foreign-policy and national-security bureaucracy, its size and the routines necessary for it to function. Recall that a rather unique national-security bureaucracy began to grow dramatically following World War II. Historically, the United States had maintained a relatively small national-security bureaucracy during times of peace; historically, during times of war the United States typically raised military troops necessary to fight the war after which it reduced its numbers, returning to a non-wartime footing. Since the 1940s, no such reduction of forces has occurred. On the contrary, a continuous growth of the bureaucracy has persisted, evolving ever-more-complex operating routines over time. It continued in the 1990s, as if the Cold War were still on, and is beginning anew in 9/11's wake.

In the United States, the basis of the fundamental relationship between the branches of government is memorialized in the U.S. Constitution. In particular, the Constitution establishes the relative foreign-policy prerogatives of the executive and legislative branches. It may surprise some readers to know — given the clear primacy of the executive branch in terms of foreign policy since the Cold War — that the Constitution actually assigns more foreign-policy prerogatives to Congress than it does to the executive branch. The Founding Fathers clearly envisaged checks and balances between the branches. Additionally, the Founders evidently sought to preclude the rise of an imperial executive branch — the so-called imperial presidency — in foreign policy by assigning more prerogatives to the legislative branch.

Article I, Section 8 of the Constitution grants Congress the following powers: to collect taxes and other monies and to provide for the defense of the nation; to define and punish piracy and other felonies on the high seas in accordance with the laws of nations (international law); "to declare War, grant Letters of Marque and Reprisal, and make Rules concerning Captures on Land and Water" (Clause 11); "to raise and support Armies, but no Appropriation of Money to that Use shall be for a longer Term than two Years" (Clause 12); and "to provide and maintain a Navy" (Clause 13). Broadly speaking, Congress holds the purse stings of the nation's treasury (Section 7), an exceptionally powerful tool, to be sure. This applies to foreign-policy initiatives as well as domestic initiatives. Clearly, without money, the executive branch can do little in either foreign or domestic policy. Congress is the branch, not the executive, that must declare war. In theory, these two prerogatives alone would proscribe the president from putting military troops in the field. Wars are to be declared before the military may be committed to battle; only the legislative branch may so declare and then fund said wars.

Thus, a president has no Constitutional basis to pay troops even if he were to find a way around the obstacle of having no declaration of war. An additional Congressional foreign-policy prerogative is the "advice and consent" responsibility for critical foreign-policy appointments. The president may not appoint many of his top foreign-policy advisors without Congressional approval. Indeed, the executive is granted relatively few foreign-policy prerogatives. Article II (Section 2) identifies the president as the commander-in-chief. In other words, once the Congress has declared war and appropriated monies for the instruments of war—war supplies, material, troops, and so on—the president takes over and is the apex of the civilian chain of command, maintaining an important founding principle of the United States: *viz.*, civilian control of the military. (The War Powers Act is an exception; see Public Law 93-148, U.S. War Powers Resolution, 68 AJIL 2 372, 1974.) Since the late 1940s, the military's own chain of command terminates with the Joint Chiefs of Staff, whose chairman is the liaison to both the secretary of defense and by extension to the president. Despite these apparent inequities, the executive branch has effectively become the dominant branch of government in terms of both foreign policy generally and military deployment specifically.[1]

The Founders intended these checks and balances so that no single branch could conduct foreign policy by fiat, thereby ensuring the accountability so fundamental to democratic theory. In particular, the Founders intended to check the executive's ability to commit troops and conduct war without Congressional authorization. U.S. foreign policy is replete with struggles over prerogatives between Congress and the executive. Prior to World War II, there was a powerful faction, principally within the Republican Party, that was doggedly isolationist. This faction historically fought tooth and nail against the United States getting involved in "Europe's" wars, including World War II. In fact, the pillars of America's pre-twentieth-century history included isolationism, commercial expansionism, and the Monroe Doctrine (1823), the latter of which specifically carved out America's sphere of influence, obviating potential European meddling. America's early foreign-policy history was distinctly isolationist. Only in the twentieth century did America partially discard isolationism (circa 1917) in favor of internationalism. After World War I, however, an isolationist renaissance reexerted itself. It would not be until World War II that the United States completely abandoned isolationism in favor of a much more active, engaged foreign policy:[2] namely, internationalism or globalism.

Prior to the twentieth century, however, isolationism played a fundamental and integral part of U.S. foreign policy, its mythology, and ethos. George Washington's farewell speech spoke to avoiding foreign entanglements. It is well worth quoting in length as it gives one the sense of how engrained isolationism was to America's early history and ethos:

> The great rule of conduct for us, in regard to foreign Nations, is, in extending our commercial relations, to have with them as little Political connections as possible. . . . Europe has a set of primary interests, which to us have none, or very remote relations. . . . Hence, therefore, it must be unwise in us to implicate ourselves, by artificial ties in the ordinary vicissitudes of her politics, or the ordinary combinations and collisions of her friendships, or enmities.
>
> Why, by interweaving our destiny with that of any part of Europe, entangle our peace and prosperity in the toils of European ambition, rivalship, interest, humor, or caprice? 'Tis our true policy to steer clear of permanent alliances, with any portion of the foreign world. (George Washington, *Farewell Address*, 1769)

John Adams said, "[We] should separate ourselves as far as possible and as long as possible from all European politics," and a somewhat pithy aphorism of the time was: "Lie down with dogs, get up with fleas."[3] Jones concedes that there was a brief "flirtation with isolationism" in the 1930s but by the beginning of the Cold War that flirtation ended (Jones 1996).

With the onset of the Cold War however, internationalism (perhaps interventionism) became the basis of U.S. foreign policy. The complexities of the Cold War eluded many Americans' understanding if not interest—in no small part, due to the U.S. government's efforts to keep Americans confused about its enemy: Communism. Americans came to know simply that Communists were "evil" and "godless" and were bent on destroying America's way of life. Americans were told, for instance, that Communists used "brainwashing" techniques (e.g., during the Korean War, during the seizure of the *Pueblo* in 1968). Given the actual threat of Soviet Communism—and by extension, its satellites in Korea, China, Vietnam, and so on—and given U.S. propaganda and mythology, Americans understandably deferred decision-making to their government leaders during much of the Cold War. After all, most Americans trusted their government in the pre-Vietnam, pre-Watergate era.

As the American public deferred to their government's "good judgment" in a complex war against insidious Communism, Congress began to sense the public mood and responded to it accordingly, conceding some of its own responsibilities. Congress too began to see the need to give the executive, under which the evolving national-security bureaucracy operated, increased flexibility. So many foreign-policy "crises" occurred in quick succession that Congress—being an unwieldy institution, intended by the Founders to deliberate issues over time—slowly stopped exercising its collective Constitutional prerogatives and simply acquiesced in virtually any and all foreign-policy initiative coming from the executive. The practical result was a new bipartisan, a Cold War consensus that lasted, at least, until midway through the Vietnam War. Once bamboozled by the Tonkin Gulf Resolution[4] and the subsequent Vietnam fiasco, Congress began to re-exert its Constitutional prerogatives by the end of the 1960s.

What is interesting following 9/11 and parallels the dynamics of the Cold War period is the way Congress has again abdicated its foreign-policy responsibilities to a large extent. Congress, as was the case with the Cold War, assiduously reads public opinion and all 535 voting members were well aware of the president's polling numbers more than a year after the commencement of Operation Enduring Freedom. As with Vietnam, Congress has yet to declare war—their Constitutional responsibility. Instead, they quickly approved a resolution supporting the president's war on terrorism. Similarly, they passed the Patriot Act in October (2001), a remarkably quick action for the U.S. Congress giving the executive branch additional and dramatic new powers.[5] In fact one of the few substantive criticisms by Democrats (the loyal opposition) having to do with the war on terrorism—and only after a lengthy respite—was whether Homeland Security Director Tom Ridge should have to testify before Congress. Rather, the Democrats have been reduced to criticizing Bush on Enron and other domestic issues and to bickering over whether or not Iraq should be considered integral to America's war on the global-terrorist hydra. Even as of this writing (spring 2003), Bush continues to be largely insulated from Congressional criticism with respect to the global war on terrorism.

Woodward and Balz's account of the week following the 9/11 attacks shows key Democrats, including Senate Majority Leader Tom Daschle "pledg[ing] bipartisanship support." Representative Gephardt told the president that he and Congress must work together to reassure the public that their government was fully functional and that the Democrats would be fully willing to participate; he asked only that the president keep Congress informed and involved. President *pro tempore*, and senior sage in the Senate, Senator Robert Byrd (D-WV) in a flair of metaphysics, told the president he was "praying for" Bush and silenced the room by telling the president he was standing there and that "Mighty forces will come to your aid."[6] (Senator Byrd subsequently led the charge against war with Iraq.)

THE LAWS OF BUREAUCRATIC POLITICS

Beyond the Constitution is another governing or constraining dynamic of U.S. foreign policy: namely the laws of bureaucratic politics. A well-known bureaucratic law—as certain as gravity—is that bureaucracies tend to grow, try to increase their spheres of influence at another bureaucracy's expense, and attempt to increase their annual budgets. Clearly, this bureaucratic law has been followed in the case of the behemoth U.S. foreign-policy and national-security bureaucracy. Congress created the National Security Act in 1947. Among the bureaucracies created by the 1947 statute—and its subsequent amendments—were the Central Intelligence Agency (CIA), the central military command structure known as the Joint Chiefs of Staff (JCS), the Department of Defense (combining two hitherto separate departments, the War Department and the Navy Department), and the National Security Council (NSC), which is directed by what has become known as the president's national security advisor. Since the 1947 statute, additional agencies have been created: the National Security Agency, which collects electronic intelligence; the National

Reconnaissance Office, which directs America's spy satellites; and various other disparate agencies. Additionally, the State Department, which historically has served as the primary focus of U.S. foreign policy, has continued to grow with tens of thousands of foreign-service officers and appointed leadership with each new administration. Similarly, the Department of Defense has grown tremendously since 1947. Together and, over time, this national-security/foreign-policy leviathan has grown into a huge bureaucracy with disparate interests, all of whose parts have to compete for a finite number of dollars appropriated by Congress. Given their disparate interests—known as parochial interests (or simply parochialism) and the competition for budget dollars—bureaucratic politics has become a powerful force in shaping U.S. foreign policy, thus properly considered as a governmental input. It is important to note that the foreign-policy, national-security bureaucracy that has evolved since 1947 falls under the control of the executive branch. Congress holds the purse strings but the president's cabinet and its directors or secretaries—those who head the various bureaucracies just discussed—serve at the pleasure of the president. The president appoints them with the "advice and consent" of the Congress.

The principal bureaucracies tasked with foreign policy/national security are: the National Security Council; the Department of State; the Department of Defense; the intelligence community; and the Justice Department. Other departments such as the Commerce Department and Treasury are involved in foreign policy but they have traditionally played a more peripheral role. In a world increasingly characterized by complex economic, political, cultural and other interconnections, other executive bureaucracies slip in and out of the foreign-policy decision-making functions. The Office of Management and Budget, the president's trade representative (during the multiyear trade negotiations over NAFTA, for example), the Department of Agriculture and, at least since 9/11, the Department of Transportation all are illustrative.

The sheer size of this collective bureaucracy is astounding. In order for the disparate parts to function and to communicate with one another, standard operating procedures (SOPs), protocols, and routines must be created. The National Security Act recognized this fact and formalized some of these routines. For example, the Director of the CIA is specified as the ultimate collector, collator, and representative of intelligence for the president; in fact, this explains why the CIA's director is known as the Director of Central Intelligence (DCI), not simply as the director of the CIA. Similarly, the 1947 statute established the military chain of command vis-à-vis the Joint Chiefs, comprised of the various service chiefs. Less formally, bureaucracies evolve their own SOPs. It is frequently these SOPs and protocols that affect foreign policy in normal times.

EFFECTS OF 9/11 ON THE GROWTH OF BUREAUCRACIES

If, in fact, the attacks of 9/11 represent a fundamentally transforming event in U.S. foreign policy, comparable to the commencement of the Cold War, then one should see a comparable terrorism-security-bureaucracy growth. That is not to say that a huge new bureaucracy must evolve. Rather, extant foreign-policy bureaucracies and newly created bureaucracies will become focused on terrorism with new clarity in mission comparable to the way they focused on the Cold War. Obviously, one cannot possibly evaluate completely so soon after 9/11 whether this had occurred. However, some observations can be made. Similarly, one should see new protocols established to coordinate communications between the new bureaucratic entities that evolve. Moreover, one should witness old bureaucracies fighting to protect their respective turfs, fighting over new foreign-policy dollars, attempting to justify their own budgets, indeed, arguing that with the mission and direction of U.S. foreign policy changing, their budgets should be increased. Again, only time will tell but we may focus on the first several months for indications of such behavior.

Terrorism had come onto the radar screen in the Clinton administration. The World Trade Center was attacked in 1993 and the two U.S. embassies in Kenya and Tanzania were destroyed in nearly simultaneous attacks. However, no comparable transforming event as 9/11 or series of events (circa 1947–1950, the beginning of the Cold War) occurred in the 1990s. The Clinton administration, nonetheless, was beginning to focus increasingly on global terrorism as a U.S. foreign-policy issue. A *Washington Post* article after 9/11 outlined the struggles within the Clinton administration over how high a priority to give terrorism as a U.S. foreign-policy threat. Clinton signed a Presidential Decision Directive (an NSC document) in March 1995. Though still classified, terrorism reportedly was defined as a "third-tier" issue. The article attributes the struggle to "bureaucratic turf" fights. Nonetheless, the Office of Management and Budget estimated that the anti-terror budget increased from $5.7 billion in fiscal 1996 to $11.1 billion in fiscal 2001, that is, it nearly doubled. The article concludes that "[b]y any measure available, Clinton left office having given greater priority to terrorism than any president before him."[7] It would take 9/11, however, to grab the foreign-policy bureaucracy, figuratively, by the throat. The question is whether 9/11 has altered U.S. foreign policy for the foreseeable future in a fundamental way as happened with the Cold War.

In the first few days following the 9/11 attacks, one would not expect to see the governmental inputs just mentioned. Rather, as discussed in external inputs in Chapter 2, during a foreign-policy crisis, individuals at the very apex of foreign-policy power can be expected to circumvent the larger bureaucracy out of necessity. The enormity of these attacks, however, caused the president to reach out to Congress, the American public, and even to his own executive agencies rather directly over the following weeks and month.

On 9/11 the president announced that the U.S. military was on maximum alert. Further, Bush ordered Naval destroyers to New York. On September 13 the Congress authorized the President to use military force against those responsible for 9/11—an extraordinary move given the political fallout of the Vietnam War and particularly the Tonkin Gulf Resolution. On September 14, President Bush spoke at the National Cathedral, symbolically alerting his Cabinet, Congress, and the public about the seriousness of the mission that lay ahead. On that same day, Bush called up fifty thousand reservists for "homeland defense." Nearly simultaneously, Congress approved the forty billion dollars requested by the president to help the victims of the attacks and to find the perpetrators. On September 16, the FBI grounded crop-dusting planes. (The FBI falls under the auspices of the Department of Justice whose director, the Attorney General, answers to the president.) Three days later, the president signed the forty-billion-dollar relief package. On September 23, President Bush signed an airline-bailout package. On October 3, the president proposed a seventy-five-billion-dollar stimulus package to preclude further negative pressures on the economy resulting from 9/11.[8]

During the initial days the sheer size of the foreign-policy bureaucracy was diminished in importance. However, after the crisis atmosphere subsided, one can find various foreign-policy bureaucracies reexerting their agendas in earnest. Put differently, when time pressures eased, the foreign-policy bureaucracies reentered the bureaucratic fray in order to protect their respective survivability. Thus government inputs eventually resurfaced as important foreign-policy variables, *after* the crisis atmosphere had diminished.

For present purposes, the government knew no further imminent threat existed for America by September 15; the government expected future attacks but nothing imminently. For example, October 7 was the beginning of the military campaign. Pentagon contingency plans, very likely, dictated the day on which the campaign began. In years to come we will doubtless read accounts of those contingency plans but we know from previous campaigns—Desert Shield and Desert Storm—that contingency plans frequently dictate when and how military campaigns commence.[9] There is no reason to doubt this, too, was the case with the Bush administration's response to 9/11.

Homeland security had been a buzz-phrase prior to 9/11. Following 9/11, however, a new government agency to focus on homeland security came to fruition. On October 8, 2001, Governor Tom Ridge was sworn in as director of the Department of Homeland Security. Again, it will be years before we can definitively compare this new agency with, say, the National Security Council created as a result of the Cold War. Tentatively, however, it appears to compare favorably. Initially, the Department of Homeland Security was created by an executive order. The executive order was subsequently codified by the statute passed by Congress and signed by the president in November 2002. Even when supported by executive order only, the Department of Homeland Security was an important, frontline government agency in the anti-terror focus of U.S. foreign policy.[10] In fact, its initial budget was more dramatic than was the National Security Council's. President Bush's proposed Homeland Security Budget for 2002 was $38 billion, which subsequently increased.

The same day Ridge was sworn in as the director of the Department of Homeland Security, the Coast Guard mobilized the largest harbor force since World War II. Not to be left behind, the FBI announced a new terrorist watch list. On October 10, FBI Director Robert Mueller released a new top-twenty-two-most-wanted list. The following day, the Senate voted 96–1 to expand the powers of the federal government to fight terrorism. Among the executive's new-found powers: roving wire taps; authority to detain "aliens" suspected of terrorism without a specific charge; and authority to spy on e-mail. On October 12, the House of Representatives voted (337–79) to pass their version of the Patriot Act.[11]

The creation of the Homeland Security Department per se will not be comparable to the NSC unless it persists over time and becomes an integral piece of American foreign policy. However, early indications are that other federal bureaucracies feel threatened by the new creation. Its director, Tom Ridge, is said to be "facing resistance to some of his ideas" by bureaucracies whose prerogatives would be affected by the Homeland Security Department. Ridge created a blueprint, which "could affect virtually every facet of federal and state government, as well as the private sector." In fact, the blueprint includes: "[s]treamlining or consolidating government agencies responsible for border security, including the Customs Service, the Immigration and Naturalization Services, the Border Patrol and the Coast Guard." Moreover, the National Security Act may be amended, in effect, by "[c]hanging the way the CIA, the National Security Agency, the FBI and other agencies gather, analyze and disseminate information."[12] (The predictions later proved accurate.)

Later in October (October 26), President Bush signed the so-called Patriot Act.[13] The Patriot Act, some 342 pages long, is a wide-ranging documentation of the federal government's response to terrorism. For instance, the Treasury Department is authorized to create a "terrorism fund" that is not subject to fiscal-year constraints. Further, it allocates the FBI $200 million to fight terrorism for fiscal years 2002, 2003, and 2004. Importantly, given the apparent intelligence failure that led to 9/11, it authorizes the agencies of the federal government to share information and intelligence, actually amending the intelligence hierarchy created by the National Security Act of 1947 as well as subsequent legislation. In particular, it amends the Foreign Intelligence Surveillance Act of 1978. Similarly in the name of security, the Patriot Act permits the federal government to intercept electronic communications. Specifically, and in the tortured prose of government lawyers, it reads: "It shall not be unlawful under this chapter for a person acting under the color of law to intercept the wire or electronic communications . . ." of potential terrorists (ibid., p. 48). Further, the act enumerates RICO-like provisions (RICO stands for Racketeer Influenced and Corrupt Organizations Act), allowing the U.S. government to seize property of persons aiding and abetting terrorists (p. 110); additionally, the act allows for several strengthened anti-money-laundering provisions (*ad passim*).

A sign that Director Ridge was gaining influence in the administration in terms of affecting U.S. foreign policy was his announcements of threat warnings. Citing a convergence of information, he warned—for the third time since October 2001— of a possible imminent attack, with the backdrop of the White House briefing room no less. If the Homeland Security Department was gaining influence, one or more other foreign-policy bureaucracies were likely to feel threatened since by the zero-sum rules of bureaucratic politics, one bureaucracy's gain is by definition another's loss. A possible indicator of bureaucratic posturing may have been the Pentagon's release of an Osama bin Laden tape in mid-December showing bin Laden taking credit for 9/11, effectively putting the Defense Department back in the spotlight. As noted, Secretary Rumsfeld had become a celebrity in his own right and was clearly enjoying it. Anyone watching his press briefings and his personal thrusts and parries with the media could see he was growing into his celebrity.

Section 904 allows the Justice Department to "defer" submittal of reports to Congress "on intelligence and various intelligence-related matters." This could prove a bit slippery. The reason the Justice Department and, in particular the FBI, have to submit such reports in the first place is to accommodate the legislative branch's oversight responsibilities: that is to say, to maintain the checks and balances the Founders found so imperative. Intelligence-related matters that the FBI engaged in during the 1950s and 1960s included antics such as compiling lists of putative liberal professors, print and electronic journalists, and political enemies of its director. Indeed, the statute actually allows the same for the secretary of defense and the DCI (ibid., Section 904, part [a]).

Another agency created quickly in the aftermath of 9/11 was the TSA (Transportation Security Agency). The agency falls under the auspices of the Federal Aviation Administration and was created to federalize airport screenings by the end of 2002. The thinking behind it seems clear enough: low-paid, undereducated airport screeners were at least partially to blame for the success the nineteen terrorists had in getting on four airplanes with box cutters on 9/11. (In reality, the rules that existed for screeners did not preclude a passenger taking a box cutter on an airplane.) Nonetheless, the U.S. government is nothing if not reactive and both the Congress and the White House rushed to create the appearance of safety. On November 19 2001, President Bush announced that for "the first time, airport security will become a direct federal responsibility." He then signed Public Law 107-71, the Aviation Security Act.[14]

Conventional wisdom asserts that the American public will not support a long war. With this in mind, and given that few American troops were dying in the war on terrorism, the Bush administration took every opportunity to note that the war would be a long-term commitment, much to the president's credit. Bush made the point during his speech before a joint session of Congress. Secretary of Transportation Norman Mineta stressed "patience" as a new form of patriotism on October 31. Secretary of Defense Rumsfeld stressed that the military would remain patient, as patient as needed to finish the job and that the job might take years, even decades. (On October 16, 2002, Ted Koppel, a prescient prognosticator, appeared on MSNBC's *Donahue* and predicted that the war on the global-terrorist hydra would take years, comparing it to the Cold War.)

Importantly, and again comparable to the commencement of the Cold War, administration officials took every opportunity to tell the American public that the war on terror would neither be simple nor painless. President Bush, for instance, used his weekly radio address on November 24, 2001, to tell the public that the nation "will face difficult times ahead. The fight we have begun will not be quickly or easily finished."[15] Just days later, on November 29, the House approved a $318 billion defense appropriation by a vote of 406-20. This would later be supplemented with additional monies. For example, President Bush announced his 2003 budget in February 2002, which included an additional $48 billion for defense and $38 billion for border security and local law enforcement. (In spring 2003, Bush requested and Congress approved a $78 billion supplemental defense appropriation for the war in Iraq.[16])

December (2001) was a month in which the war coverage overshadowed visible governmental inputs. The heavy coverage of the Tora Bora campaign crowded other news stories off the pages of the four major papers from which data was collected. Similarly, the cable-news talk or punditocracy programs, CNN's *Inside Politics, Wolf Blitzer Reports,* MSNBC's *Hardball,* and so forth, focused almost uniformly and singly on the bombing campaign, the subsequent cave-to-cave search, and "where's Osama?"[17]

EFFECTS OF 9/11 ON THE DEPARTMENT OF DEFENSE BUDGET

By the end of 2001, the Taliban regime was finished. The al Qaeda camps in Afghanistan were destroyed. The war on terrorism continued in Afghanistan — in a quasi-mopping-up fashion — while expanding worldwide. As it turned out, another bombing campaign in eastern Afghanistan began early in the new year, causing some to wonder whether or not the Afghan phase of the war *was* finished, especially given the geographic expansion elsewhere. Recall that in early 2002, the war on global terrorism began expanding its activities to some eighty countries from the Americas (including Canada and South America) to Europe, and Central, South, and Southeast Asia. The expansion necessarily put additional budgetary pressures on both federal and state treasuries.[18] Where budgetary pressures exist, one should perforce expect to find evidence of increased bureaucratic turf wars as well. In the following pages we shall see whether, in fact, this was the case.

President Bush had previously increased the defense budget from the Clinton era. After 9/11, however, the budget increased significantly. As previously discussed, after 9/11 President Bush called for a $48 billion increase in the Defense Department's budget.[19]

> The cost of fighting terrorism at home and abroad will require so much money in 2003 that President Bush plans to propose a budget with little or no growth in most other areas of government, according to administration officials.
>
> Administration officials said discretionary, or non-mandatory, spending is expected to grow by 9 percent, up from 4 percent last year. But when defense and homeland security spending is excluded, the figure drops to 3 percent, barely ahead of inflation.[20]

Clearly the budget priorities changed following 9/11; the question is whether U.S. foreign-policy priorities had changed. Though we shall discuss this question in the conclusions, it is worth quoting the president's own words in early 2002. President Bush clearly felt the need to respond to criticisms, "embarrassing" or not — in part due to budget pressures and in part due to the Democrats highlighting the same. When Bush talked about the issue, he did so in terms of U.S. foreign-policy priorities.

> Defeating international terrorism and defending Americans in our homeland are imperative duties of the federal government, *above and beyond all its other*

*activities. . . . *We must provide for these increases and fund other necessary pro-
grams without letting total spending rise unacceptably. We must demand proof of
value from programs of lesser priority."[21]

EFFECTS OF 9/11 ON THE SPEED OF BUREAUCRATIC PROCESSES

Government bureaucracy is notorious for looking dynamic yet being, in reality, slow
to change. Moreover, the Department of Defense is among the most notorious. The
September attacks on America provided a new kind of impetus, however. Prior to
9/11 the secretary of defense had focused on a two-fold approach to his job. First,
Rumsfeld had undertaken a comprehensive review of the Pentagon and its budget.
Second, the secretary had publicly called for abrogating the Anti-Ballistic-Missile
(ABM) treaty and implementing a reduced vision of the Strategic Missile Defense.
Both tracks became somewhat obscured by 9/11. The 9/11 attacks allowed missile-
defense detractors to mount an attack on missile defense generally. The *New York
Times* reported that an unclassified version of the intelligence assessment, known as
the National Intelligence Estimate (NIE), said that for the first time, "the United
States is 'more likely to be attacked with [weapons of mass destruction] using *non-
missile means*' than conventional weapons systems" (italics added).[22] (As the NIE is
the DCI's job, this may have been a bureaucratic ploy by DCI Tenet to improve his
standing, given Rumsfeld's rising star and Tenet's recent grilling before Congressional hearings.)

Given that 9/11 represented such a new kind of threat, the federal government
had to improvise and create new SOPs. One that became controversial was the im-
prisonment of "detainees" at Guantanamo, Cuba, and whether they would be classified as prisoners of war, illegal combatants, or detainees. Not surprisingly, with
more than four months' time passing, bureaucratic battles were becoming increasingly evident in Washington. In late January, a *New York Times* article reported that Secretary of State Powell was fighting a rear-guard action with respect
to the issue of "detainees." Attorney General Ashcroft and Vice President Cheney
were said to be on one side with Secretary Powell reportedly urging the president
to reconsider the decision. That Bush was being pulled in different directions was
evident in his own words when he said "We're in total agreement on how these
prisoners—or detainees, excuse me—ought to be treated."[23]

Uncharacteristically, change was even occurring in the inner rings of the Pentagon. The Pentagon, one could plausibly argue, was still poised to fight the Cold
War well into 2001. The Pentagon is a national-security bureaucracy, unmatched
in sheer size, that typifies incremental change during normal times. Even in the
Pentagon—normally characterized by inertia—9/11 provided new emphasis for
bureaucratic change. For some fifty-plus years, America's principal foreign-policy
goals were containment and deterrence. Operationally, these goals were equated
with being able to fight two (at times two and a half) wars simultaneously and deterring nuclear attack on America, a policy known as mutually assured destruction

(MAD). In early 2002, the Pentagon was said to be developing "new doctrine": "In the military's graduate schools and think tanks, strategists and students are coming to terms with this new world."[24]

Other government bureaucracies, not typically associated with U.S. foreign policy, were adjusting to the new realities as well. The Secret Service, for instance, an agency under the auspices of the Treasury Department, was created to prevent forgery of American currency and to protect the president. As an agency, it has historically played only a marginal foreign-policy function. The *Christian Science Monitor* reported in early February that its role and budget had been expanded as a result of 9/11.[25] Apparently, the Secret Service too would be getting a bigger role in foreign policy in President Bush's "new world."

Understanding the bureaucratic rush to transform their missions such that said missions fit the war on terrorism, President Bush's budget director, Mitchell Daniels, sought to forestall inappropriate transformations of missions—a bureaucratic ploy of excessively reshaping bureaucratic missions—while granting that new missions meant new budgets in America's war on terrorism. The *Washington Post* reported that "Sources said the budget [2003] will double spending on homeland security from about $15 billion to $30 billion." and further that "The budget is so focused on national and domestic security that agencies throughout government suddenly tried to redefine programs in those terms. 'From the get-go, we realized that everyone would put this uniform on if we let them,' Daniels said."[26]

By the new year, the Department of Homeland Security discovered the realities of federal bureaucratic turf battles firsthand. After all, there are finite dollars available and infinite claims on them. Ridge's goals included streamlining border security—bringing disparate parts under one agency, notably led by the Department of Homeland Security—changing the way the FBI, CIA, NSA, and others collect and disseminate intelligence, and creating a national alert system. One article reported that "Less [sic] than four months after taking office, [Ridge] is preparing initiatives that would create a new border security agency, revamp the way intelligence is gathered and distributed throughout the government, and impose national standards on agencies that respond to terrorist acts." It continued, however, that Ridge was running into "resistance to some of his ideas, forcing him to apply the brakes on key elements of his agenda and raising questions about how much he can accomplish."[27] As of May 2002, the only initiative accomplished by the Department of Homeland Security was the new agency's color-coded alert system. (Subsequently, Ridge was able to make Homeland Security a cabinet bureaucracy with an annual $50-billion budget.)

Comparable fights occurred early in the history of the NSC as well. In John Prados' history on the NSC, he reported that Truman's special assistant on national security, Admiral Souers, prepared a memorandum for an NSC meeting in 1949. Included among the statutory members of the NSC is the secretary of defense. Truman's secretary of defense, Louis Johnson, reflected the tensions that may exist between heads of bureaucracies as noted in the following anecdote:

> Johnson listened, chair tilted back, gazing at the ceiling, seemingly calm and attentive. Suddenly he lunged forward with a crash of chair legs on the floor and

fist on tables. . . . No one, he shouted, was going to make arrangements for him to meet with another Cabinet officer . . . and be told what he was going to report to the President.[28]

Thus, that Ridge found himself running into bureaucratic hurdles is neither surprising nor a particular indication that the Department of Homeland Security is an easily outmaneuvered bureaucratic entity due to its newness. Indeed, one could plausibly argue that the attention it was getting from potential bureaucratic rivals was an indication of its potential power. After all, unlike the State and Defense Departments, the Homeland Security Department was specifically created for the war on terrorism. Another comparison with the early NSC is staff. The NSC staff was initially a skeleton staff and only grew incrementally over several administrations and as the Cold War gained momentum. In fact, it was not until Eisenhower and Kennedy that the NSC staff reached a hundred or slightly higher. (When Kennedy actually took office he reduced the size of the staff, albeit temporarily.) The Homeland Security Department already has some eighty employees and was expected to have some one hundred and twenty staff employees in 2002.[29]

An additional indicator of governmental inputs affecting foreign-policy in fundamental ways may be seen in the CIA's maneuvering. As any "successful" bureaucracy knows, seizing the day may be a particularly effective ploy. The *New York Times* reported that "before September 11 the agency had largely been out of the spy business for years, not hiring new agents and avoiding delicate inquiries for fear of embarrassing itself, other nations, or the White House." Not any longer. 9/11 "changed the C.I.A.," with it hiring scores of new operatives and opening relations with regimes and leaders hitherto considered *persona non grata*.[30] Interestingly, and pertinent to the previously noted turf battles, Director of Central Intelligence George Tenet made a trip to Pakistan and surrounding countries in the fall of 2001 and apparently neglected to coordinate with or even inform the Department of Homeland Security Director Ridge.

As noted, the budget is reflective of whether the government has actually embarked on a new direction in foreign policy. It is therefore worth exploring in more detail the 2003 budget that Bush submitted to Congress in February 2003. Already increased from an average of some $270 billion (in constant 1996 dollars) annually since 1950—a sizable annual budget directly linked to fighting the Cold War—Bush had already asked for a significant increase for 2002 ($311 billion), more than a 15 percent increase over the Cold War average. But as the war on terror progressed, as the war in Afghanistan continued to consume roughly $1 billion daily, and as said war expanded into Uzbekistan, the Philippines, Georgia, Yemen, and so forth, Bush requested a defense budget of $379 billion in 2003, a 50 percent increase over the pre-Bush Cold War average. Moreover, his plans called for an annual defense appropriation of $451 billion by 2007, more than a 67 percent increase over average Cold War budgets. Recall the threat that drove historic Cold War defense budgets: a huge Soviet conventional military force coupled with tens of thousands of nuclear weapons, *and* being able to fight a second "major" war simultaneously. (See Table 4.1 on page 98 for comparative defense appropriation data.) The two largest

TABLE 4.1   OMB FIGURES ON U.S. DEFENSE SPENDING

FISCAL YEAR	DOLLARS IN CONSTANT 1996 U.S.$	INCREASE/ PREVIOUS FISCAL YEAR	FISCAL YEAR	DOLLARS IN CONSTANT 1996 U.S.$	INCREASE/ PREVIOUS FISCAL YEAR
1947	$99.40		1978	$230.60	0.17%
1948	76.50	−23.04%	1979	236.70	2.65
1949	109.10	42.61	1980	236.70	3.63
1950	113.90	4.40	1981	259.30	5.71
1951	186.10	**63.39**	1982	282.30	8.87
1952	352.40	**89.36**	1983	305.00	8.04
1953	372.10	5.59	1984	309.20	1.38
1954	341.40	−8.25	1985	330.50	6.89
1955	285.40	−16.40	1986	353.70	7.02
1956	265.30	−7.04	1987	360.50	1.92
1957	270.40	1.92	1988	364.50	1.11
1958	267.20	−1.18	1989	369.70	1.43
1959	267.70	0.19	1990	354.70	−4.06
1960	273.00	1.98	1991	310.10	−12.57
1961	274.20	0.44	1992	327.40	5.58
1962	287.30	4.78	1993	314.30	−4.00
1963	281.50	−2.02	1994	298.10	−5.15
1964	286.50	1.78	1995	282.00	−5.40
1965	264.50	−7.68	1996	265.80	−5.74
1966	292.30	10.51	1997	264.80	−0.38
1967	346.90	18.68	1998	259.90	−1.85
1968	379.10	9.28	1999	260.50	0.23
1969	361.00	−4.77	2000	270.80	3.95
1970	338.50	−6.23	2001	278.50	**2.84**
1971	308.50	−8.86	°2002	306.90	**10.20**
1972	282.60	−8.40	°2003	328.00	**6.88**
1973	255.30	−9.66	°2004	335.00	**2.13**
1974	244.90	−4.07	°2005	346.50	**3.43**
1975	240.70	−1.71	°2006	353.00	1.88
1976	231.60	−3.78	°2007	358.40	1.53
1977	230.20	−0.60			

*Represents "estimates" of the Office of Management and Budget.

Source: Office of Management and Budget (OMB), *Budget of the U.S. Government,* "Historical Tables," Fiscal Year 2003, Tables 3.1, 3.2, and 4.1. (Washington, D.C.: U.S. Government Printing Office, 2003). All figures are U.S.$ billions. Note that the bold data are compared in the text, in particular, the *actual* versus *estimated* post–9/11 data. Also note that supplementals are excluded.

increases from one year to the next—during the 1947–1952 period—are roughly 64 and 89 percent respectively.)

The proposed budget is said to reflect what Secretary Rumsfeld requested in order to realign the Pentagon to "a significant expansion in intelligence-gathering capabilities, Special Forces equipment and protective measures that [the secretary] says are needed to combat terrorists and battle unconventional adversaries in the 21st century."[31] Compare this to the change in military appropriations in the late 1940s to the early 1950s. As will be seen, beginning in 1950 defense appropriations rose to significantly higher levels over the previous three years, followed by relatively constant defense budgets over the subsequent Cold War years; further, said budgets remained relatively constant well into the 1990s, as if the Cold War were still being contested between the superpowers. Recall further that the Cold War and its defense-budget increases resulted from a dramatic series of events: the Turkey-Greece "crisis" (1946–1947); the year-long Berlin Airlift "crisis" (1948); the victory of a Soviet "surrogate," the PRC, and the resulting fleeing of China's KMT to Taiwan (1949); and North Korea's invasion (another Soviet "surrogate") of America's ally South Korea (1950). In other words, an incredible series of extraordinarily threatening events caused the dramatic increase in defense spending as the Cold War commenced. Thus, the 2003 actual increase and the even more dramatic estimated increase intended by 2007 are more startling.

As implied previously, the CIA in particular began reasserting its bureaucratic muscle in the war on terror. We have already cited that some believed the CIA had lost its focus during the 1990s. The events of 9/11 breathed new life into the agency. In February (2002), it was reported that the CIA was working with the military in unprecedented ways, carrying out military operations, actually using high-tech drone airplanes to fire on groups of suspected Taliban and al Qaeda groups,[32] prior to the military's own use of the same planes, effectively out-militarizing the military.

The CIA, however, also released a NIE (National Intelligence Estimate) in January effectively diminishing the import of a national missile defense to America's security. This move was dramatic for at least two reasons. First, any missile defense would fall under the umbrella of the Defense Department; indeed, it was known to be a Rumsfeld pet project. Second, President Bush, Vice President Cheney, and Secretary of Defense Rumsfeld were all strongly on record as supporting a national missile defense. Even following 9/11 this troika continued to insist that missile defense was imperative. Thus it was curious, and perhaps indicative of bureaucratic posturing by the CIA, that the agency would release an NIE questioning the need for missile defense. Demonstrating incredible bureaucratic deftness—if not outright brazenness—the CIA leaked the estimate effectively discounting missile defense's efficacy against the global-terrorist hydra.[33]

Americans also learned in February that the war on terror was expanding into the Philippines. It is unclear how closely related the indigenous *Abu Sayyaf* is to al Qaeda, but the administration apparently wished to show it was following terrorists to the corners of the globe. Many reports characterized *Abu Sayyaf* as "mercenaries" willing to kidnap anybody who might fetch a bounty, though others have linked them in a loose coalition with al Qaeda.[34] *Abu Sayyaf* was also said to be providing sanctuary to al Qaeda members on the run. Clearly, deputy Secretary of Defense Wolfowitz believed the latter. He made that clear in a hastily arranged trip to the Philippines in June (2002) where he announced that he felt the United States ought to "expand" its mission in the Philippines.[35]

Given the confirmed al Qaeda connections in Singapore and Malaysia, a cynical observer might be tempted to conclude that the U.S. expansion into the Philippines was a diversionary tactic. The United States could not simply march into Singapore or Malaysia; by contrast, it was effectively invited into the Philippines. Moreover, some of the first negative press concerning the war on terrorism was suspiciously close in terms of timing to the introduction of American troops in the Philippines. For instance, on February 12, the *New York Times* published a story raising the specter of poor coordination and micromanagement of the drone planes firing Hellfire Missiles. While the article did have some positive things to say about cooperation between the CIA and the military, its overall tenor was negative.[36] What is clear in the article is that various CIA and Pentagon sources cited in the article were attempting to attribute SNAFUs to their opposite agency, indicating down-and-dirty turf fights. On the same day, the same newspaper published a story announcing that "[t]he House and Senate intelligence committees are set to begin a joint investigation into U.S. intelligence gaps. . . ."[37] As will be seen later, discussion of intelligence failures eventually created bureaucratic battling at the highest levels.

During times of foreign-policy crisis, the national-security bureaucracy may be temporarily circumvented. Over time, however, foreign-policy bureaucracies catch up with events and reexert their normal influence. As we have seen, said bureaucracies had begun to reexert their influence with respect to U.S. foreign policy within weeks—the newly created Homeland Security Department began to get in the "game" by the end of September. Further, the military campaign, begun in early October, indicated that the Pentagon had successfully regained the initiative and was reexerting its influence at high levels. Perhaps no better indication that government inputs were becoming increasingly crucial was an article in February 2002. The *Los Angeles Times* published a story reflecting how integral Pentagon lawyers had become in the prosecution of the war in Afghanistan. The article reported: "There are lawyers in the top-secret operations center, called the Tank, deep inside the Pentagon, 24 hours a day, seven days a week, signing off on the legality of raids and strikes." It further stated that it was leading to "growing tension." Though it may have been causing tension, the unconventional and unprecedented war on terrorism had made the legal thicket even more dense.[38]

Though special-interest groups were properly discussed in societal inputs in Chapter 3, it is also worth mentioning here that by 2002, defense contractors too were getting their pound of government pork. The *Boston Globe* reported that "Defense contractors are trying to be war profiteers and are unfairly manipulating a nation in distress." While identifying defense contractors specifically, clearly the government too was complicit. Recall that this relationship is characterized as the military-industrial complex, sometimes the iron triangle—where government is an integral partner with defense contractors.[39] As an industry, the defense-contractor sector of America's economy comprises a unique special-interest group, though just one of many that affects U.S. foreign policy.

Post-9/11 government agencies not normally associated with foreign policy were being tasked with new anti-terror activities. Witness the Winter Olympics in

February 2002. As the Olympics opened on February 9, some ten thousand security personnel blanketed Salt Lake City making it "one of the safest places in the world," according to Homeland Director Ridge. Perhaps most interesting was not that the FBI and National Guard comprised the bulk of the security force but, rather, that the Secret Service was used in a major way. In order to carry out its new mission, the service necessarily had to work with foreign governments, thus affecting U.S. foreign policy in new ways hitherto unseen.

During times of crisis, there are far fewer opportunities for bureaucratic infighting since decisions must be made in a shortened time horizon. Once crises are over, however, bureaucratic infighting returns. If, as we are attempting to determine, U.S. foreign policy is taking a new direction in which new agencies and bureaucracies will be created and during which new monies are up for grabs, we should therefore expect to see some particularly hardy bureaucratic posturing following the post-9/11 period.

In February we learned that a debate within the administration had erupted over how to handle the taking of American hostages overseas. "After a protracted debate that pitted the State Department against the Pentagon, the Bush administration . . . adopted a new policy that requires the federal government to review every kidnapping of an American overseas for possible action." The policy-review group was directed out of the National Security Council (NSC). Condoleezza Rice, putatively a Powell protégé and moderate, is of course the head of the NSC. Against the moderates, apparently, were "[o]pponents of the policy, particularly at the Pentagon." The NSC evidently fashioned "a compromise . . . which on balance favored the State Department's position." The full policy was issued in a Bush administration National Security Presidential Directive (NSPD) that remains classified.[40]

Interestingly, Ashcroft's Justice Department carved out for itself a good deal more influence in foreign policy than during past administrations. (Due to nepotism, the Kennedy administration may be an exception.) One need not be a student of political science to discern the high profile this Justice Department has had since 9/11 relative to past Justice Departments. Attorney General Ashcroft, for instance, has given regular press briefings ranging from FBI activities—the FBI is under the Justice Department—to the handling of "detainees," to the canvassing and questioning of Muslims living in the United States in order to develop intelligence for foreign-policy use to the department's controversial TIPS program. New routines, not surprisingly, have therefore been created necessarily in response to 9/11. For example, of the hundreds of Arabs and other Muslims rounded up following 9/11, Ashcroft refused to release information about them or allow them access to lawyers—a truly dramatic change in standard operating procedures. Of the hundreds of such detainees still being held in late 2002, Justice Department officials "acknowledged a great reluctance to release" them, or even release their names according to one *New York Times* piece. "Most of the detainees are Arabs or Muslims, and many have spent more than 100 days in jail waiting to leave the country, with no end to detention in sight. Nearly all were jailed after being picked up on visa violations at traffic stops or because of neighbors' suspicions,"[41] perhaps demonstrating the efficacy of the Justice Department's TIPS.

As one might expect, these actions have been controversial among civil libertarians as well as others. One ACLU lawyer characterized the changed policies this way: "The government has effectively reversed the presumption of innocence. They are holding people for months once their immigration cases are concluded while they look to see if there is a reason to bring other charges." A lawyer trying to help detainees said, "It reminds you of the famous Kafka story of 'The Trial'" (ibid.). The reader may decide for himself or herself how draconian these measure are but they clearly reverse a trend in the United States over the past few decades, arguably reflecting the changes in U.S. foreign policy hypothesized here.

The Defense Department has demonstrated similar creativity in adapting to a potentially "new world" in U.S. foreign policy. Even more than Ashcroft, Secretary Rumsfeld has become associated with daily news briefings. This is striking given the fact that prior to 9/11, Rumsfeld was characterized as having little interest in speaking to the media. Prior to 9/11, Rumsfeld was working on a top-down review of America's defense policies that was characterized by great secrecy. What is more, Rumsfeld was said to have offended many of his own top military leaders with his "authoritarian" manner and secrecy.[42] Despite the enemies Rumsfeld had made in the administration, within his own Pentagon, and with the media, in the post-9/11 era, the secretary has become a press-briefing *cause célèbre*. In February, the shine of his celebrity became slightly, albeit temporarily, tarnished. As discussed earlier, it was about mid-February when Rumsfeld's office announced their new internal agency, the Office of Strategic Influence (OSI). One interesting aspect was that the money for the new agency would come from the special $10 billion supplemental appropriation Congress had authorized the Bush administration.[43] A bureaucratic law is that an agency grabs additional dollars whenever it can. That Secretary Rumsfeld would do so for his bureaucracy is, therefore, unsurprising. More controversial, however, was its purpose: to spread disinformation. It was unclear whom the department had in mind for its disinformation, domestic or foreign audiences. Though proposed as a way to get America's defense message out abroad, many in the media wondered if such information might find its way back into the United States (known as "blowback"); some wondered if that might not be the real motivation. In any event it caused an uproar for a couple of weeks. Apparently Rumsfeld neglected to clear the OSI with the White House, again indicative of bureaucratic posturing.

We have seen that Rumsfeld had made enemies within his own shop, particularly in the top uniformed, command structure. The day after the OSI was announced, an article appeared that suggested disagreements in the Pentagon.

> The dissension at the Pentagon over the new information effort, which was first reported in yesterday's *New York Times*, focuses on the intention of some officials to operate in peacetime as well as wartime. The military has long tried to influence public opinion in countries at war under the title "psychological operations." *But the new office apparently plans to extend such operations into nations in which the United States is not a combatant.* (italics added)[44]

Certain persons within the Pentagon were already distancing themselves from their bosses, Secretary Rumsfeld as well as his deputy, Paul Wolfowitz.

Whether the White House was upset over not having Rumsfeld's OSI fully vetted by Bush's political advisors, or whether it simply felt upstaged, one thing was clear: The White House was unhappy. "In a rare airing of disagreement within the Bush administration, White House aides were furious about the Pentagon proposal that could have led to the feeding of false stories to foreign journalists." Apparently Bush had his own information office in mind: "President Bush has decided to transform the administration's temporary wartime communications effort into a *permanent office of global diplomacy* to spread a positive image of the United States around the world and combat anti-Americanism" (italics added).[45] Surely Rumsfeld—as a member of the NSC principals and war cabinet—was aware of the administration's plans, again suggesting barely latent bureaucratic rivalries at work.

Finally, after months of nearly lock-step bipartisanship, Congress began criticizing the budget and the direction of the war effort, albeit indirectly. The criticism focused on the administration's missile defense plans. As noted, there was bipartisan support for the mammoth increases in the defense budget. Prior to 9/11 the administration had requested $311 billion for 2003. In itself this represented a sizable increase over the roughly $270 billion average over the past several decades.

As is normally the case, Congress wrestled, figuratively, over the increase, particularly given the administration's desired tax cut. Following 9/11, the administration asked for an increase for 2003 of $379 billion (a sixty-eight billion dollar increase or nearly 30 percent higher than its previous request, *supra*). Both parties fell all over themselves to approve the post-9/11 increase. By late February, however, some Democrats began questioning the budget. Why, they asked, did the administration continue to insist on billions of dollars for missile defense when the United States, according to Bush's own words and the CIA's recent assessment, had a global-terrorist war to fight? Democrats questioned the administration's priorities and, implicitly, its leadership when criticisms were "voiced in both the Senate and in the House during a hearing on missile defense. . . ."[46]

Back at the Pentagon, busy planners continued to come up with new ideas to spend new-found dollars. "[T]he Defense Department has begun laying the groundwork to ban non-U.S. citizens from a wide range of computer projects." On the face of it this may seem a reasonable idea. The problem is that the U.S. government, including the Defense Department, uses an increasing number of contract workers who perform functions from payroll to writing software for U.S. systems. Again, Rumsfeld evidently failed to clear the idea with the White House, since President Bush's cyber-security advisor, Richard Clarke, viewed the restrictions "as a misguided priority."[47] Nonetheless, the Defense Department bureaucracy was a juggernaut on a roll. The following day an article was published outlining the department's potential revision of U.S. nuclear strategy. For decades, since the 1960s, U.S. nuclear strategy had been based on deterrence. Deterrence as a policy simply means preventing another nation from doing what it might otherwise do. In nuclear terms, this equates to preventing another country—the USSR during the Cold

War—from doing what it might otherwise have done: launch a nuclear first strike against the United States or its allies. In operational terms, deterrence meant mutually assured destruction (MAD). The United States had ample nuclear warheads and had them protected in a "strategic triad" (submarine-based, land-based, and air-based delivery platforms). Thus even had the then USSR been foolish enough to attempt a first strike, the United States would retain sufficient warheads to ensure a devastating second-strike capability, thereby deterring the Soviets. Consequently, no rational actor would attempt a first strike since it would assure that actor's own destruction. The Soviets adhered to the same policy. In effect, and perversely given the hundreds of billions of dollars consumed by MAD as strategy, the buildup of nuclear forces on both sides was with an explicit view toward never using them.

The "nuclear posture review," which was leaked to the *Los Angeles Times*, arguably turned deterrence, a long-honored Cold War strategy, on its head. Rather, it identified seven countries against which the United States might use nuclear weapons under certain scenarios. The potential targets: China, Russia, Iraq, Iran, North Korea, Libya, and Syria. The policy review directed the military "to prepare contingency plans to use nuclear weapons against at least seven countries and to build smaller nuclear weapons for use in certain battlefield situations." In other words, the review was suggesting supplanting deterrence with its nuclear opposite, "compellence": causing a country to do what it otherwise would not do. How this would be useful against terrorism was not clear given that al Qaeda and other terrorist groups had no countries, per se, to threaten.[48] In fact, Bush had made it *clear* that deterrence and compellence were integral to Phase I of the global war on terrorism. There appeared to be a communications breakdown between the White House and the Defense Department.

Tom Ridge had been accused of being too timid for the position for which Bush had appointed him. It was therefore interesting to see him avail himself of the Defense Department's recent woes. Into the breach went Ridge in a bold move to establish bureaucratic power for his agency. The newly created Homeland Security Department's director had issued a few alerts in the fall (three by October) and early spring. Yet despite the fact that his shop was the glamour agency, it really had failed to gain any power. It had a budget, some $40 billion, and some office space in the Old Executive Office Building—which meant proximity to the president—but had very little to do in actuality. Its bureaucratic newness alone made it vulnerable to overt attacks by other foreign-policy bureaucracies. Further, the Homeland Security Department had been criticized in the media as an agency with nothing to do officially. Moreover, Director Ridge had been sitting by for months watching the FBI, the Justice Department, the CIA, and the Defense Department all put forth new plans to get a piece of the war-on-terror pie. In early March Ridge announced his new color-coded threat assessment schematic, with great fanfare.[49] Ridge was learning the vicissitudes of bureaucratic politics in Washington, D.C. As will soon be seen, he had a considerably bolder move up his sleeve.

Rifts within the White House cabinet continued to appear from time to time as well. As we have discussed, there were hawks, or neoconservatives, and doves, or moderates within the president's cabinet. These "factions" had split early over whether to abrogate the Anti-Ballistic Missile (ABM) treaty in order to proceed with missile defense. Since 9/11, what to do about Iraq had become a recurring debate between factions as well. More prosaically, another post-9/11 debate was the extent to which the United States would participate in peacekeeping in Afghanistan once the military objectives were accomplished. This obviously turned principally on the length of time the United States would stay in Afghanistan. The hawks were in favor of completing military objectives, then moving on to Iraq. The doves, who were somewhat dubious about going to war in Iraq in the first place, felt the United States was obligated to stay in Afghanistan. Their concern was more than merely humanitarian: History had repeatedly demonstrated that if left to its own devices, Afghanistan would return to anarchy. If Afghanistan devolved into chaos, the United States would eventually have to return militarily. The hawks felt the stabilization of Afghanistan could and should be left up to others, notably the British. To complicate matters, Bush had campaigned *against* "nation building," and, clearly, remaining in Afghanistan to stabilize Afghanistan had the whiff of nation building to it. "During the visit of Afghan leader Hamid Karzai to Washington . . . he appealed to the Bush administration to approve a substantial enlargement of the force" in order to bring a quick conclusion to the chaos. Karzai and "[f]oreign diplomats and some of the administration, especially in the State Department, . . . also pressed for more peacekeepers. . . ." However, "Cheney said the best prospect for stability in Afghanistan would come from the creation of strong national institutions, including a military."[50] The Bush administration is well known, among other things, for being a tight ship and controlling information carefully, perhaps better than any modern administration. That these differences were appearing in the media demonstrated that factional and bureaucratic tensions were growing, very much in earnest.[51]

Anybody who has crossed the U.S.–Mexico border before and after 9/11 knows how much things have changed. Southern Californians who live close to the border have occasion to cross the border fairly routinely. The San Ysidro crossing in San Diego—the busiest border in the world—is a common crossing point for Southern Californians. Prior to 9/11, one could expect to spend ten to fifteen minutes to walk across the border. Since 9/11, that expectation has changed dramatically. A more realistic expectation now is a wait of two hours. The point is this: Secure borders are an integral part of homeland security. It was not surprising then when President Bush proposed, in March, "to merge the nation's major border-guarding forces into a single super-agency." The plan reportedly "combines the 20,000-member Customs Service with the 35,000-member Immigration and Naturalization Service (including the Border Patrol),"[52] a trial balloon floated by Mr. Ridge. Various bureaucracies naturally felt threatened by the potential for such major changes.

It took some time for said bureaucracies to mount counteroffensives, but by July they had begun to mobilize as the wisdom of the plan began to be debated on Capitol Hill. What none of the affected agencies could have possibly known was that Bush's political advisor, the president himself and, importantly, Tom Ridge, were preparing an even more dramatic reorganization that would stymie many of the bureaucratic moves then occurring behind the scenes. This core group of insiders began meeting secretly in April and May (2002) to consider strengthening homeland security, a reorganization that would become clear only in June. All these new programs, agencies, and missions did not come without a substantial price tag. We have already noted the hefty increases in appropriations requested and approved by Congress following 9/11. What with all the new agencies (the Homeland Security Department, the TSA, the Super-Border Agency, and so forth) and missions (airport screening, interrogating Muslim Americans, new strategies for guarding the nation's borders, and so forth), even the increased appropriations did not go far enough. President Bush requested, in late March, an additional appropriation. According to the *Washington Post*, the Bush administration "asked Congress for an additional $27.1 billion for military, domestic security and other needs stemming from the September 11 attacks, an indication that the counterterrorism war at home and abroad is costing more than anticipated." The requested appropriation included an additional $14 billion for the Defense Department and the intelligence bureaucracies. The Homeland Security Department and even the Federal Emergency Management Agency (FEMA) were in line for additional dollars.[53]

Again, when the budget pie is increased, one should expect to see indications of various bureaucracies vying for what they perceive as their proper portion. Such activities are not necessarily going to be direct budget battles. Rather, it is more likely that the bureaucracies in question will simply attempt to raise their profile — show the public (and key individuals within the White House) that they are imperative to America's foreign-policy focus. In fact there was a flurry of such activity following President Bush's request. We have discussed many such activities already. We also know that there were existing tensions between the State and Defense Departments and were unaware which agency would ultimately most influence the president and resultant foreign policy. Some of these tensions may have been of a personal nature — between, say, Rumsfeld and Powell there were subtle hints from time to time — while others were philosophical: neoconservatives versus moderates. Within days of Bush's request, Secretary Rumsfeld changed his hard line on the issue of U.S. troops remaining in Afghanistan after military operations were concluded. Indeed, Secretary Rumsfeld "assigned the American military a complex new mission in Afghanistan today as he announced that Special Forces troops would begin training the new Afghan army within the next six weeks." If it was intended as a preemptive strike against the moderates, it was a bold and classic bureaucratic move. It is unclear whether this was vetted at the White House; what is clear is the move effectively undercut Powell and other moderates. Rumsfeld went on to say that the United States would work with other nations to raise funds to create and train an Afghan military to make certain the country stayed stable.[54]

Next came the Justice Department, demonstrating Ashcroft's bureaucratic deftness. Two days after Rumsfeld's announcement, according to the *Los Angeles Times*, the Justice Department told a court that it would seek the death penalty against Zacarias Moussaoui, the only person charged in the September 11 terrorist attacks against New York and Washington. Again, it is impossible to say whether this was Ashcroft grandstanding. The article mentioned the timing: "The decision came after weeks of deliberations inside the Justice Department and carries international implications, especially in Europe, where the terrorism investigation continues in several countries that oppose capital punishment."[55] France, in particular, had threatened to be less than helpful in gathering evidence for the prosecution if the United States asked for the death penalty. Moussaoui is a French citizen; therefore, France could be instrumental in the case. In another bold move by the Justice Department, the FBI (under the Justice Department) soon made news by doing something it had never done before, and pulling off a coup in the process: "FBI agents joined Pakistani police officers in the pre-dawn raids that scooped up 26 suspected al Qaeda and Taliban fugitives. . . ."[56] Pakistan's President Musharraf had insisted, prior to this event, that U.S. personnel would not violate Pakistani sovereignty.

Noticeably absent from the budget sweepstakes was the State Department. Secretary Powell had recently announced a trip to the Middle East but had demonstrated little success in getting even preliminary concessions from either the Palestinians or the Israelis, making Powell look ineffective. This may have led to Powell losing ground to the neoconservatives in the Defense Department who had argued, in contrast to the State Department, that the United States ought not to bother brokering anything until Arafat was gone. What is more, the hawks in the Defense Department appeared to have had recently swayed the president to their position. Some support for this proposition appeared in early April. White House spokesman Ari Fleischer seemed to minimize the prospect of Powell meeting with Arafat on his trip to the region. Shortly after Fleischer's announcement, Powell made a meeting seem more likely. The *Washington Post* noted that during "the Bush administration's first 15 months, the president has refused to receive Arafat, and Vice President Cheney balked at meeting him during a Middle East tour last month. As Secretary of State, Powell had met Arafat three times, including twice in the West Bank."[57] Powell's star appeared in decline.

Cheney has frequently been identified as being in the neoconservative camp with Rumsfeld and Wolfowitz. It would be interesting to discover who gave the information to the *Washington Post* journalists—Cheney and/or Rumsfeld or Wolfowitz or their respective minions are logical candidates—and whether it was an actual attempt to make Powell look weak. At a minimum, there were communication problems between the White House, Justice, Defense, and State Departments. Just months earlier, Powell had been the administration's foreign-policy golden boy. Powell's decline was further suggested given that Condoleezza Rice, a Powell protégé and ally, had seemingly disappeared from the radar screen, again suggesting the neoconservatives were in the ascendancy. Additional support for said thesis appeared in the *Washington Post* two days later: "The Pentagon is seeking broad congressional authority to spend tens of millions of dollars on military assistance to unspecified foreign countries or 'indigenous forces,' authority that traditionally has rested with the State Department. It appeared that Defense officials were now contending that they "need the new authority to cover extraordinary situations triggered by the Bush administration's global war on terrorism."[58] If Powell had lost stature in the administration, and there was mounting evidence that he had, his bureaucratic rivals were taking advantage of it.

Powell's silence was deafening. Where was his counteroffensive? Instead, the bad news kept coming. A week after the article asserting that the Defense Department was attempting to usurp the State Department's prerogatives, another article was published—again by the *Washington Post*—whose subject was Deputy Defense Secretary Wolfowitz and his suspicions of Hans Blix, the chairman of the UN team tasked with inspecting Iraq's weapons of mass destruction. Apparently, Wolfowitz was suspicious that Blix was too soft on Iraq, so suspicious, in fact, that Wolfowitz had the CIA investigate Blix! The article made clear reference to the bureaucratic struggle going on in the administration between the neoconservatives and the moderates. Wolfowitz's highly unusual action was said to "illuminate the behind-the-scenes skirmishing in the Bush administration over the prospect of renewed U.N. weapons inspections in Iraq." "The inspection issue has become 'a surrogate for a debate about whether we go after Saddam,' said Richard N. Perle [a well-known neoconservative], an advisor to Defense Secretary Donald H. Rumsfeld as chairman of the Defense Policy Board." In a background quote—meaning the person leaking would not go on record by name—a source stated: "The hawks' nightmare is that inspectors will be admitted, will not be terribly vigorous and not find anything."[59] Though budget battles were never mentioned in the article, it is clear that going to war with Iraq would equate to additional dollars and prestige for the Defense Department, while diplomatic solutions to Iraq would represent more dollars and prestige for the State Department. As just discussed, Rumsfeld had recently made a request for additional appropriations.

Another law of bureaucracies is that one never gives up any of its responsibilities to another agency. (That was one of the principal reasons, as noted, the Defense Department's attempt to usurp the State Department's responsibilities was so critical and indicative of Powell's descent.) True to form Attorney General Ashcroft fought tooth and nail to prevent the INS being removed from the Justice Department. As seen, President Bush had recently proposed a new super agency for border security. Subsequently, Congress had taken up the issue and as Congress is often wont to do, started to come up with ever-more creative ways to reconstitute the various agencies. Despite the fact that the president himself had initially proposed it, and Congress had taken its turn at it, Ashcroft resisted it, demonstrating the seriousness with which bureaucracies take their prerogatives. The *New York Times* reported that "Attorney General John Ashcroft said the administration still objected to some of the bill's details, mainly the new associate attorney general's relative lack of authority."[60]

It is unclear who the source of the leaks to the *Washington Post* was and whence said leaks originated (the White House, the Defense Department, or other sources). What is clear is the leaks were increasingly detrimental to Powell. We have seen several indirect and implied swipes at Powell and the State Department. In late April the *Washington Post* published an article that explicitly and directly identified the rifts within the administration. This article is worth quoting in some length.

> State Department officials say Secretary of State Colin L. Powell has been repeatedly undercut by other senior policymakers in his effort to break the Middle East deadlock, warning this has left U.S. diplomacy paralyzed at an especially volatile moment. These officials say that Powell's return from the Middle East a week ago with few concrete results has left them more discouraged than at any time since the Bush administration took office.[61]

The author noted that State Department officials "partly fault what they said was the administration's unwillingness to stand behind Powell," as Powell attempted to work toward peace in the Middle East.

> Powell has displayed little public frustration. But his employees' complaints, reflecting their own exasperation . . . reveal the depth of divisions inside the administration, *especially between the State Department and the Pentagon*. Many in the State Department cite resistance to their diplomatic efforts coming from Defense Secretary Donald H. Rumsfeld, who has more of a voice in shaping Middle East policy than his predecessors. (ibid.; italics added)

To be sure, diplomatic policy—such as working on Middle East peace—has historically been the purview of the State Department, not the Defense Department. The exasperation was therefore understandable.

It noted furthermore that "the opinions of Rumsfeld and his key lieutenants, notably Deputy Defense Secretary Paul D. Wolfowitz . . . figure prominently because the Pentagon has been given a seat at interagency discussions over the Middle East conflict." Rumsfeld and his advisors have advocated giving Sharon wide latitude to press his military operations, viewing the Israeli campaign as a cognate of America's war on terrorism. At the same time, they saw little value in trying to engage Palestinian leader Yasser Arafat in renewed negotiations.

> Powell and his team have a different view. They sympathize with Israel's need to defend itself but worry that the unprecedented Israeli offensive is fostering greater Palestinian hatred and destroying the Palestinians' ability to govern themselves. While the Powell camp shares the disdain for Arafat, it believes he remains central to any settlement. (ibid.)

The article continued, "The rift in President Bush's inner circle, some State Department officials said, has left the administration's policy 'dead in the water.'" Interestingly, the article also cited the CIA as being in the Powell camp (i.e., the moderates), in opposition to the neo-conservatives. This may have resulted from its director, George Tenet, who had been so involved in Middle East negotiations in the previous administration. Tenet was a holdover and may have been suspect for that reason alone, though several articles have suggested that Bush has an excellent working relationship with Tenet.

The article then addressed both Cheney and National Security Advisor Rice. As for Cheney, the article noted that Vice President Cheney and his staff largely shared the Pentagon's perspective. "With respect to Condoleezza Rice, it noted her function was "primarily to broker discussions among senior officials and promote Bush's view." Importantly, however, the article also asserted that "she played an important part in the decision to step up the administration's engagement and dispatch Powell to the region." Hence she was still, apparently, working in Powell's behalf, albeit quietly. Finally, the article mentioned one of Rice's deputies for Middle East affairs, Flynt Leverett, and noted that he "is considered suspect by the more hawkish policymakers because of his pedigree as a CIA employee who also worked for the State Department" (ibid.). So what had been hinted at for months was now out in the open. It was getting interesting for students of politics. Inside Washington, D.C., this was big news, grist for the inside-the-beltway rumor mill. It made most of the major talking-head programs: *Hardball, Crossfire,* Russert's *Meet the Press,* and several others. Still little in the way of a counteroffensive from Powell could be seen.

It was time for the Department of Transportation to get back in the game. They had been relatively quiet since the Department's earlier TSA announcement. The TSA (discussed earlier) made news in early April and proved a law of bureaucracies. It seems its initial budget would not do. Nor would the number of employees it had been authorized to hire. In fact, Secretary Mineta now envisioned a TSA that would ultimately be larger than the FBI. The *Los Angeles Times* noted that Transportation Secretary Norman Mineta said that "the TSA will be bigger than the FBI, Drug Enforcement Administration, and Border Patrol combined. The agency may have to hire more than 50,000 employees . . . a 25 percent increase over previous estimates of about 40,000 workers."[62] As we shall see, Secretary Mineta would make a subsequent bureaucratic move to enlarge his agency and budget in late July but, comparatively speaking, he has proved a bureaucratic lightweight in post-9/11 bureaucratic posturing.

Another series of stories that began to circulate in the spring had to do with intelligence failures and the fact that the White House itself had information about the forthcoming 9/11 attacks as early as May. It is difficult to gauge how much influence these stories had on policy, though it is worth summarizing a few. One story noted that the same sort of attack had been planned in 1995 in France, though it had been thwarted. The French shared the information with both the Clinton and Bush administrations and both apparently ignored it. Another dealt with a similar scenario in India that the intelligence community had ignored. Yet another had the FBI's controversial e-mail snooping program, "Carnivore," mishandling al Qaeda's planning so that those persons tasked with watching what al Qaeda was up to failed to get the information.[63] Clearly persons in high places were leaking to the *Washington Post* but it is difficult to attribute any foreign-policy outcomes directly to these leaks. Nonetheless, the leaks were illustrative of bureaucratic turf battles that likely affected policy in unseen ways. (It should be noted that as of spring 2003, Congress decided to hold hearings on potential intelligence failures.)

Some desired good news for the administration came in May: "The House passed the biggest increase in military spending in decades early Friday to help fight the war on terrorism. . . . Lawmakers voted 359–58 to send the $383 billion measure outlining 2003 defense spending to the Senate." It further made an interesting comparison, adjusting for inflation it noted that this represented "the largest real boost" in Defense spending since 1966.[64] Recall that in 1965 the United States introduced U.S. troops into Vietnam at Da Nang, which officially began the Americanization of the Vietnam War. (See "Conclusions" in Chapter 7 for additional analysis of Defense Department appropriations.)

Most of the bureaucratic posturing, as we have seen, has occurred between the Defense and State Departments. To be more precise, a group whom we have called the neo-conservatives (hawks) formed one camp or faction. Most of this faction resides in the civilian leadership at the Defense Department, though a few hawks are sprinkled throughout the White House and Vice President Cheney is, by all accounts, in this group. A second group whom we have called the moderates (doves) exist principally at the State Department and within the National Security Council, elements of the CIA, and some top military brass. The basis of the two factions' disagreements is philosophical, perhaps ideological. However, the fact that they represent large national-security bureaucracies makes them bureaucratic rivals who compete for the portion of the U.S. budget devoted to national security and foreign policy. Each faction leaks when it sees it as advantageous. Nor are bureaucratic rivalries unique to the Bush administration. Rather, bureaucratic politics is a time-honored tradition and can be seen in every administration, at least for the past thirty years, both during the Cold War and since its demise.

Other bureaucracies who compete for these finite dollars also behave parochially. In late May—interestingly enough, after some negative publicity in Congress and in the media—the FBI announced that the United States should expect suicide bombers just as Israel regularly experienced and that future terrorist attacks were "inevitable."[65] Was Director Mueller simply telling the truth? Was he responding to negative publicity? Or was Mueller attempting to usurp the Department of Homeland Security's newly-won prerogatives? Senator Shelby (R-AL) began criticizing the FBI and Director Mueller by name. Shelby had been quoted on NBC's *Today* show as saying the FBI could have done a better job in warning the president of terrorist intentions, and so forth. And at least two important Democrats made similar remarks. Whatever Mueller's motives were, his comments grabbed headlines and news programs for several days, diverting negative attention away from the director, if not the entire FBI.

The same day the *Washington Post* reported on problems Congress was having in putting together a panel to look into intelligence failures associated with the 9/11 attacks. The article focused on the partisan bickering occurring on Capitol Hill but also noted that both the CIA and FBI were throwing up roadblocks to an investigation. The article even noted that the Justice Department was dragging its feet on the release of certain documents. The article added: "The panel's troubles come amid . . . questions about whether the CIA, FBI and other agencies misread warning signs about a possible attack against the United States."[66]

A week later, what had largely been a hidden battle between the CIA and the FBI came out into the open: "It began with the CIA and the FBI hissing and scratching at each other like alley cats, renewing one of the Capital's oldest back-fence feuds."

> Now, as it has spread deep into the FBI itself in the last few days, the controversy over who knew what in the days and weeks before September 11 threatens to explode into the kind of unpredictable melee most politicians dread—raging across party lines to drag Congress, the White House and other government institutions into a conflict none can control.[67]

The authors suggested "the debate is a hardball contest of leaks and spin, fought by the agencies themselves but also by partisans on the Hill, in news media and in the policy establishment." It went on to outline the actions and reactions of both agencies. For instance, the article noted that the FBI had sought to place any intelligence failure at CIA's doorstep while "[t]he CIA also aimed elbows at the FBI." The CIA, it seems was gleeful about FBI headquarters failing to act on a memo from one of its own agents in Phoenix who had warned of inordinate numbers of Middle Easterners taking flying lessons (i.e., the "Rowley" memo). "Within a day, the FBI anonymously declared that it *had* shared at least portions of the memo with the CIA" (ibid.; italics added).

If one considers the article that appeared two days later as an indication of the intelligence agency making progress in bureaucratic battles, the CIA was ahead on points. According to one piece, "Evidence of FBI missteps" was generating political pressures to reshape the crime-busting bureau," and dividing it up into different shops: one that fights crime; one that fights terrorism. The Rowley memo was further highlighted. It seems that the Rowley memo, an in-house criticism by an FBI lawyer that had been sent to Director Mueller, leaked. The overall thrust of the article showed a director under siege. The following day Director Mueller announced changes in the FBI. Certainly it is possible that the director had been planning these changes for some time, though as we know, he was appointed only in late 2001. Those inclined to be somewhat suspicious of coincidental timing in Washington politics may well see ulterior motives at work. It is therefore not unreasonable to suspect a bureaucratic motive behind the announcement: namely, it may have been intended to preempt the spate of plans circulating that would carve up his agency in what the FBI would see as undesirable.[68]

Cited earlier was a "bold bureaucratic move" by the Department of Homeland Security's Tom Ridge. Similarly, references to his detractors were cited—in particular, his political rivals within the administration and some of his critiques in the media were briefly discussed. Ridge's next move—and it was as dramatic as it was surprising—came in early June. President Bush and a small core of inside advisors advanced an extraordinary bureaucratic coup. Instructively, the core of advisors consisted of his chief-of-staff—in effect the president's top political advisor and importantly the "gatekeeper" who determines who gets to speak with the president—

Andrew Card, Jr., White House Counsel Alberto Gonzalez, Office of Management and Budget (OMB) Chief Mitchell Daniels, *and* Mr. Ridge. Pundits who had predicted that Ridge's personal relationship with the president would prove decisive were apparently prescient, in contrast to the Cassandras who had described Ridge as too timid for Washington politics.

Evidently, the president—perhaps sensing the writing on the walls of Congress—began a process of considering a massive reorganization of the executive branch in April and May. During those two months this core group of insiders—and note, neither Powell, Rice, nor Rumsfeld had been included—met in total secrecy to discuss said reorganization. In effect, they planned to reorganize the federal government, in terms of fighting global terrorism, completely and decisively! The proposal that came from the White House "was designed largely by just four of President Bush's most trusted senior aides, meeting for 10 days in a bunker-style, secure conference room beneath the White House." Senator Lieberman (D-CT), author of legislation "much like the White House's proposal, got a call from the Department of Homeland Security Director Tom Ridge on Wednesday night [June 5, 2002] asking about the details of the senator's bill—but Ridge didn't give a hint as to what was coming in the morning."[69]

Clearly, Ridge's bureaucratic acumen had been underestimated by his detractors. In one bold move, his new bureaucracy (a bureaucracy that will potentially have extraordinary influence on foreign policy) usurped portions of some twenty-two departments and/or agencies. The entire exercise showed extraordinary discipline, focus, political and bureaucratic prowess, and boldness. In the past, the Bush Administration had typically submitted only broad principles to Congress for a given initiative. By announcing, then quickly giving a blueprint to Congress, the administration preempted a great deal of potential Executive-Legislative wrangling. What cabinet head or director could go either to the White House or the Congress effectively to lobby for its own interests if said interests conflicted with the blueprint? While Ridge was yet to be announced as the Director of the new cabinet-level position, he clearly had shaped it—indeed, was the only person in the group with foreign-policy responsibilities, other than the president—and had an inside position from which to maneuver. For some two months, this core group had met and nothing had leaked, an extraordinary feat, inasmuch as virtually everything leaks in Washington. That fact alone distinguished the administration's move: "a seven-week deliberative process secret even by the standards of the Bush administration known for its discipline and control" (ibid.). Affected bureaucracies and agencies were now left in the position of playing catch-up.

Politics in Washington is an iterative game. As has been witnessed time and again, bureaucratic politics is nothing if not a dynamic process of moves and countermoves. If Mueller had experienced a couple of bad weeks, by early June he was coming out of it with his star arguably rising again. Ironically, the Bush blueprint may have actually taken the focus off Mueller for a time. After discussing some of his woes—the *Wall Street Journal* actually called for his resignation and *Time* published a cover story entitled "How the FBI Blew the Case"—the *Washington Post* nonetheless asserted that he came out of it in good shape: "Mueller may have finished the week in a stronger position than where he started it." Politics in the nation's capital is a full-contact sport; what is more, it is a zero-sum game in which one agency's gain is perforce another agency's loss. Indeed, just a few days later a piece came out in the *New York Times* in which it was reported that the CIA had actually been tracking al Qaeda operatives, some of whom turned out to be 9/11 hijackers, months earlier than it had hitherto reported, making the CIA look incompetent and prone to covering its mistakes, if not down right duplicitous.[70]

As Congressional hearings on potential intelligence failures loomed, the intensity of parochialism increased. Scheduled to begin Tuesday, June 4, Senator Bob Graham (a presidential hopeful in 2003) and Representative Goss, chairs respectively of the Senate and House Intelligence committees, were working out the ground rules. (Goss, incidentally, is a former CIA case officer—i.e., an actual "spook.") The *New York Times* reported that "on Tuesday they will begin joint oversight hearings to examine the painful subject of a colossal intelligence failure and who in the government knew what before the attacks on the World Trade Center and the Pentagon." The author continued: "Finger pointing, some pitting the F.B.I. against the C.I.A., already threatens to overshadow the joint committee's actual hearings." Despite the gravity of the hearings, the hearing's seriousness

> has not halted the typical Washington cycle of leak and counter-leak. Today, the C.I.A. responded to charges that it had waited too long to notify the F.B.I. about two hijackers by disclosing that it had found e-mail traffic between C.I.A. and F.B.I. employees showing that the bureau *was* notified that a man named Khalid al-Midhar was about to attend a meeting in Malaysia.
>
> The C.I.A. passed along Mr. Midhar's name and Saudi passport number to an F.B.I. official, according to agency records. In a January 6, 2001, e-mail message between a C.I.A. employee and an F.B.I. official working for the counterterrorism center at C.I.A. headquarters, the C.I.A. employee noted that the bureau already had the information about Mr. Midhar. (italics added)[71]

Midhar was integral to planning and executing the 9/11 attacks and indeed turned out to be one of the hijackers. Yet another piece noted: "The intense Congressional scrutiny has already forced two old rivals, the C.I.A. and F.B.I., into an increasingly bitter exchange of charges and countercharges about 'two al Qaeda associates who later turned out to be among the 19 hijackers.'"

> In another development today, the C.I.A. acknowledged that it had first received a report from a third country in March 2000 about a man who was later identified as one of the hijackers. The report said Mr. Alhamzi, had visited Jordan and then flown to Los Angeles on January 15, 2000.

Alhamzi had come to the United States after leaving a meeting in Malaysia with other suspected al Qaeda members in January 2000,[72] making another embarrassing link to the Malaysia fiasco. Though the article does not attribute the CIA's admission to governmental leaks, it was rumored at the time that someone at the FBI intentionally leaked the story in order to cause the CIA to have to acknowledge its failure and, in the process, obfuscating the negative focus the FBI had so recently endured.

Thus far we have focused principally on intra-executive-branch parochialism. Inter-branch turf battles are yet another governmental input. The architecture of Congress—535 voting members—the division of responsibilities between the House (purse strings), and the Senate (specific foreign-policy responsibilities), requires a complex choreography of protocols for foreign-policy decision-making. Multiple Congressional committees and subcommittees have a "hand" in various parts of foreign-policy output. To name the most obvious, there exist Senate and House Committees and Subcommittees on International Security, International Relations, Defense, and Intelligence. Additionally, a "seniority" system exists whereby those who have managed to stay in Congress the longest enjoy seniority on the committees on which they serve and ultimately chair.

Indeed, that is why it is common for most readers to associate certain names with foreign-policy issues. When Sam Nunn was a Senator, he was associated with defense because he had moved up to be either chair or the ranking member, depending upon which party held the majority, of the Senate Armed Services Committee. During 2002, Representative Henry Hyde (R-IL) was the chair of the House Committee on International Relations. Senators Bob Graham (D-FL), and Richard Shelby (R-AL) were the chairman and ranking Republican respectively of the Senate Select Committee on Intelligence. Similarly, Senators Carl Levin (D-MI) and John Warner (R-VA) were the chairman and the ranking Republican on the Senate Armed Services Committee. Senator John McCain (R-AZ), whom the media routinely interview on foreign-policy, was the third-ranking member of the Senate Armed Services Committee. (In 2003, McCain is now the second-ranking Republican on said committee.) Of the one hundred senators, two represent each state in the Union and fight for that state's interests. Of the four hundred thirty-five voting members of the House, each represents a district within a state that has unique interests.

The point is that parochialism is not limited to the executive branch; it is alive and well within the legislative branch as well. Within the Senate, Senator Shelby was said to be concerned that the close friendship between Senator Graham and Representative Goss might proscribe the in-depth and "freewheeling" investigation into potential intelligence failures that Shelby desired. As ranking Republican on the Select Committee on Intelligence, Shelby apparently did not care for his lack of input in terms of setting the ground rules. Additionally, he had been a critic of DCI George Tenet in the past. And in a relatively rare display of partisanship—when it comes to the war on the global-terrorist hydra—Senator Tom Daschle, majority leader of the Senate, was identified as preferring an independent commission to investigate the matter separately, implying he feared potential cover-ups.[73] Other Congresspersons had complained, to the contrary, that the hearings would be used to attack the Bush administration solely, without attributing appropriate blame, as they saw it, to the Clinton team. This was eventually solved by an agreement to investigate intelligence failings and communication problems between various bureaus going as far back as 1986. Even President Bush joined the fray briefly admitting that both the CIA and FBI were guilty of intelligence failings and that, obviously, neither agency had sufficiently communicated with one another prior to 9/11, perhaps seeking to put an end to the public bickering.[74]

When Bush first proposed homeland security, he did so by executive order. By contrast, the NSC was created by Congressional statute (the 1947 National Security Act). Now the Department of Homeland Security too would be a product of Congressional statute, making the similarity between the Department of Homeland Security and the National Security Council even clearer. The piece reported that "the White House billed it as the biggest reorganization of the government since restructuring by President Harry Truman in 1947, when the War and Navy Departments were combined into the Defense Department." Recall, that the 1947 National Security Act and its amendments also created the CIA and eventually created the Joint Command structure of the military. The new department included "parts of eight current departments—Agriculture, Commerce, Health and Human Services, Justice, State, Transportation and Treasury as well as the Federal Emergency Management Agency."[75] Bush had resisted making this move for months, as several senators and representatives called for just such action. Bureaucratically, the White House was seizing the initiative and making a virtue out of necessity in a fairly deft political move.[76]

One cannot be certain of Ashcroft's precise motivation, but the Justice Department announced the same day that henceforth it planned to "fingerprint and photograph more than 100,000 visa holders who pose 'national security concerns,' taking another step in its efforts to keep track of foreign visitors to the United States." One could speculate that Ashcroft pined for the publicity he had received earlier, under the theory that *any* publicity is good publicity. Or perhaps like the proverbial moth to the flame, he is simply attracted to controversy. Less cynically, it may simply be a case of coincidence, though coincidence is a rare commodity in Washington politics. Whatever the reason, his announcement did result in more scrutiny and managed to anger immigrant groups: "The initiative immediately angered immigrant groups and some members of Congress, who accused the government of racial and ethnic profiling of hundreds of thousands of Middle Eastern students, workers and tourists."[77]

As already noted, Ashcroft is literally FBI Director Mueller's boss. Whether coordinated or not, Director Mueller made a dramatic move the same day. As noted, the CIA and the FBI had been "fingerpointing" at each other over the previous couple of months. Nonetheless, using one of the boldest bureaucratic maneuvers around, Mueller told Congress that he needed a bigger budget and more agents. Turning a sow's ear into a silk purse, as it were, he actually cited the intelligence failures by which his agency had recently been tainted to justify the increases.[78] Minimally, one has to give him credit for his sheer brazenness.

Congress was evidently feeling unappreciated. Bush's blueprint allowed Congress and many of the 535 voting members to get in on the action in one way or another. Some 88 Congressional committees and subcommittees would now have a piece of the Department of Homeland Security puzzle. "As the House opened hearings on *Mr. Bush's ambitious plan to reorganize the government,* House and Senate leaders embraced the broad concept of a new department but made clear that Congress intended to put its own stamp on it" (italics added). Being bipartisan, as Congress had nearly uniformly been since 9/11, did not mean that those who represent the American public on Capitol Hill had to check either their egos or parochial interests at the door. Nor would Bush's plan necessarily sail smoothly through the Congressional processes irrespective of the fact that many in Congress had been clamoring for much of Bush's blueprint. One reporter noted that "Despite the bipartisan desire to create the homeland security department swiftly, the House hearings today provided a glimpse into possible difficulties ahead. Lawmakers raised concerns about aspects of the president's plan as varied as its authority over full Immigration and Naturalization Service and role of the National Guard." Over the following days additional issues would emerge: For instance, would the Department of Homeland Security have authority over portions of FBI and CIA or would it be a customer of those agencies?[79]

Big-league posturing must surely have been occurring behind the scenes. "Senior CIA and FBI officials have begun to question," reported one author, "whether members of Congress and the Bush administration . . . may be promising too much and going too far in providing them [the Department of Homeland Security] tools to fight terrorism."[80] Over the next several days several variations on the Department of Homeland Security–CIA–FBI relationship were circulated and debated. Some in Congress thought either one or both agencies ought to be moved into the Department of Homeland Security. Others spoke of carving off pieces of each agency. What seems to have emerged (as of this writing) was that the new department would have access to intelligence information, which, notably, was the favored position of the White House. "The decision to give the department [Homeland Security] such unambiguous powers to collect intelligence information and protect the nation seemed to placate some in Congress who had been concerned that the department was incomplete without the F.B.I and the C.I.A. under its umbrella." The CIA and FBI managed to guard their respective turfs to some extent; had they been placed under the Department of Homeland Security they would have lost some of their independence. Instead, the "bill does not require the agencies to turn over raw intelligence material like tapes or transcripts of clandestine conversations." Rather, they would be allowed to "scrub" the intelligence, thereby protecting some of their sources and methods. The Department of Homeland Security could "request" raw intelligence under certain circumstances, with the White House being the final arbiter if disagreement arose.[81] The Department of Homeland Security would be a "consumer" of intelligence while the FBI and CIA retained most of their respective prerogatives. (It will be interesting to see over the next few years whether the CIA will attempt to use the Department of Homeland Security against the FBI and vice versa.)

In announcing his plan, the president effectively likened it to the national-security apparatus that resulted from the Cold War. "He [Bush] said generations of Americans would look back on the bill submitted . . . *as the foundation for an eventual triumph over global terrorism.*" Director Ridge went even further. He visited Capitol Hill and in "an unusual bipartisan appearance," with members of both chambers said: "As history has shown, when the Congress of the United States and the president of the United States unite, no challenge is too great, no cause is out of reach, no dream is impossible, *whether it's winning a world war, a cold war, a war on terrorism*" (ibid.; italics added).

Two final events occurred in late July, both of which should properly be discussed under the rubric of governmental inputs. One involved Secretary of Transportation Norman Mineta. Recall that in the aftermath of 9/11, a good deal of attention was paid to airport security. As described earlier, this resulted in a new agency being created in the Transportation Department: the TSA. The idea was that by "federalizing" airport security and screening, and by hiring federal employees who would receive government benefits and salaries, a better quality of security would result. From a bureaucratic standpoint, this was a positive for Mineta and his Department of Transportation. Unfortunately for Mineta, his increased budget came with strings. One was that deadlines were given for Mineta's department to accomplish its hiring, training and staffing, and so forth. In late July, Mineta testified before the House Transportation Committee (actually its subcommittee on aviation) and explained that without an additional $1 billion, he would not be able to meet the deadlines. Mineta had not demonstrated the bureaucratic acuity comparable to, say, Ridge or Rumsfeld. This ploy, however, was not bad for a department that historically has had little to do with U.S. foreign policy and whose budget has never been comparable to the big-league, foreign-policy bureaucracies.[82] (Note: In spring 2003, TSA fired thousands of recently hired employees as a result of too hastily conducted background investigations.)

The second involved President Bush's earlier public call for the "toppling" of Saddam Hussein. Indeed, he had talked about preemptive strikes to take out regimes building weapons of mass destruction and regimes who have ties to terrorists.[83] This actually caused a row for a couple of days in June 2002. On successive weekends (July 21 and July 28) the *New York Times* published U.S. military plans; the articles attributed their sources to the Pentagon. Clearly the leaks were coming from frustrated military planners who either disliked specific plans or simply wished not to go to war in Iraq. Meeting with troops at Fort Drum, New York, the president "renewed his vow that the United States [would] strike preemptively against countries developing weapons of mass destruction. . . . Theretofore Mr. Bush had said relatively little about the strategy of preemptive action that he first described in a speech in June at West Point."[84]

Clearly the president has the right to announce U.S. military and foreign-policy plans any time he wishes; he is, after all, the commander-in-chief. However, that he would do so was curious inasmuch as both the White House and the Defense Department, specifically Secretary Rumsfeld, had been complaining bitterly over the previous months' "leaks," most of which were landing on the pages of the *New York Times*. When one plan was leaked, Secretary Rumsfeld responded by telling a press briefing that if he identified who was leaking he would have the person(s) prosecuted legally.[85] After the June 29 article leaked the Pentagon's most recent plan (called the inside-out attack) Rumsfeld again displayed anger at leakers in his own shop. Oddly, White House spokesman Ari Fleischer similarly complained about Defense Department leaks at his daily press briefing!

The basis of their complaints was that Pentagon leaks precluded surprise: It put Saddam on alert that the United States was coming and allowed him to prepare for any such eventuality. CNN's *Wolf Blitzer Reports* devoted a substantial portion to the leaks and the complaints by Rumsfeld in particular. Why the president effectively "leaked" the same thing, is therefore hard to comprehend. It may be that he was simply playing to his audience. More cynical, perhaps, were the inexplicable bureaucratic machinations behind his announcement, for instance, preparing the public for what eventually became Operation Iraqi Freedom (2003). In any case, let us now consider the president and other key individuals as inputs into U.S. foreign policy.

NOTES

1. U.S. Constitution, Articles I and II, *ad passim*.
2. Walter S. Jones, *The Logic of International Relations* (1996), pp. 49, 51–52.
3. Charles W. Kegley, Jr. and Eugene R. Wittkopf, *American Foreign Policy: Pattern and Process*, 5th ed. (New York: St. Martin's Press, 1996), p. 33.
4. Incidentally, the Tonkin Gulf fiasco eventuated in the War Powers Act, which allows the president to put troops in the battlefield for sixty days without a declaration of war and allows for the possibility of a thirty-day extension.
5. See HR 3162, 107th Cong., 1st sess., October 24, 2001.
6. Dan Balz and Bob Woodward, "America's Chaotic Road to War, Part I," *Washington Post*, 27 January 2002.
7. Barton Gellman, "Struggles inside the Government Defined Campaign," *Washington Post*, 20 December 2001, p. A-1.
8. Brookings Institution Chronology, http://www.brook.edu/dybdocroot/fp/projects/terrorism/chronology.htm.
9. See Bob Woodward, *The Commanders* (1991).
10. For example, see "Text: Bush on Homeland Security Development," eMediaMillWorks, January 24, 2002.
11. Brookings Institution Chronology, op cit.
12. Eric Pianin and Bill Miller, "For Ridge, Ambition and Realities Clash," *Washington Post*, 23 January 2002, p. A-1.
13. Patriot Act, op. cit.
14. Quote comes from White House press release, "President Signs Aviation Security Legislation," November 19, 2001, http://www.whitehouse.gov. For the Aviation Act that creates the Transportation Security Administration, see Public Law 107-71, November 19, 2001, 115 Stat. 597. Available at: http://www.tsa.dot.gov.
15. Brookings Institution, op cit.
16. Richard Simon, "House, Senate Panels Back Funds for War," *Los Angeles Times*, 2 April 2003.
17. These are second-tier pundits, using Eric Alterman's criteria. See Eric Alterman, *Sound and Fury*, 1997, especially "Operation Pundit Storm."
18. See Adam Clymer, "Ex-Operative Writes of the Decline at C.I.A.," *New York Times*, 26 January 2002.

19. Fredricke Kunkle, "At Pentagon, Healing and Rebuilding," *Washington Post,* 22 January 2002, p. A-1. Budget figures from Richard W. Stevenson, "Bush Budget Links Dollars to Deeds with New Ratings," *New York Times,* 3 February 2002.
20. Mike Allen and Amy Goldstein, "Security Funding Tops New Budget," *Washington Post,* 20 January 2002, p. A-1.
21. Richard W. Stevenson, op. cit. "Bush Budget Links Dollars to Deeds with New Ratings," *New York Times,* 3 February 2002.
22. Bob Drogin, "Missiles Not Biggest Threat, Report Says," *Los Angeles Times,* 12 January 2002.
23. Katharine Q. Seelye and David E. Sanger, "Bush Reconsiders Stand on Treating Captives of War," *New York Times,* 29 January 2002.
24. Esther Schrader, "Military Fuses Old, New to Create a Lethal Force," *Los Angeles Times,* 10 February 2002.
25. Abraham McLaughlin, "Secret Service Dons New Role for a New Era," *Christian Science Monitor,* 6 February 2002.
26. Mike Allen and Amy Goldstein, "Security Funding Tops New Budget," *Washington Post,* 20 January 2002, p. A-1.
27. Eric Pianin and Bill Miller, "For Ridge Ambition and Realities Clash," *Washington Post,* 23 January 2002, p. A-1.
28. John Prados, *Keepers of the Keys* (New York: Morrow, 1991), p. 38.
29. NSC info from Prados, ibid; Homeland Security numbers from Pianin and Miller, op. cit.
30. Adam Clymer, "Ex-Operative Writes of the Decline at C.I.A."
31. Bradley Graham, "Bush to Propose Sustained Rises in Military Spending," *Washington Post,* 3 February 2002, p. A-6.
32. Terrance Neilan, "Pentagon Faces More Questions on Afghan Raid, Plus C.I.A. Role," *New York Times,* 12 February 2002.
33. Bob Drogin, "Missiles Not Biggest Threat, Report Says," *Los Angeles Times,* 12 January 2002.
34. Nicholas D. Kristof, "Sleeping with Terrorists," *New York Times,* 12 February 2002.
35. Eric Schmitt, "Wolfowitz, in Philippines, Looks to a Greater U.S. Role," *New York Times,* 4 June 2002.
36. Terrance Neilan, op. cit.
37. *New York Times,* "Lawmakers to Investigate U.S. Intelligence Failures," 12 February 2002.
38. Ether Schader, "War, on Advice of Council," *Los Angeles Times,* 15 February 2002.
39. Eric Miller, "More Money Won't End the War," *Boston Globe,* 5 February 2002, p. A-11.
40. Judith Miller, "U.S. Plans to Act More Rigorously in Hostage Cases," *New York Times,* 18 February 2002.
41. Christopher Drew and Judith Miller, "Though Not Linked to Terrorism, Many Detainees Cannot Go Home," *New York Times,* 18 February 2002.
42. Stories accusing Rumsfeld of authoritarian behavior and not listening to his top military brass have proliferated. While editing this text, a one-day, CNN and MSNBC cable-news story circulated in mid-October 2002.
43. James Dao and Eric Schmitt, "Pentagon Readies Efforts to Sway Sentiment Abroad," *New York Times,* 19 February 2002.
44. Thomas E. Ricks, "Defense Dept. Divided over Propaganda Plan," *Washington Post,* 20 February 2002, p. A-10. Also see Thomas E. Ricks and Vernon Loeb, "Rumsfeld and Commanders Exchange Briefings," *Washington Post,* 3 March 2002, p. A-19.
45. Mike Allen, "White House Angered at Plan for Pentagon Disinformation," *Washington Post,* 25 February 2002, p. A-17. Elizabeth Becker and James Dao, "Hearts and Minds," *Christian Science Monitor,* 19 February 2002. Represents "Estimates" of the Office of Management and Budget.
46. Vernon Loeb and Bradley Graham, "Democrats Criticize Budget, Anti-Terror War," *Washington Post,* 28 February 2002, p. A-8.
47. Charles Piller, "U.S. to Curb Computer Access by Foreigners," *Los Angeles Times,* 7 March 2002.
48. Paul Richter, "U.S. Works Up Plan for Using Nuclear Arms," *Los Angeles Times,* 9 March 2002.
49. Bill Miller, "Ridge Close to Unveiling New Terror Alert System," *Washington Post,* 9 March 2002, p. A-13.
50. Alan Sipress, "Peacekeepers Won't Go Beyond Kabul, Cheney Says," *Washington Post,* 20 March 2002.
51. Rumsfeld began to soften his position a short time later. See Thom Shaker, "The Military," *New York Times,* 26 March 2002.

52. Abraham McLaughlin, "Bush Plans Super-Agency to Improve U.S. Border Control," *Christian Science Monitor,* 25 March 2002.
53. Dana Milbank, "Bush Seeks $27.1 Billion More for Military, Security, Relief Efforts," *Washington Post,* 22 March 2002, p. A-7. Subsequent supplemental appropriations were passed in spring 2003, *supra.*
54. Thom Shaker, "The Military," *New York Times,* 26 March 2002.
55. Larry Margasak, "U.S. to Seek Death Penalty," *Los Angeles Times,* 28 March 2002.
56. Kamran Khan and Karl Vick, "FBI Joined Pakistan in Staging Raids," *Washington Post,* 30 March 2002, p. A-13.
57. Alan Sipress and Dan Balz, "U.S. Seeks Arab Role in Reviving Peace Talks," *Washington Post,* 6 April 2002, p. A-1.
58. Bradley Graham, "Pentagon Seeks Own Foreign Aid Power," *Washington Post,* 8 April 2002, p. A-1.
59. Walter Pincus and Colum Lynch, "Wolfowitz Had CIA Probe U.N. Diplomat in Charge," *Washington Post,* 15 April 2002, p. A-1.
60. Eric Schmitt, "Vote in House Strongly Backs an End to I.N.S.," *New York Times,* 26 April 2002.
61. Alan Sipress, "Policy Divide Thwarts Powell in Mideast Effort," *Washington Post,* 26 April 2002, p. A-1.
62. Ricardo Alonso-Zaldivar, "Cost of Fortifying Airports May Top $6 Billion in 2002," *Los Angeles Times,* 26 May 2002.
63. Dan Eggen, "'Carnivore' Glitches Blamed for FBI Woes," *Washington Post,* 29 May 2002, p. A-7. Mike Allen, "Questions Swirl around Bush over 9-11 Attacks," *Washington Post,* 16 May 2002.
64. Jennifer Loven, "House Passes Defense Spending Bill," Associated Press, 10 May 2002.
65. Mike Allen, "Questions Swirl around Bush over 9-11 Attacks," *Washington Post,* 16 May 2002. For Mueller's comments see Associated Press, "F.B.I. Says Suicide Bombers Likely in U.S.," 20 May 2002.
66. Dana Priest and Walter Pincus, "Strife, Dissent Beset Hill's September 11 Panel," *Washington Post,* 20 May 2002, p. A-1.
67. Richard T. Cooper and Josh Meyer, "CIA-FBI Feuding Relentless. Intelligence," *Los Angeles Times,* 26 May 2002.
68. Abraham McLaughlin, "Pressure Mounts to Overhaul the FBI" *Christian Science Monitor,* 28 May 2002. See Susan Schmidt, "Mueller Announces a New Focus for FBI," *Washington Post,* 29 May 2002.
69. Dana Milbank, "Plan Was Formed in Utmost Secrecy," *Washington Post,* 7 June 2002, p. A-1.
70. David Von Drehle and Susan Schmidt, "Mueller May Be Stronger after Tough Week," *Washington Post,* 2 June 2002, p. A-1; David Johnston and Elizabeth Becker, "C.I.A. Was Tracking Hijacker Months Earlier Than It Had Said," *New York Times,* 3 June 2002. The *Time* article can be found at: http://www.time.com/time/nation/article/0859924999400.html.
71. James Risen, "Rifts Plentiful as 9/11 Inquiry Begins Today," *New York Times,* 4 June 2002.
72. David Johnston and Don Van Natta, Jr., "Congressional Inquiry into 9/11 Will Look Back as Far as 1986," *New York Times,* 5 June 2002.
73. James Risen, "Rifts Plentiful as 9/11 Inquiry Begins Today," op. cit.
74. *Washington Post* Staff Writers, "Bush Cites CIA-FBI Breakdown," *Washington Post,* 5 June 2002, p. A-1.
75. *Washington Post* Staff Writers, "Bush to Propose Security Cabinet Position," *Washington Post,* 6 June 2002. Also, Elisabeth Bumiller and David E. Sanger, "Bush, As Terror Inquiry Swirls, Seeks Cabinet Post on Security," *New York Times,* 7 June 2002.
76. Patrick E. Tyler, "White House Acts to Regain the Initiative," *New York Times,* 7 June 2002. Also, "Bush Urges Congress to Move Quickly on Cabinet Post," Associated Press, 7 June 2002.
77. *Washington Post,* "U.S. to Track Visitors Deemed a Security Risk," 6 June 2002, p. A-1.
78. *Washington Post,* "Mueller Says Criticism Underscores Need for FBI Changes," 6 June 2002.
79. The figure on committees and subcommittees comes from "Bush Urges Congress to Move Quickly on Cabinet Post," Associated Press, op. cit. The quote comes from Allison Mitchell and Carl Huse, "Congress Seeking to Put Own Stamp on Security Plan," *New York Times,* 12 June 2002. The information on how to associate the Department of Homeland Security with CIA and FBI is from Jim VandeHei and Dan Eggen, "Hill Eyes Shifting Parts of FBI, CIA," *Washington Post,* 13 June 2002.
80. Walter Pincus, "Congress to Postpone Revamping of FBI, CIA," *Washington Post,* 13 June 2002, p. A-1.

81. David Firestone and Allison Mitchell, "Congress Gets Bill Setting up Security Dept.," *New York Times*, 19 June 2002.

82. "Mineta Says Spending Bill 'Undermines' Airline Security," Associated Press, 23 July 2002, http://www.airportnet.org/depts/federal/press/articles.ap30723.pdf.

83. See Bob Woodward, "President Broadens Anti-Hussein Order," *Washington Post*, 16 June 2002, p. A-1.

84. David E. Sanger, "Bush Renews Pledge to Strike First to Counter Terror Threats," *New York Times*, 20 July 2002.

85. See, for example, "Battle Plans for Iraq," *New York Times*, 6 July 2002.

INDIVIDUAL AND ROLE
INPUTS TO U.S. FOREIGN POLICY

Individual

Just three days removed from these events, Americans do not yet have the distance of history. But our responsibility to history is already clear: *to answer these attacks and rid the world of evil.* War has been waged against us by stealth and deceit and murder. This nation is peaceful, but fierce when stirred to anger. The conflict was begun on the timing and terms of others. It will end in a way, and at an hour, of our choosing.

> —President George W. Bush, Washington, D.C., the
> National Cathedral, September 14, 2002 (italics added).

Role

Defending our nation against its enemies is the first and fundamental commitment of the federal government.

The gravest danger to freedom lies at the crossroads of radicalism and technology. When the spread of chemical and biological and nuclear weapons, along with missile technology—when that occurs, even weak states and small groups could attain a catastrophic power to strike great nations. Our enemies . . . declared this very intention, and have been caught seeking these terrible weapons. They want the capability to blackmail us, or harm our friends—and we will oppose them with all our power.

> —President George W. Bush, "Preamble" to the "National
> Security Strategy of the United States of America,"
> and West Point, New York, June 1, 2002, respectively.

Recall Chapter 1's brief discussion regarding the problematic nature of attributing a person's actions to his or her beliefs, life experiences, ethos, and so on, from behavior or actions that result from role expectations. Clearly, these two inputs are essentially the opposite sides of the same coin. Specifically, role theory suggests that persons at the apex of foreign-policy decision-making and their idiosyncratic behavior is proscribed, constrained, and altered by long-held expectations of the office they occupy. These expectations are from various sources: expectations derived from the U.S. Constitution; expectations held by elites, particularly in the foreign-policy decision-making bureaucracy; and expectations held by the American public.

A simplistic but illustrative example is that of Master Drill Sergeant Hartmann from the popular film *Full Metal Jacket.* One would be hard pressed to find a more offensive, abusive, objectionable individual. Role theory suggests that Gunny Hartmann is "play acting" to achieve a certain effect. Now let us assume that Gunny Hartmann has a family to whom he returns home, if not nightly on some semiregular basis. Clearly, if Gunny Hartmann returned home to his family and behaved the way he behaves in training new Marines, he would soon be divorced, without a family, and very likely behind bars for spousal and child abuse.

Bill Clinton, one could argue, pushed the boundaries of the role of the president. In addition to appearing on MTV and "nonserious news programs," he answered a question about his underwear, stretching the boundaries of the presidential role. Needless to say, his behavior with Monica Lewinsky in the Oval Office shattered widely held role expectations of presidential behavior. Interestingly, his infidelity was not the crux of his violation of role expectations. Several presidents have apparently behaved similarly. Rather, his infidelities were committed *in* the White House—the Oval Office—while he conducted the nation's business. Thus, it was actually the brazenness with which he committed said infidelities and the fact that he prevaricated about them to the nation instead of showing (or even feigning) remorse.

Further, consider the Cuban Missile Crisis of October 1962. Whatever else one thinks about the Kennedy administration's handling of the crisis, at one point—according to the transcripts that were released in the early 1990s—the president believed the role of the presidency required that he do something. In other words, role precluded a "do-nothing" option. Doing nothing, in President Kennedy's view, would have been an impeachable offense according to transcripts. From the same era, newspaper accounts from conversations between Lyndon Johnson and any number of Congressional and personal friends make clear he could not pull out of Vietnam, despite his early realization of the war's futility. The role of the presidency rendered a unilateral withdrawal impossible. Role expectations, as indeed the oath of office to defend the Constitution and nation, simply did not permit such actions.

The point is that role theory holds very specific expectations for various key decision-makers. The role expectations vary for the military versus civilian leaders as well. And of course, the National Security Council (NSC) principals—what has currently been called President Bush's war cabinet—is comprised of both types of role. One might expect the secretary of defense's role to be nearly the opposite of the secretary of state's. Specifically, one would expect the former to be much less reluctant to use military instruments as first resort based on role. Among other reasons, the secretary of defense is the chief of the defense establishment: the military, the civilian employees, and, to some extent, the defense-industrial complex. The annual budget, furthermore, is a finite number of dollars and a law of bureaucracy is that each bureaucracy seeks a greater share of said dollars. Since the total pie is finite, any additional dollars the Defense Department obtains are at the expense of other national-security bureaucracies: It is, in other words, a zero-sum game. Additionally, as discussed in Chapter 4, there are bureaucratic rivalries that may have little to do with budgets. Anecdotally, in early summer (June 2002), stories were leaked by both the CIA and the FBI blaming the other for dereliction regarding the 9/11 intelligence. These are not necessarily indicative of evil, insidious persons but, rather, evidence that Washington, D.C. politics is a "contact sport." The individuals who hold high office in the various national-security bureaucracies are infamous for having enormous egos. The fact is, they like to have the president's ear and they like to win. Winning is getting the president to adopt their views over their bureaucratic rivals.

Simplistically, one could hypothesize behavior, based simply on role expectations of the bureaucracy its director leads. The president is the chief executive of the nation; practically speaking, his principal role is commander-in-chief. The secretary of state, currently Colin Powell, is the chief diplomat of the United States. One would expect him to seek to resolve conflicts via diplomacy and to be amenable to using military instruments as a last resort. The DCI is the chief intelligence officer and also the person most directly associated with paramilitary and/or covert operations. Though the president's chief of staff is not specifically a foreign-policy advisor, at least since the Eisenhower administration the chief of staff has become instrumental in policy decisions, including foreign-policy decisions: He is the official gatekeeper and determines who sees the president and when; similarly, his proximity to the president gives him unusual influence in policy. The vice president traditionally has had little influence in foreign policy. Since the Carter administration, however, vice presidents have enjoyed increasing influence in foreign policy, beyond attending funerals of foreign dignitaries. In the case of Vice President Cheney, his former positions as secretary of defense in the first Bush administration and chief of staff in the Ford administration, doubtless, increase his foreign-policy influence. National Security Advisor Condoleezza Rice is the president's top foreign-policy advisor and one would expect her to mediate, somewhat, the contrasting roles of the secretaries of defense and state. Role theory suggests the office shapes the individual more than the individual shapes the office. Of course personal idiosyncrasies, one would expect, would surface from time to time but, ultimately, those personal proclivities are eclipsed by the role expectations associated with the office. Impressionistically, a few observations can be offered. Dr. Rice is said to be a trusted and valued member of the president's inner circle or war cabinet. Whether she simply goes out—during press conferences and interviews—and repeats what the president believes or whether she actually initiates what the president says is unclear. Bush did, after all, come into office with virtually no foreign-policy experience. Before becoming president, he had very little travel experience and little exposure to disparate cultures. And despite his service in the Texas National Guard during the Vietnam War, George W. Bush avoided going to Vietnam, reminiscent of Clinton, and in stark contrast to the president's father, a genuine war hero.

Role theory applies, presumably, to virtually all of the important decision-makers who surround the president as well. That might include speechwriters, informal advisors, close friends and confidants, and others. Given the limited space of this text, it will not be possible to identify every important presidential confidant, much less his or her specific role, socialization history, and personal histories. Instead, the assessment of role expectations and relevant personality histories of Bush's so-called "war cabinet" will be somewhat limited: President Bush, Defense Secretary Rumsfeld, Vice President Cheney, Secretary of State Powell, National Security Advisor Rice, and DCI Tenet.[1] In other words, this assessment will confine itself to the "NSC principals" and a few second-tier advisors where relevant.

Many of these roles are associated with protecting the bureaucracies headed by the various secretaries and advisors. The various military chiefs, for instance, need to justify their budgets and missions. One would therefore expect the secretary of the Navy—and its civilian director—to be quick to propose naval components of any military campaign. The same would be true of the Air force, the Army, and the Marines. It is important to note here, however, that often roles get confused and personalities and specific idiosyncrasies supplant the roles to which one might expect specific decision-makers to conform. That is when individual inputs become paramount.

Individual inputs are very nearly the opposite of role: *viz.*, the individual imposes his or her personality on the office. Obviously this happens during unique decision-making settings. On the other hand, individual personalities and idiosyncrasies are frequently overshadowed by the sheer size and routines of the various foreign-policy bureaucracies. The sheer size of the governmental bureaucracy and its SOPs can quickly, in "normal" times, negate individual inputs. Individuals can only accomplish so much through the bureaucracy that supposedly works for him or her.

Gelb and Halperin discuss a version of the diminutive effect top officials may have on the larger bureaucracy. They labeled it *bureaucratic sabotage*; it occurred during the Cuban Missile Crisis of 1962.

> [The bureaucracy chose] to obey the orders it liked and ignore or stretch others. Thus after a tense argument with the navy, Kennedy ordered the blockade line moved closer to Cuba so that the Russians might have more time to draw back. Having lost the argument with the president, the navy simply ignored his order.
>
> When Kennedy began to realize he was not in full control, he asked his secretary of defense [McNamara] to see if he could find out just what the navy was doing. McNamara then made his first visit to the navy command post in the Pentagon. In a heated exchange, the chief of naval operations suggested that McNamara return to his office and let the navy run the blockade.[2]

As mentioned, times of crisis are among those rare occasions wherein individuals at the apex of foreign-policy decision-making have a greater chance to affect policy directly. Among other reasons, this is due to the short time in which to respond. As the previous example illustrates, however, even during crises individuals may have only a marginal effect. This phenomenon will be discussed in more detail subsequently when process is considered.

The point is that it is often difficult to differentiate individual inputs—personality, education, socialization, and so forth—from role. For this reason, in this chapter, role and individual inputs will be considered together. If and when a clear distinction between individual and role inputs can be made, said distinction will be made. Presently, we will illustrate the president's role based on his own words during his remarks at the National Day of Remembrance and his remarks to the nation from the White House Treaty Room when he informed the nation that the military campaign, Operation Enduring Freedom, had commenced. In those speeches there exist some relatively clear examples of presidential role: the sorts of things any president would be expected to say during a similar situational context.

INDIVIDUAL AND ROLE INPUTS: THE FIRST DAYS

One of the few articles that addresses Bush's "worldview" directly was published well after the 9/11 attacks.[3] While it is difficult to judge how accurately the author plumbs Bush's personality, it is at least worth quoting some of the author's observations before moving on to individual-role inputs more chronologically. Mufson begins by discussing a Bush visit to Camp David prior to 9/11. Accordingly, he took a book with him by Robert Kaplan entitled *Eastward to Tartary*. The book is a "political travelogue" through the region from Bulgaria and Romania to the oil-rich region of the Caspian Sea. Mufson claims Bush "immersed" himself in the book over the weekend. Mufson further claims that Bush was enamored with the book and that the book jibed with Bush's own "evolving" worldview, so much so that Bush asked his staff to invite Kaplan to the White House.

> Bush's interest in the book—and the somber views of its author, Robert Kaplan—reveals something about the intellectual journey of a president who nearly a year later is consumed with a campaign against "evildoers" and the dangers posed by the "axis of evil." Though September 11 *may have altered Bush's presidency, it probably didn't fundamentally alter his view of the world as a place populated by complicated, ancient feuds and dozens of dangerous groups. These groups must be confronted and, if necessary, vanquished, Bush has made clear.* (ibid.; italics added)

The author goes on to compare the current President Bush with his father. He argues that former President Bush thought in terms of the nation's self-interests in achieving freedom and prosperity. In "stark contrast,"

> Bush's darker view—which the events of September 11 reinforced—*is now driving U.S. policy on everything from civil liberties to federal spending to foreign policy.*

Military spending is projected to outstrip non-military discretionary spending within a few years. . . . Countries with whom relations have been tense are asked to
choose sides. In a battle against the forces of darkness, it's dangerous to remain in
the shadows. (ibid.; italics added)

Mufson argues that Bush's view contains a religious component. He quotes
Bush: "We've come to know truths that we will never question: Evil is real, and it
must be opposed," and that Americans are "facing danger together," and finally vis-
à-vis his religiosity, "many have discovered again that even in tragedy—especially in tragedy—*God is near.*" Mufson believes that "Bush would say that the greater
goal is to drive the barbarians away from the gates of the civilized world" (ibid.;
italics added).

Subsequent to Mufson's piece another author penned an article entitled "The
Soul of George W. Bush."

> But Mr. Bush brings something to the job that makes country-club conservatives
> quiver with unease. He is a *moralist*. I think this was true before September 11, but
> the attacks have *galvanized his inner missionary*. More precisely, September 11
> confirmed for him that God had chosen him for a purpose, and showed him what
> that purpose is. (italics added)[4]

Having briefly highlighted what others have interpreted to be the worldview of
President George W. Bush, let us now turn to a chronological examination of individual and role inputs. The reader may decide for himself or herself how accurate the previous observations are and whether they properly relate to role-theory
or individual inputs.

Whether role or individual inputs, the Balz and Woodward series presents a very
detailed account of the president and his advisors during the first few days following 9/11. As established earlier, this text takes the position that the first few days following the attacks are properly characterized as a foreign-policy crisis. (The reader
may wish to refer to Chapter 2 in which foreign-policy crises and Charles Hermann's definition thereof are discussed.) Keeping the relevance of foreign-policy
crises in mind, it is worth quoting the Woodward and Balz series—an "insider's"
view of the first week following 9/11, which was published in January 2002.[5]

> In the first hours after the terrorist attacks of September 11, Bush and his top ad-
> visors had been preoccupied with *the crisis at hand*, assessing additional threats,
> grounding airplanes, moving government officials to safety, mobilizing emergency
> rescue crews, measuring the scope of the devastation in New York and Washing-
> ton, determining who might be responsible. (ibid., Part I; italics added)

The early events surrounding the 9/11 attacks have already been examined in
the section on external inputs in Chapter 2. Rather than recount those events here,
a couple of points are in order. Anybody who watched the horrors unfold on television that day will recall occasions during which Bush's aides whispered into the

president's ear while Bush read to children in a Florida school classroom. The first message was from senior advisor Karl Rove who told the president "a small, twin-engine plane" had hit the Twin Towers, and that "it appeared to be an accident." This occurred at about 8:30 A.M. (EDT). In subsequent interviews the president recalls thinking it must have been pilot error and that perhaps the pilot had suffered a heart attack. President Bush assumed it was an accident and continued reading to the schoolchildren. The next message President Bush received was much more grave. At just past 9:00 A.M., the president's chief of staff, Andrew Card, was seen on television whispering in the president's ear. The message: "a Boeing 767 smashed into the South Tower of the Trade Center. Bush was seated on a chair in the classroom when Card whispered the news: 'A second plane hit the second tower. America is under attack.'"

President Bush looked, to put it indelicately, as if someone had punched him in the gut. It is probably fair to say that any president in the same circumstances would react similarly. Nevertheless, it was not the president's finest hour. And indeed, his deer-in-the-headlights performance continued for most of the first day. Recall, for instance, that the president's first remarks—just prior to being spirited away on Air Force One—were anything but comforting to the public at large. In fairness, the president's top advisors were scattered hither and yon. Vice President Cheney and National Security Advisor Condoleezza Rice were both in Washington, D.C.; Secretary of State Powell was in Peru; Secretary of Defense Rumsfeld was in his Pentagon office; DCI George Tenet, the lone voice in the administration who had been warning of something big from al Qaeda for some months, was breakfasting with former Senator Boren, the former Chair of the Select Committee on Intelligence.

Surrounded only by domestic-political advisors, the president's first words before embarking on Air Force One were shaky.

> At 9:30 A.M. the president appeared before television cameras, describing what had happened as "an apparent terrorist" and "a national tragedy." He appeared shaken, and his language was oddly informal. He would chase down, he said, "those folks who committed this act."
>
> Bush also said, "Terrorism against our nation will not stand." It was an echo of "This will not stand," the words his father, George H. W. Bush, had used a few days after Iraq invaded Kuwait in August 1990—in Bush's opinion, one of his father's finest moments. (ibid.)

Not only were his remarks seemingly incongruous, his entire demeanor seemed to be that of a president who was dazed and confused. What this says about the president's personal idiosyncrasies is unclear. However, it is important to note his initial response, given the remarkable transformation that had taken place in the president's demeanor by the time he arrived in Washington later than evening. Whatever early stumbles he may have exhibited, by Tuesday evening—and particularly over the next several days—a hitherto "wobbly" president had become a decisive, war-time president and leader of the nation. He had in fact accepted—or had foisted upon him—the role of a war-time president. After a shaky start, President Bush became a president whom some 70–90 percent of the public have consistently viewed as a great leader. (This continues in 2003.)

The Balz and Woodward account of Bush's activities while flying from Florida to Barksdale Air Force Base in Louisiana, and to Offutt Air Force Base, Nebraska, actually portrays a president who was beginning to get things under control. Cheney had already made comments in the president's behalf from the Capital that day. The implication of the account is that Bush's own government was concerned about his lack of looking presidential (i.e., role). It is worth noting that Bush's personal advisor, Karen Hughes, was in Washington, D.C.; so too was his chief speechwriter, Mark Gerson. Nonetheless, the president made several phone calls from Air Force One, beginning to direct his government and beginning to behave as expected, given his role as president.

At about 3:30 P.M., from Nebraska, President Bush held his first National Security Council meeting via secure video link. Bush began to take control of his national-security team. For example, after hearing a report from DCI Tenet, Cheney voiced concern that additional attacks could be forthcoming. Tenet commented that all the attacks had occurred by 10:00 A.M. and that he doubted any more would be coming that day. "Get your ears up," the president told Tenet and the others. *"The primary mission of this administration is* to find them and catch them" (ibid.; italics added).

How much of this was Bush's personality, life experience, upbringing, and so forth and how much was his foreign-policy team reminding the president of his role is difficult to discern. Nonetheless, it seems plausible to posit that at least part of this metamorphosis was due to Bush's individual characteristics and the *gravitas* he had imputed to the attacks. The president had made a brief statement from Barksdale Air Base that was less than reassuring.

> When Bush finally appeared on television from the base conference room, it, similarly, was less than reassuring. He spoke haltingly, mispronouncing several words as he looked down at his notes. When he got to the last sentence he seemed to gain strength. "The resolve of our great nation is being tested," he said. . . . The entire statement consisted of just 219 words, and the president took no questions. (ibid.)

While his words may have failed to instill much confidence in the nation, his actions were beginning to reflect his growing resolve.

DCI Tenet—not an NSC principal but an advisor by statute—had been characterized by some as "obsessed" with Osama bin Laden and al Qaeda and in his zeal to put the issue on the radar may have actually prevented Bush's top advisors from taking Tenet seriously. In effect, he had "cried wolf" so often that no one took his warnings seriously since he had made so many without anything of substance actually happening. As he left former Senator Boren, in a moment of prescience, he said "I wonder if this has anything to do with this guy taking pilot training," referring to Zacarias Moussaoui, who had been detained in August after attracting suspicion when he sought training at a Minnesota flight school—one at which we subsequently learned he requested to learn how to fly a jumbo jet but not how to take off or land it.

Hitherto, Tenet had apparently been a relatively lone voice in the administration. Bush and his foreign-policy team had a deep suspicion of anything that smacked of Clinton foreign policy. Reportedly, the Bush administration had even come up with a clever initialization: *ABC*, "anything but Clinton." But Tenet was the sole political appointee (in the war cabinet) who was a holdover from the Clinton days. He had been working the terrorism angle since at least 1995 when Clinton signed Presidential Decision Directive 35 (still classified), which put terrorism on the priority list—albeit third.[6] Thus it was a combination of things—an aversion to Clinton foreign policy and Tenet being a holdover who had worked the issue for some six years—that led Tenet to be the only foreign-policy principal who had a feel for terrorism and specifically Osama bin Laden. Indeed, in the breakfast discussed previously, as he left former Senator Boren sitting there, he uttered: "This has bin Laden all over it; I've got to go."

Balz and Woodward describe Tenet's state:

> Through much of the summer, Tenet had grown increasingly troubled by the prospect of a major terrorist attack against the United States. There was too much chatter in the intelligence system and repeated reports of threats were costing him sleep. His friends thought he had become obsessed. Everywhere he went, the message was the same: Something big is coming. (Woodward and Balz, Part I, January 21, 2002)

In any case with many of the foreign-policy principals out of town, and with Bush temporarily ineffective, first reactions fell to those in town: Condoleezza Rice (national security advisor), Tenet (DCI), and Vice President Cheney. And Cheney is nothing if not forceful and confident. It was perhaps fortuitous that Bush's handlers flew him around the country while he regained his presidential composure. Bush's absence left it to Vice President Cheney to reassure a horrified and nervous nation, something Bush's brief speeches earlier had failed to do. It is difficult to differentiate Cheney's role as the Vice President—perhaps more importantly, the former civilian head of the Defense Department as well as a former chief of staff in the Ford administration—from his personal idiosyncrasies, but he was clearly quite comfortable filling in while the president flew from one secure location to another. While Bush was on Air Force One, the Secret Service sequestered Cheney, and eventually Rice, in the secure Presidential Emergency Operations Center (PEOC) (ibid.).

But Cheney's actions speak to both his role and his personality. He spoke to the president by secure link as the president flew to a secure base. The military, per SOPs, had already "ordered up the airborne command post used only in national emergencies." Moreover the Pentagon had raised U.S. defense readiness to DefCon3, the highest it had been since the 1973 Yom Kippur War. The question was:

What are the rules of engagement? Under what circumstances could they shoot down an airliner that was presumed to be heading for another target? As it turned out, this was more than an academic exercise since United Flight 93 had made a U-turn and was heading back toward Washington. Cheney told President Bush that they needed rules of engagement. Incredibly, the vice president (in a role normally the brunt of jokes and seen as a ceremonial figure at best) proved an exceptionally competent surrogate. "Cheney recommended that Bush authorize the military to shoot down any such civilian airliners—as momentous a decision as the president was asked to make in those first hours." Bush acceded to Cheney's recommendation (ibid.).

The decision would shortly cause serious duress. Soon thereafter a military aide reported that a plane was some eighty miles out from Washington. The aide reported that they had a fighter in the area and asked Cheney whether the military should engage. "Yes," Cheney replied without hesitation.

> Around the vice president, Rice, deputy White House chief of staff Joshua Bolten and I. Lewis "Scooter" Libby, Cheney's chief of staff, tensed as the military aide repeated the question, this time with even more urgency. The plane was now 60 miles out. "Should we engage?" Cheney was asked.
>
> "Yes," he replied again.
>
> As the plane came closer, the aide repeated the question. Does the order still stand?
>
> "Of course it does," Cheney snapped. (ibid.)

Soon the president was en route back to Washington. Bush was reported to be getting angry as the day went on and to be gaining resolve. He deputized Karen Hughes to make a brief statement from the White House, on behalf of the president, reassuring the nation that the president would be speaking to them soon. Meanwhile, Gerson and Hughes were working on the speech the president would give to the nation later that evening upon returning to Washington (ibid.).

Bush soon decided he wished to return to Washington post haste. Some of Bush's advisors, and specifically the Secret Service, recommended that the president not return until the dust had settled. Secretary Rumsfeld said: "Terrorists can always attack; the Pentagon is going back to work tomorrow." Cheney weighed in that he too thought the president should return. "I'm coming back," Bush said. He was making it clear that he would not allow his government to be cowed by terrorists (ibid.). This was likely the product of both presidential role and Bush's own personal idiosyncrasies, the latter reflected in his growing anger and resolve over the course of the day.

It has become nearly axiomatic since the Truman administration that subsequent administrations would be associated with so-called "doctrines." Recall that in response to Soviet behavior in Turkey and Greece, Truman enunciated the Truman Doctrine. In effect, it alerted the Soviets and their patrons that the United States would not sit idly by while Communists made gains in other nations—whether by external (read Soviet meddling) or internal insurgencies. The Carter

Doctrine effectively defined the Persian Gulf region as an American strategic interest over which the United States would risk war to secure oil for the West. The Reagan Doctrine temporarily altered America's containment strategy to include more proactive means of forestalling Soviet success, even survival. That evening, the Bush Doctrine was created.

An interesting reality of foreign-policy decision-making is how serendipitous the promulgation of said doctrines can be. Reagan, as has been well documented, rarely said anything that was not written out on cue cards and/or reflected off a Teleprompter. What became the Bush Doctrine actually has a interesting history. As noted, both Gerson and Hughes were in Washington and not with the president. Throughout the day Hughes kept in contact with the president by secure phone and with Gerson—who was at home—via e-mail. Gerson had been working on a draft based on his communications with Hughes and the latter's communications with the president. "The president's chief speechwriter, Michael Gerson . . . had e-mailed Hughes a rough draft, which she substantially reworked, based on her conversations with Bush." As speechwriters often do, Gerson went back to reread a speech candidate Bush had made on national defense in 1999. In the 1999 speech, at the Citadel, Bush had warned of a "devastating" response to those, including terrorists, who would do harm to the United States. According to the draft text Gerson sent to Hughes that day, he had written:

> We will make no distinction between those who planned these acts and those who permitted or tolerated or encouraged them. "That's way too vague," Bush complained, proposing the word "harbor" as an alternative. In final form, what the White House came to call the Bush Doctrine was put this way: "We will make no distinction between the terrorists who committed these acts and those who harbor them."

Woodward and Balz describe this as a "huge step for the administration."

> Although he had talked about the idea in the campaign and aides had been working for months on a new policy for dealing with Osama bin Laden, Bush had never enunciated his anti-terrorism policy as president. *What he outlined that night from the Oval Office committed the United States to a broad, vigorous and potentially long war against terrorism*, rather than a targeted retaliatory strike. *The decision to state the policy that night was made without consulting most of his national security team, including Cheney and Powell.* (ibid.; italics added)

President Bush had gone from being the nominal commander-in-chief to being the actual commander-in-chief and a war-time president in about twelve hours. Condoleezza Rice and Cheney appear to be the only two national-security principals whom the president consulted during the day of 9/11. Again, this appears to reflect both his personality and his sense of the role of the presidency.

Another anecdote illustrative of Bush's individual style, perhaps role as well, is what happened later that night after the First Family had retired for the evening.

The Secret Service woke the president around midnight telling him and the First Lady that they had to go to the secure bunker. Apparently, intelligence was collected that suggested potential new threats to the White House. They complied, evidently making their way to the bunker in their bedclothes. Bush recorded the following in his journal about the incident. "We cannot allow a terrorist a thug to hold us hostage," presumably referring to bin Laden, a personal comment perhaps reflecting the Texan in Bush. Then in a moment of reflection that may be suggestive of his role of the leader of the world's single superpower: "My hope is that this will provide us an opportunity to rally the world against terrorism" (ibid.).

As noted, certain role expectations are associated with positions in government. Years ago an aphorism used to characterize this proposition was: Where one stands depends upon where one sits. In other words, the secretary of defense's stand on a particular position is going to be affected disproportionately by where he sits (*viz.*, in the Pentagon). Of all of President Bush's top national security decision-makers, Condoleezza Rice is arguably the most enigmatic. National Security Advisor Rice seems to fit the role of national security advisor especially well. The president is said to trust her judgment and to confide in her. Bush apparently values her intelligence as a former academic and as one capable of fighting turf wars on the way up; and she seems to go out of her way to stay out of the public light. As noted, she was one of the few NSC principals whom the president consulted prior to enunciating the Bush Doctrine.

Moreover, President Bush (not unlike former President Reagan) showed little compunction in terms of surrounding himself with foreign-policy experts smarter than him—to his credit. What is more, since Dr. Rice is often in the shadows—arguably an important criterion of a good NSC advisor—it is therefore problematic to get a specific fix on her personality. She is frequently cited as a Powell ally, that is, a moderate in contrast to the so-called neoconservative hawks in the administration. It is worth considering whether she influences the president's foreign-policy thinking rather than vice versa. Thus it is worth examining some of the few things we *do* know about her personality, style, and the role of the NSC advisor.

Just days after the 9/11 attacks, Dr. Rice held a press briefing. One theme Dr. Rice sounded was that America's problem was not with Islam per se or Arabs. You may recall that just days earlier, President Bush had referred—in an ill-considered, impromptu comment—to America's war as a "crusade." Bush seemed surprised by the response caused by his crusade remark; it seemed he failed to comprehend the significance of crusade in Islam's history. This created a stir in the Islamic world, including, importantly, among the Islamic and Arab countries, those very same nations that America was hoping to cobble together in its overlapping coalitions. Importantly, President Bush was meeting with Indonesia's president that very day. In response to a question, speaking on behalf of President Bush, Dr. Rice said everyone must understand "that America believes that the terrorism that we experienced is not the work of Islam, is not the work of Islamic people, it is not the work of Arabs, it is the work of extremists." Giving some insight into how Bush NSC meetings work—whether the president is aloof (e.g., Reagan) or, arguably, too hands on (e.g., Carter)—she spoke of NSC mechanics. She noted the president had held an NSC meeting that morning. "The pattern is that he meets with his National Security Council in the morning. He chairs those meetings himself. And the principals reassemble later in the day to share notes, to consult and coordinate and to prepare the next day's National Security meeting. The clear impression is the president is not uncomfortable allowing his NSC principals—the experts as it were—basically to set the agenda for NSC meetings.[7]

The president struck several themes in his remarks in the first few days following 9/11. As was detailed earlier, his chief speechwriter Gerson and confidante Hughes wrote the words he uttered the evening of September 11 and the following couple of days. If one reads the texts, specifically Bush's remarks at the National Day of Prayer and Remembrance, it is quite interesting to note *what he did not say*; particularly since after a series of NSC meetings—where Rice presumably influenced the president directly—and the Presidential Address to the Nation (his announcement that he had initiated Operation Enduring Freedom (October 7, 2001), he scarcely mentioned the patience that would be needed, or that the American public must not turn its ire toward Arabs and or Muslims (or those who looked like either). But Bush would soon begin publicly to address those themes. While one cannot conclusively prove that Rice is responsible for Bush picking up these themes, it is worth noting that following Rice's numerous meetings with Bush over the first couple of weeks after 9/11, Bush began stressing the themes Dr. Rice had previously stressed.

In Dr. Rice's press briefing on September 19, 2001, she recognized the stress under which Americans were operating and noted that Americans would need to be patient at least twice: She noted that the president believed patience would be necessary, and that the campaign could "not be hurried." Similarly, she commented several times that this campaign would not be a short-term engagement. Rice noted that the president would talk to the nation about "the sustained nature of this campaign," and she made other statements alluding to the length of the campaign: "We're in this for the long haul"; the campaign will have "several phases . . . and this has got to go on for a long time"; after the initial phase "there will be other phases that will go on for a long time"; it will be "a long struggle"; "this is not going to be over in a few months." In an extraordinary statement that Dr. Rice actually repeated, she used the dreaded "S" word: *sacrifice*. Since former President Carter asked the nation to sacrifice for energy independence and Reagan made political hay of it, no administration who hopes to serve more than one term has used the "S" word. In contrast, Rice responded to a reporter's question about whether the president's plans would entail sacrifice for Americans. In response, she said, "[E]very American understands that life changed" on 9/11 and Americans would need to adjust accordingly, and "yes, this is going to be a time of sacrifice." In response to yet another question she said that Americans understand that "this is going to be a time of sacrifice" (ibid.). Hence, given that President Bush began taking up those themes following Dr. Rice's press briefing, it is not implausible to suggest that Dr. Rice's initial influence on President Bush proved considerable. She may be enigmatic, but she appears to be very influential.

Secretary Rumsfeld is a fascinating bureaucratic player and NSC principal. After all, he is of a different generation than virtually any of the top Bush people. Like Cheney, Rumsfeld has served in various positions in the U.S. government. One could reasonably posit this fact as a potential cause of friction between the defense secretary and the president, the former believing his political and intellectual acumen superior to the latter. Prior to appointing Rumsfeld secretary of defense, Bush had interviewed Rumsfeld to get a sense of what sort of working relationship they might have: which goals and objectives they shared and which they did not share, which direction they thought the Defense Department ought to be going in (*viz.*, modernizing, including dumping ABM and moving ahead with a modified missile defense), and so forth.

> Bush had spoken to his prospective secretary of defense . . . about their shared belief that America's deterrent strength had been eroded through misapplication of the country's military power. Rumsfeld recalls saying to Bush that whenever the United States was attacked or threatened, the Clinton administration had followed a pattern of "reflexive pullback." *Rumsfeld said he believed that U.S. power was needed to help discipline the world.* (italics added)[8]

By temperament and by position, he seems to fit the role one would predict for his position perfectly. He views the military as an instrument of U.S. foreign policy. Clearly, the military is not the only tool of policy: A large "toolbox" of foreign-policy instruments exists but, when the military is the most efficacious instrument, Rumsfeld is not reluctant to use said option. Further, he was reportedly quite confident in his own judgment. He had actually got out in front of the administration in public utterances, for example, with his talk of abrogating the ABM Treaty. Prior to 9/11, a raft of rumors about Rumsfeld's arrogance and his penchant to act, effectively, as commander-in-chief swirled. "Rumsfeld had irritated lawmakers on Capitol Hill and many of his senior military officers at the department with his brusque and sometimes secretive style of management" (ibid.).

Secretary Powell's personality and personal style and role as the U.S. chief diplomat might at first blush seem incongruous. After all, he is a former Chairman of the Joint Chiefs of Staff (JCS). Previously, he was a general, had fought as an officer in Vietnam and had been integral to the former Bush administration's military actions in Panama and the Gulf. What is more, he had been Reagan's national security advisor, albeit for a short time near the end of Reagan's tenure. The reality, however, is that he is well suited to the office of secretary of state. As Woodward's *The Commanders* documented, Powell has almost always been a voice of caution and patience. He had, for instance, supported giving sanctions more time to work before going to war against Saddam Hussein in 1991. Indeed, while Chairman of the JCS, he was reported to keep a quote from the Athenian general-cum-historian Thucydides on his desk. The quote: "Of all manifestations of power, restraint impresses men most."[9]

As one would expect from his role as chief diplomat—as well as his own personality, such as we know it—Powell was put in charge of cobbling together the coalition that President Bush felt was needed to wage a comprehensive war on terrorism. Much of the work of assembling an international coalition was left to Powell, but on that day alone Bush called the Russian president a second time and also spoke with French President Jacques Chirac, German Chancellor Gerhard Schroeder, Canadian Prime Minister Jean Chretien, and Chinese President Jiang Zemin (Balz and Woodward, Part I). Bush felt it imperative to make these important calls initially to establish personal rapport with these leaders. Thereafter, however, Powell adhered to the role expectations of the principal diplomat: working the coalition and keeping it unified.

The president held his second NSC meeting upon returning to Washington Tuesday evening.[10] Over the next several days, more meetings were held with NSC principals (whose statutory members include secretaries of state and defense, the vice president, and, of course, the president), with the NSC advisor, the Chairman of JCS, and the DCI included as advisors; additionally, there was at least one NSC "deputies" meeting on Wednesday. As the name implies, the deputies are the second-tier representatives of the NSC principals. At an afternoon NSC principals meeting on Wednesday, the discussion turned to how broad the goals were and what a U.S.-led coalition should look like ultimately. Regarding the former, the question was whether this war was a war against al Qaeda or broader, including states that are associated with terrorists. Regarding the latter, the question was how the United States could put together a coalition that would hold up should the war broaden beyond just al Qaeda (ibid.).

It was Secretary Powell who reportedly proffered the idea of what became known as overlapping coalitions. The way he put it in the NSC meeting was "variable geometry."

> Powell offered what a colleague later described as the "variable geometry" of coalition-building. The coalition should be as broad as possible, but the requirements for participation would vary country by country. (ibid.)

Vice President Cheney commented that the "mission should define the coalition, not the other way around"—not a particularly unique notion. Rumsfeld responded that "they wanted coalition partners truly committed to the cause, not reluctant participants," another rather self-evident proposition.

An NSC principals meeting held on Wednesday afternoon—the third war-cabinet meeting since 9/11—proved an important meeting for at least three reasons. First, what had begun as a foreign-policy crisis had arguably begun to evolve into a more deliberative decision-making setting: High threat was beginning to diminish. Second, the president had seemingly seized control of his own government and was truly acting as the commander-in-chief. What had been several disparate statements and opinions now began to emanate from the president as the chief executive; and his senior advisors clearly sensed that. Third, Attorney General Ashcroft emerged, at least for the time being, as an insider, in effect a default NSC principal.

This third NSC meeting proved crucial in terms of deciphering roles and personalities in the Bush administration. In fact, one gets a feel for the interactions between competitive national-security bureaucracies and the extent to which respective personalities and roles affected the foreign-policy decision-making in response to the 9/11 attacks. "Bush convened his National Security Council in the Cabinet Room and declared that the time for reassuring the nation was over," clearly acting in his role as chief executive and commander-in-chief. In a similar indication of presidential role, Bush noted that "the enemy hides in shadows and runs."

> The United States would use all its resources to find this enemy, but it would entail "a different kind of war than our nation has ever fought." He said that he was confident that if the administration developed a logical and coherent plan, the rest of the world "will rally to our side." At the same time, he said, he determined not to allow the threat of terrorism to alter the way Americans lived their lives. "We have to prepare the public," he said, "without alarming the public. (ibid.)

Evidently, the meeting began with FBI Director Mueller describing the investigation that was underway, what they knew, and where the investigation was heading. He stressed the need to avoid tainting evidence so that criminal prosecutions would not be jeopardized. Mueller's boss, Attorney General Ashcroft, quickly interjected that this issue was not criminal prosecutions but running terrorists to ground.

In this instance, the attorney general's role appeared to be metamorphosing, perhaps being outright supplanted by Mr. Ashcroft's own personal predilections.

> The president had made clear to Ashcroft in an earlier conversation that he wanted to make sure an attack like the ones on the Pentagon and World Trade Center never happened again. Now, Ashcroft was saying, the focus of the FBI and the Justice Department should change from prosecution to prevention, a fundamental shift in priorities.
>
> "It was made very clear to me" by Bush, Ashcroft said in an interview, "that we had a responsibility to do everything in our power and to find ways to do things that we might not otherwise think there are ways to do, to curtail the likelihood, to reduce the risks, to prevent this from happening again."
>
> "My instruction was this: to think outside the box. . . . We can't think outside the Constitution, but outside the box. . . . If there's a question between protecting a source and protecting the American people, we burn the source and we protect the American people. That's just the way it has to be." (ibid.)

In fairness to Mr. Ashcroft, he appears to have taken his cue from the president. On the other hand, his own words demonstrate an unusual situation: a strong personality type lacking shyness about changing the mission of a bureaucracy that is primarily a domestic policy institution and molding it to President Bush's war on terrorism.

Once the NSC meeting ended, President Bush held a truncated NSC meeting with a smaller group of senior administration officials. Included were the vice president, the Secretaries of State and Defense, and apparently Condoleezza Rice. Per his role, Secretary Powell commented that he was prepared to take the president's message (*viz.*, you're either with us or against us) to the Taliban and to Pakistan's Musharraf and the latter's powerful intelligence service. Reflecting his role as the civilian chief of the Department of Defense and, in particular, reflecting his direct representation of the military service chiefs, Rumsfeld interjected, "It is critical how we define goals at the start, because that's what the coalition signs on for." Additionally, the authors report that Bush said, "Other countries want precise definitions." "Do we focus on bin Laden and al Qaeda or terrorism more broadly?" Rumsfeld asked rhetorically (ibid.). The JCS, whose interests Rumsfeld is supposed to represent, have historically been reluctant to get involved in military interventions without clear objectives, measurable milestones, and a sense of the exit strategy. In effect, Rumsfeld was cleverly co-opting Powell's portfolio to make a point important to the Pentagon.

Powell reportedly argued that the goal was terrorism in the broadest sense, but that the focus must first be on al Qaeda; in other words, Powell was tacitly challenging Rumsfeld's and his deputy Paul Wolfowitz's position. This may have been a clever bureaucratic maneuver, going on record appearing not to be too cautious while directing attention toward a narrow focus. Cheney was next. His line was the hardest of the group. "To the extent we define our task broadly," Cheney said, "including those who support terrorism, then we get at states. And it's easier to find them than it is to find bin Laden" (ibid.).

As is well known, President Bush was elected under somewhat dubious conditions and had, consequently, gained—fairly or unfairly—the reputation as a president without a mandate. Additionally, his reputation was that of a president with little foreign-policy experience: a bit of a hollow suit, at least, in terms of foreign policy. An objective analysis would have to question the accuracy of that reputation. In a display of unusual perspicacity and bureaucratic agenda setting, he seized the discussion and announced what U.S. policy would be, henceforth.

> "Start with bin Laden," Bush said, "which Americans expect. And if we succeed, we've struck a huge blow and can move forward." He called the threat "a cancer" and added, "We don't want to define [it] too broadly for the average man to understand." (ibid.)

He similarly showed a grasp and comfort with the challenges a president faces in the Pentagon. Predictably, the various branches of the military and the defense contractors associated with them form a strong lobby with which many a president has butted heads. (The anecdote cited earlier during which President Kennedy and Secretary McNamara arguably faced a form on insubordination during the Cuban Missile Crisis provides an example.)

> Bush said he knew the military would resist committing force to an ill-defined mission. But he also believed he needed to push the Pentagon to think differently about how to fight this war. "They had yet to be challenged to think on how to fight a guerrilla war using conventional means," he said. "They had come out from an era of strike from afar—you know, cruise missiles into the thing." (ibid.)

In other instances, Bush's personality (individual input) seemed to dictate role. Following the Wednesday morning NSC meeting, on which Bush had placed his personal *imprimatur,* he prepared to make another television appearance. Calming the nation is clearly a function of role as it relates to foreign policy. Just before 11:00 A.M. he appeared in a blue suit in the Cabinet room of the White House. "[Bush] wanted to escalate his rhetoric from the previous night's pronouncement"— likely a function of Bush's style and personality rather than role. "The deliberate and deadly acts that were carried out yesterday against our country were more than acts of terrorism," the president stated, "They were acts of war." "This is an enemy that tries to hide, but it won't be able to hide forever." Preparing the public for the war on terror, he said ". . . we will be focused, and we will be steadfast in our determination." His peroration: *"This will be a monumental struggle between good and evil. But good will prevail"* (ibid.; italics added).

By virtually any measure, the first few days had been an incredible decision-making setting. Even during the first days—those days that can properly be considered a foreign-policy crisis—bureaucratic posturing reared its head, albeit on a small scale. A secretary of state who was publicly popular but whose recent media accounts had suggested his overshadowing by the neoconservative hawks in the Defense Department and elsewhere, had emerged as a key figure in the NSC and a Bush confidant. Most importantly, a president who had been considered a foreign-policy lightweight had emerged as a strong, determined, war-time president. Woodward and Balz describe it thusly:

> By the end of the second day, some of those concepts were taking shape. The war would be comprehensive, employing all instruments of national power, not just conventional military forces; building a coalition was essential, but other nations would not dictate the terms of battle; the targets would be terrorists and terrorist states; they would seek to destroy al Qaeda worldwide, starting in Afghanistan. (ibid.)

INDIVIDUAL AND ROLE INPUTS: THE MONTHS FOLLOWING 9/11

Over the next several months President Bush filled his presidential role as prescribed by public expectations. He held news conferences and gave numerous speeches. He entertained a veritable caravan of world leaders, giving important world leaders in America's war on terrorism valuable face time and photo opportunities. He traveled the country speaking in venues in which the war on terror and his message could easily be fitted into the day's speech. Importantly, he took every opportunity to remind the American public that the war on the global-terrorist hydra would in fact be a long struggle. It would not be won in months; it may even be analogous to the Cold War. It is an important role of the president—more specifically, of the commander-in-chief—to tell the nation what lay ahead and what it would cost America in both treasure and blood. This may be an unpopular role of the president; many presidents have outright lied about it (Kennedy, Johnson, Nixon, and others). But it is an important role and one for which the president should receive due credit.

The president, again in his role as commander-in-chief, used his secretary of defense as the conduit to the Pentagon and effectively told them to throw out old contingency plans and to come up with creative roles to go after al Qaeda. In contrast to the president, Secretary of Defense Rumsfeld demonstrated fewer proclivities to fit role expectations, at least visibly. In addition to protecting the Pentagon, its programs, defending the nation when diplomacy fails, and an array of other roles, he is supposed to stay behind the scenes for the most part. Recall that during the Persian Gulf War (1990–1991), while then Secretary of Defense Dick Cheney was a key decision-maker, he rarely held news conferences (Woodward, *The Commanders*). Secretary Rumsfeld, by contrast, had become a bit of a celebrity in his own right. His frequent news conferences (that continue as of 2003) have seemingly taken on the appearance of a dog-and-pony show with laugh lines and jostling back and forth with the media.

Uniquely Role Inputs?

Earlier it was argued that role and individual inputs may be indistinguishable in *praxis:* It is frequently difficult to distinguish where individual proclivities, personalities, life experiences, and predilections end and where role expectations and constraints begin. In *theorem*, one should be able to differentiate the various inputs. However, the analyst would minimally need detailed psychohistories of the principal decision-makers to attempt such precise delineation. This section, however, presents some obvious instances in which role expectations clearly were either compelling the president to act in specific ways or constraining him from acting in others. To the extent that these examples affected U.S. foreign policy, the independent variable "role" must be given due weight in the analysis.

One of the roles that has become associated with being president is to console the nation during times of national tragedy. Consider FDR's fireside chats during trying times for the United States. Carter similarly attempted to console the nation after the hostages were seized in Iran, albeit less successfully than FDR. President Clinton attempted to console the nation several times: after Columbine, following the tragedy in Somalia that became known as *Black Hawk Down*, and so forth. The scope of the tragedy of the 9/11 attacks made the presidential role daunting. Arguably, President Bush performed this role in an exemplary fashion. On the National Day of Remembrance, at the National Cathedral in Washington, Bush surprised many critics with sensitivity to this role and acuity in pulling it off. It is worth quoting in some detail:

> We are here in the middle hour of our grief.
>
> . . . .
>
> On Tuesday, our country was attacked with deliberate and massive cruelty.
>
> . . . .

They are the names, lists of casualties we are only beginning to read. . . . They are the names of people who faced death, and in their last moments called home to say, be brave, and I love you.

They are the names of passengers who defied their murderers, and prevented the murder of others on the ground. They are the names of men and women who wore the uniform of the United States, and died at their posts.

. . . .

To the children and parents and spouses and families and friends of the lost, we offer our deepest sympathy of the nation.[11]

Another presidential role is to play on America's myths and ethos. All nations have mythologies that are part of their national identities. Mythology does not necessarily means fabrication: Typically there are bits and pieces of a people's actual history that have been embellished over time and help to form a nation's self-perception and resultant ethos. Earlier, Jones was quoted on pillars of pre-twentieth-century American foreign policy. Jones argues that America's mythology includes a unique definition of freedom in political terms, social contract, the great Western emigration from Europe to the Americas to escape tyranny, and so forth. In terms of foreign policy, according to Jones, this translates into America's feeling that it has recurrently and only reluctantly been dragged into wars and only to protect the freedoms of dispossessed peoples and peoples subjugated by tyrants (Fascism, Communism, now *Jihadism*) and to prevent world tyrants from being successful. There is a tremendous continuity in presidents embracing themes along these lines in the last century, especially from World War II forward. It has become integral to the presidential role. President Bush's speech played brilliantly on these presidential-role themes:

War has been waged against us by stealth and deceit and murder. This nation is peaceful, but fierce when stirred to anger. This conflict was begun on the timing and terms of others. It will end in a way, and at an hour, of our choosing.

. . . .

America is a nation full of good fortune, with so much to be grateful for. But we are not spared from suffering. *In every generation, the world has produced enemies of human freedom. They have attacked America, because we are freedom's home and defender.* And the commitment of our fathers is now the calling of our time. (ibid.; italics added)

On October 7, 2001, his role of commander-in-chief came through in his remarks to the American people announcing the commencement of Operation Enduring Freedom.

Good afternoon. On my orders, the U.S. military has begun strikes against al Qaeda terrorist training camps and military installations of the Taliban regime in Afghanistan.

Since the decision had been made to seek overlapping coalitions in this campaign, he included language to demonstrate that the United States led a broad-based coalition in a just cause.

> We are joined in this operation by our staunch friend, Great Britain. Other close friends, including Canada, Australia, Germany, and France, have pledged forces as the operation unfolds. More than 40 countries in the Middle East, Africa, Europe and across Asia have granted air transit or landing rights. Many more have shared intelligence. We are supported by the collective will of the world.
>
> . . . .
>
> I'm speaking to you today from the Treaty Room of the White House, a place where American Presidents have worked for peace. *We're a peaceful nation. . . . In face of today's new threat, the only way to pursue peace is to pursue those who threaten it.*
>
> *We did not ask for this mission, but we will fulfill it. . . .* We defend not only our precious freedoms, but also the freedom of people everywhere to live and raise their children free from fear.

Near the end of the speech, speaking to the military directly, he told them that their mission was clearly defined, and "your goal is just" (italics added).[12]

For illustrative purposes contrast these words—scripted by presidential speechwriters just as all presidents' words are scripted—with Bush's improvisation upon his first visit to Ground Zero in New York, just after the attacks. While Bush's movements, stops, visits, and so forth, were choreographed, he was clearly acting as George W. Bush when he put his arm around the fire worker on a pile of rubble, grabbed a megaphone and made his famous remarks about being able to hear the workers and suggesting that those who had destroyed the Twin Towers would soon hear from "all of us."

Over the next couple of months, Bush was almost strictly a war-time president. He had a host of *consiglieres*. As discussed earlier in societal inputs in Chapter 3, the president and indeed the entire administration was provided wide berth by Americans and the media. His popularity soared to record heights and remained high. December's and January's media coverage focused, understandably, on the day-to-day war coverage. The bombing campaigns in eastern Afghanistan eclipsed coverage of exogenous inputs in day-to-day decision-making. Role inputs reduced simply to commander-in-chief. Indeed, General Franks, the Commander-in-Chief, Central Command (the general in charge of the war in Afghanistan and subsequently in Iraq) and Secretary Rumsfeld garnered more media attention, perhaps understandably, than the president.

By February, the president began making news again. Bush took an Asia junket making the obligatory stop in South Korea. The president uttered strong words from South Korea vis-à-vis North Korea, a common role expectation for presidents since the 1950s. In another action that has become part and parcel of presidential role, Bush did the DMZ tango.

> The DMZ, which President Bill Clinton called "the Cold War's last divide" and the scariest place on Earth, has been a frequent backdrop for American presidents

since shortly after the armistice [1953]. Presidents Dwight D. Eisenhower, Lyndon B. Johnson, Gerald R. Ford, Jimmy Carter, Reagan and George H. W. Bush all visited troops there. Clinton went three times.[13]

The United States keeps some 37,000 troops there as a trip wire: deterrence to the North Koreans. Nobody believes that 37,000 American troops, even with their South Korean counterparts, would be able to stop the one-million-strong North Korean forces. Rather, the trip wire metaphor suggests that should the North Koreans ever invade South Korea again, the full force of America's military would automatically be triggered. The DMZ tango is thus where the president visits the troops on the line of demarcation between North and South Korea. Over the years there have occurred several incidents that have threatened to erupt into war. On any number of occasions, the North Koreans have tunneled under the DMZ. In the 1960s, they shot down an American helicopter near the DMZ. On another occasion, North Koreans hacked up American troops who were attempting to cut down a tree in the DMZ: the Poplar Tree incident of 1976. In short, the DMZ is a place of great tension. Thus, presidents visit troops there since it is presumed to demonstrate their fearlessness as commander-in-chief.

Another role function of the commander-in-chief is to help the nation properly mourn the death of American troops who have been sent into harm's way. Once the war began on October 7, 2001, it was a certainty that the military would lose troops. America's war-fighting methods have changed since Vietnam. The U.S. military employs far more airpower for a far longer period than it has in the past. (Recall a number of times when President Clinton punitively used cruise missiles from ships to respond to attacks on U.S. troops.) Nonetheless, at some point ground troops are invariably used in war. In March 2002 when the United States launched an attack on the cave complexes in eastern Afghanistan, some of America's troops were ambushed and killed. At such times presidents may be expected to mourn properly their soldiers' deaths while concomitantly showing firm resolve. That is exactly what President Bush did. "President Bush said yesterday that he was saddened but undeterred by those losses. 'I am just as determined now as I was a week ago or three months ago to fulfill this mission, and that is, to make sure our country is safe from further attack,' he said on a visit to Minneapolis."[14]

The secretary of defense plays a similar, somewhat redundant, role at such times. Whereas the president speaks to the nation, the secretary's audience is the military itself. Accordingly, Secretary Rumsfeld cautioned on May 4, 2002 at the Pentagon: "This will not be the last such operation in Afghanistan," he said. "I think we have to expect that there are other sizable pockets, that there will be other battles of this type" (ibid.). Secretary Rumsfeld was effectively telling his troops that additional casualties would be forthcoming.

Any president's principal diplomat is his secretary of state. (The one exception may be President Nixon whose national security advisor, Henry Kissinger, overshadowed his secretary of state, William Rogers. Kissinger eventually became secretary of state and actually held both portfolios for a time.) The secretary of state normally speaks for the president on foreign-policy matters. The exception to this rule is when the president himself goes on the road. The president is the one person who has more "juice" in matters of diplomacy and foreign policy generally. President Mubarak of Egypt came to Washington, D.C. in March to see the president face to face. It was not a rebuke of Powell's trips—or for that matter, Vice President Cheney's then upcoming trip—to the Middle East but, rather, a symbolic indication of how grave the matters needing attention were: another expected presidential role. As one description characterized the visit, "Mubarak came to Washington to appeal for more active U.S. intervention . . ." with respect to the Israeli–Palestinian conflict.[15]

One role that is personified by the president but might more accurately be described as the role of the United States in the post–World War II period, is world superpower. There were, of course, two superpowers from 1945 until the beginning of the 1990s. Since then, the United States has played the unique role of world leader. It too is the world's leading coalition builder. While a candidate, and during the first year or so of Bush's administration, the president abdicated this role to a large degree and became a unilateralist actor in international politics. Since 9/11, the Bush administration has again seized its America-leads-the-civilized-world role in earnest. The long-rumored attack on Iraq (or as it was euphemistically called, "regime change") is one such example. In spring 2003, Bush apparently assigned this role to his subordinate. Robin Wright, a well-respected journalist and author on Middle Eastern affairs, described Vice President Cheney's trip to the region. "Vice President Dick Cheney's ambitious 11-nation swing through the Middle East, which begins today, has one of its critical goals lining up a consensus on what to do about Iraq."[16]

A presidential role related to his commander-in-chief function is an obvious one. To explain to the nation what America's interests are and why and when it warrants spending America's treasure and blood to go to war. This Bush did dramatically following the 9/11 attacks; we have already considered his National Cathedral, his State of the Union, and other early speeches. As the six-month commemoration came round, Bush again addressed the nation and clarified America's national interests, objectives, and the instruments for achieving same. As noted elsewhere, America's ethos includes seeing itself as thwarting tyranny. America sees itself, rightly or wrongly, as the only nation with the moral and material wherewithal to stop tyranny. It therefore tends to see foreign policy in terms of right and wrong with little moral ambiguity. The Fascists of Germany and Italy and expansionist Japanese imperialism, for instance, were tyrants bent on subjugating weaker nations. The Soviet Union, originally an ally in World War II, became an even more threatening tyrant following the war's conclusion. Muslim fundamentalism that has become radicalized—*Jihadism*—is seen as the latest of the world's great tyrants, necessitating U.S. action. Additionally noted was Bush's own worldview. Accordingly, he too sees the world in terms of right and wrong, black and white. There is little room for nuance or shades of gray. Bush's worldview contains a religious component, ironic in a sense, given that the war on terror is indirectly against the Muslim faith in its most extreme form.

It is therefore worth considering his six-month commemoration speech for indications of either role and/or individual inputs into the Bush administration's foreign policy since 9/11.

> We have come together to mark a terrible day, to reaffirm a just and vital cause, and to thank the many nations that share our resolve and will share our common victory. Six months separate us from September the 11th. Yet, for the families of the lost each day brings new pain; each day requires new courage. . . . America will not forget the lives that were taken, and the justice their death requires.[17]

Note the president mentions "vital" interests, "just," and "justice" all in one paragraph. America's ethos requires its actions to be just. What is more "just," after all, than thwarting terrorism, aiding a people (Afghanis) who are being subjugated by tyrants?

> We face an enemy of ruthless ambition, unconstrained by law or morality. The terrorists despise other religions and have defiled their own. And they are determined to expand the scale and scope of their murder. (ibid.)

Though the president fails to use the word *tyrant*, he has outlined a fairly clear definition of tyranny. As already noted, vilification of America's enemies is integral to America's thwarter-of-tyranny mythology. The president then goes on to put 9/11 in historical context. He furthermore puts America's response in the context of a coalition of civilized nations, the implication being that those whom the United States opposes are not only tyrants but also uncivilized.

> History will know that day not only as a day of tragedy, but as a day of decision — when the civilized world was stirred to anger and to action. And the terrorists will remember September 11th as the day their reckoning began.
> A mighty coalition of civilized nations is now defending our common security. (ibid.)

The president then addresses those, led by the United States, whom the coalition of civilized nations was freeing from the yoke of tyranny. In a nice touch, the president worked in the fact that while all of the Afghanis were subjugated by the tyrants, women in particular were the target of extraordinary oppression.

> Part of that cause was to liberate the Afghan people from terrorist occupation, and we did so. Next week, the schools reopen in Afghanistan. They will open for all — and many young girls will go to school for the first time in their young lives. (ibid.)

Another presidential role the president fulfills in his speech is to demonstrate, not just that America has resolve — rallying the American people to the cause — but that the president himself is decisive as commander-in-chief. Later in the speech, the president reiterates this point.

> Every nation should know that, for America, the war on terror is not just a policy, it's a pledge. I will not relent in this struggle for the freedom and security of my country and the civilized world. (ibid.)

Finally, there is another portion of the speech that is particularly interesting. The predicate has been set throughout the speech that America is, as has been its tradition, freeing peoples from tyranny. And he has sufficiently vilified the enemy against whom the civilized coalition is arrayed. But recall that early in the speech he also mentioned America's "vital" interests. Relatively late in the speech he gives the public a sense of what those vital interests are.

> At the same time, every nation in our coalition must take seriously the growing threat of terror on a catastrophic scale—terror armed with biological, chemical, or nuclear weapons. America is now consulting with friends and allies about this greatest of dangers, and we're determined to confront it.
>
> Here is what we already know: Some states that sponsor terror are seeking or already possess weapons of mass destruction; terrorist groups are hungry for these weapons, and would use them without a hint of conscience. And we know that these weapons, in the hands of terrorists, would unleash blackmail and genocide and chaos.
>
> These facts cannot be denied, and must be confronted. In preventing the spread of weapons of mass destruction, there is no margin for error, and no chance to learn from mistakes. Our coalition must act deliberately, but inaction is not an option. Men with no respect for life must never be allowed to control the ultimate instruments of death. (ibid.)

A deft speech, to be sure, as were his earlier addresses. One of the reasons that the president's speeches have been so well received, with the exception of his first two brief speeches on the day of the attacks, is that the president's own worldview, one might argue, meshes so well with America's ethos and mythology about America's history. Clearly both individual inputs (the president's and his inner circle's idiosyncrasies) and role inputs (expectations associated with position) have affected U.S. foreign policy in fundamental ways since 9/11. Clearly too, in retrospect, the president was preparing the nation and others for what would soon follow vis-à-vis Iraq. Let us now consider the final piece of the puzzle: process.

NOTES

1. Unless otherwise identified, the quotes, chronologies, and accounts come from Dan Balz and Bob Woodward in an eight-part *Washington Post* expose of the weeks following 9/11. Dan Balz and Bob Woodward, January 27, 2002–February 3, 2002, *Washington Post*. The series ran with the following titles: Part I, "America's Chaotic Road to War," 27 January 2002; Part II, "We Will Rally the World," 28 January 2002; Part III, "Afghan Campaign's Blueprint Emerges," 29 January 2002; Part IV, "A Pivotal Day of Grief and Anger," 29 January 2002; Part V, "At Camp David, Advise and Dissent," 31 January 2002; Part VI, "Combating Terrorism," 1 February 2002; Part VII, "A Presidency Defined in One Speech," 2 February 2002; and Part VIII, "Bush Awaits History's Judgment," 3 February 2002.

2. Quoted in Kegley and Wittkopf, *American Foreign Policy* (New York: St. Martin's Press, 1996), p. 488.
3. Steven Mufson, "The Way Bush Sees the World," *Washington Post*, 17 February 2002.
4. Bill Keller, "The Soul of George W. Bush," *New York Times*, 23 March 2002.
5. Balz and Woodward, *op. cit.*
6. Barton Gellman, "Struggles inside the Government Defined Campaign," *op. cit.*
7. Condoleezza Rice, "Text: National Security Advisor," September 19, 2002, eMediaMillWorks.
8. Dan Balz and Bob Woodward, "America's Chaotic Road to War," Part I, *Washington Post*, 27 January 2002, Part II, p. A-1.
9. Woodward notes that former Chairman of the JCS, General Colin Powell, kept Thucydides's quote on his desk. Bob Woodward, *The Commanders* (New York: Pocket Books, 1991), p. 128.
10. The first NSC meeting was held on Tuesday via secure video link as the president flew from base to base.
11. Presidential Remarks at National Day of Prayer and Remembrance (www.whitehouse.gov), released September 14, 2002.
12. Presidential Address to the Nation (www.whitehouse.gov), October 7, 2001.
13. Mike Allen, "President Has Tough Words for N. Korea," *Washington Post*, 20 February 2002, p. A-1.
14. Thomas E. Ricks, "Battle Sends Broader Message of U.S. Resolve," *Washington Post*, 5 March 2002, p. A-15.
15. Robin Wright, "Bush, Mubarak Vow to Redouble Efforts for Peace," *Los Angles Times*, 6 March 2002.
16. Robin Wright, "An Iraqi Campaign Faces Many Hurdles," *Los Angles Times*, 10 March 2002.
17. George W. Bush, "President Thanks World Coalition for Anti-Terrorist Efforts, 11 March 2003, at www.whitehouse.gov/news/releases/2002/03/20020311-7.html.

PROCESS

The president and his advisors started America on the road to war that night without a map. *They had only a vague sense of how to respond, based largely on the visceral reactions of the president.* But nine nights later, when Bush addressed a joint session of Congress, many important questions had been answered.

> —Dan Balz and Bob Woodward, "America's Chaotic Road to War," *Washington Post*, 27 January 2002, p. A-1; italics added.

Kegley and Wittkopf remind us that process is the final and crucial variable affecting U.S. foreign policy. The reasons are multiple. First, we presented the clusters of independent (X or exogenous) variables in a more or less random and arbitrary order: That external was presented first and individual/role last was not intended to convey the relative importance of the clusters of independent variables. Second, process is truly distinct: It is where various exogenous variables come together in assorted and sundry ways, depending upon type of external threat/opportunity, issue area, and an array of other factors. Third, and similarly, process is where the exogenous clusters of variables establish their relative weight in a given foreign-policy situation or event. Fourth, process is more than a simple independent variable. It is an intervening variable: a unique type of exogenous variable. Finally, process can be a rather messy area of U.S. foreign policy, subject to controversy and various interpretations. Consider that four of the five categories of independent variables are domestic variables. It is unsurprising then that process may make discussion of foreign policy "political" in the pejorative sense of the word. Indeed, of the five clusters only external-systemic is the historical purview of international-relations analysis. The external-systemic cluster represents a set of variables that, in the historical tradition of international-relations scholarship, encompasses the theory of state behavior known as *realpolitik*. Process is a unique exogenous variable: It represents the interaction of other independent variables, one with another.

The reader will recall that Kegley and Wittkopf figuratively viewed process as a distinct, intervening variable. The visual metaphor was a funnel of foreign-policy inputs with process at the bottom of the funnel or spout through which all the independent inputs pass and intermingle, however slightly, with one another. Figure 1.2 displayed the authors' graphic representation of inputs, process, and output (namely, U.S. foreign policy). In this text the decision was made to simplify the framework by combining individual and role inputs. The rationale rested on the difficulty in distinguishing where role inputs ended and individual ones began. This analysis found it difficult to make a clear distinction. Put differently, in *theorem*, Kegley and Wittkopf (and for that matter, Rosenau) clearly differentiate where the demarcation belongs. Yet, in *praxis*, it is frequently confusing to distinguish individual versus role inputs. Thus, with slight modification to Kegley's and Wittkopf's funnel of foreign-policy causality, the funnel could be visualized as presented in Figure 6.1.

Previously, the foreign-policy process has been visualized in a different way—two ways actually. The first, as noted, is a rather crude but effective metaphor. Recall

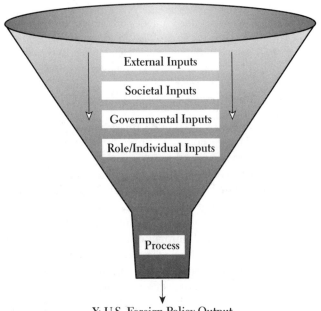

Y: U.S. Foreign Policy Output

FIGURE 6.1   ADAPTED FUNNEL OF CAUSALITY

This funnel illustrates exogenous (X) inputs and endogenous (Y) output (Rosenau's framework) *viz.* U.S. foreign policy.

Note: The funnel has been adapted so that individual and role inputs are combined.

Source: From Wittkopf, Kegley, and Scott, *American Foreign Policy, Sixth Edition*. © 2003. Reprinted with permission of Wadsworth, a division of Thomson Learning: www.thomsonrights.com. Fax 800-730-2215.

that foreign-policy process is similar, figuratively, to a sausage-making machine. Various ingredients are pushed in through the top. It is likely that several of these ingredients, if seen by an individual observer, would wrench the observer's stomach. Yet the hopper—the process or intervening variable in this metaphor—serves its purpose. It mixes the inputs until the correct composition of mixture has been attained. At that point, of course, the mixed ingredients are pushed through the hopper as the finished product. Voila': One has sausage that may well taste delicious but whose fabrication one may be loathe to observe. Rather, it is the finished product (output or endogenous, Y-variable) one wishes to experience.

A second metaphor is that of concentric circles. The idea of the circles being concentric is that each inner circle may be either attenuated or intensified by the proximate circles representing independent-variable clusters. Two visualizations illustrate. First, in Figure 6.2, from the side-on view one notes that the circles, if compressed as envisaged, would look tubular or spherical. The first representation simply illustrates the X-variables disaggregated through which stimuli pass. Note: The stimuli enter the slices—representing clusters of X-variables. Some stimuli are opportunities and others are threats. In the second illustration (Figure 6.3 on page 152), the same idea (i.e., concentric circles) is illustrated as a cross section view. The reader must visualize some stimulus or stimuli on the Z-plane; since paper effectively illustrates only two dimensions.

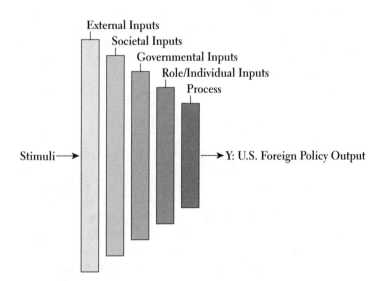

FIGURE 6.2   CONCENTRIC CIRCLES, DISAGGREGATED

This figure gives a visual representation of U.S. foreign policy: concentric circles, side view (i.e., turned on side). The rank ordering of X clusters is a function of situational context. Given a particular situational context, societal might precede external, individual-role might precede societal, and so forth.

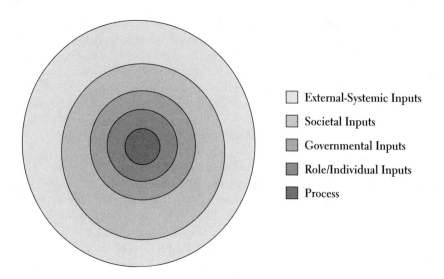

External-Systemic Inputs

Societal Inputs

Governmental Inputs

Role/Individual Inputs

Process

FIGURE 6.3   CONCENTRIC CIRCLES, COMPRESSED CROSS SECTION

This figure shows a cross section of concentric circles, constraining and/or exacerbating other exogenous (independent—X) variables. Stimuli (Z plane) are not represented.

The point is not how one chooses to visualize U.S. foreign policy, or for that matter any other nation-state's foreign policy given the generalizable nature of the comparative foreign-policy framework. Rather, the point is the relative importance of process as an intervening (i.e., a special type of independent variable) in terms of foreign-policy output.

DECISION-MAKING PHASES

The importance of process may be illustrated in terms of decision-making phases as well. First, let us assume that there exist minimum steps in foreign-policy decision-making. Recall the conceptual definition of U.S. foreign policy. As discussed in Chapter 1, U.S. foreign policy may be defined as the *goals* U.S. decision-makers wish to attain abroad, the *values* that give rise to those goals, and the *instruments* employed to achieve said goals. Three principal concepts comprise the definition. For each—goals, values and instruments—one could conceivably find indicators and/or exemplars of each to measure change quantitatively. Irrespective of quantification, note that the definition specifies "the goals U.S. decision-makers wish to attain abroad." Thus, U.S. decision-makers are obviously an integral aspect of U.S. foreign policy. It is necessary to stress the concepts and the principal actors (U.S. decision-makers) in order to introduce additional issues germane to process (i.e., the phases of decision-making).

What are the minimum steps decision-makers take to formulate foreign policy? The first step is *recognition* of a challenge (threat) or opportunity. Second, decision-makers must convene the preliminary decision-making unit (DMU), what we might call *convocation* of the DMU for the sake of continuity in language. Third, an option must be chosen; let us call this step the *selection* of option(s). Fourth, the selected option must be implemented—*implementation* of option. Finally, ideally there ought to be some sort of feedback so that the DMU might know whether the chosen option is working or whether a different course of action needs to be undertaken.[1] Feedback may be called *evaluation* of outcome. Finally, the entire process may go through subsequent iterations.

Now let us consider examples of different types of foreign-policy decision-making processes. The first scenario involves "foreign-policy crises." Recall that foreign-policy crises are characterized by a high threat to the survival of the state (or DMU); second, they are characterized by a short time in which the DMU must respond before the foreign-policy event changes, in particular, worsens; third, the DMU is surprised by the stimulus or stimuli.[2] During a foreign-policy crisis, the DMU—being surprised—has neither useful contingency plans to pull off the shelf nor, perhaps, contingency plans of any particular relevance on which to rely. Failure to anticipate the threat or opportunity causes the foreign-policy decision-makers to focus elsewhere, obviating normal contingency planning typically available to the U.S. foreign-policy decision-makers during more routine times. In short, foreign-policy crises cause U.S. foreign-policy decision-makers to improvise. Similarly, the timeframe in which the DMU may take action is short. Consequently, the convocation of the DMU is exclusive, small in size relative to other types of foreign-policy events; seen previously, proximity of principal decision-makers (i.e., who is actually in town) may also be relevant to the convocation of DMU. Obviously, that the survival of the nation—and/or the DMU—is at stake causes a hasty convocation of the initial DMU—that is, high threat compels the DMU to convene initial meetings when, under more routine circumstances, the DMU might otherwise wait to convene. What are the consequences of such a foreign-policy crisis?

While convening the DMU and selecting option(s) during crises, the composition of the DMU is likely to be very different than, say, during the multiyear, two-administration-long negotiations for NAFTA. During crises, potential expertise from the NSC, the State Department, and the Pentagon—and possibly elsewhere—are perforce excluded from those steps because there is simply too little time in which to assemble a larger DMU. The broader bureaucratic expertise may well become involved, subsequently, during implementation of the selected option. However, by that time, the shape of U.S. foreign policy may have been demonstrably altered in unexpected ways. Over time, if the foreign-policy crisis metamorphoses into a routine foreign-policy event, the larger bureaucracy may well become involved but will have a marginal effect with the altered direction already set in motion. Let us consider whether this was indeed the case with September 11.

PROCESS SINCE 9/11: DAY ONE

Clearly, the discussion of the "type" of foreign-policy event is more than an academic matter. The attacks of 9/11 began as a foreign-policy crisis (at least for the first few days) and evolved into something less than a crisis: what Charles Hermann might call a "reflexive situation."[3] During the first couple of days, the DMU was indeed small. Thus far, the most definitive source of the early days of activity in the executive branch is that of Balz and Woodward, cited in the previous chapter.[4]

As many have seen on television *ad infinitum*, and as described in the previous chapter, on the morning of 9/11, President Bush was sitting with schoolchildren in Florida, reading to them. The president had begun the morning by rising early and running around the White House golf course for some four miles. The day's schedule called for a "soft event," meaning a campaign junket for his brother's reelection bid and meeting with an uncritical crowd—children. The reader will recall from television that one of the president's most trusted political advisors and friends, Karl Rove, was seen whispering in the president's ear that a plane had hit the World Trade Center. Bush, as was the case with many, initially thought the plane was small and the incident accidental. Bush responded to Rove, "This is pilot error," and recalls thinking that the pilot "must have had a heart attack."[1]

More memorable was the president's response to the news that a second plane had rammed into the Trade Center complex: "At 9:05 A.M., [the second plane] smashed into the South Tower. . . . [Andrew Card, Chief of Staff] whispered the news: 'A second plane hit the second tower. America is under attack.' Bush remembers exactly what he thought: 'They had declared war on us, *and I made up my mind at that moment that we were going to war*'" (ibid.; italics added). Recall the president's face upon receiving the news: His lip quivered then stiffened, and he began shaking his head affirmatively as if he were processing the enormity of what was happening. In fact he looked gaunt, as would most of us in similar circumstances. The potential for revisionism in postevent interviews notwithstanding, Balz's and Woodward's account is consistent on the president making the "broad" decision early on and simply informing his "war cabinet" as he encountered them (Balz and Woodward, Parts I–VIII, 2002, *ad passim*).

Thus, if we take Bush at his word, the first convocation of the DMU and the broad selection of options consisted of one person: the president. It is not difficult to believe given what we know of the phases of decision-making and the effects of a foreign-policy crisis. After all, the president's foreign-policy decision-making team was scattered. Secretary of State Powell was in Lima, Peru, only to return later that night. Secretary of Defense Rumsfeld was in the Pentagon where, incidentally, he was instructed to go to a safe place but instead helped with rescue efforts, perhaps saving lives. Both Vice President Cheney and National Security Advisor Rice were in their respective West Wing offices. The then chairman of the joint chiefs of staff (JCS) was halfway across the Atlantic Ocean on his way to Europe. (General Richard Meyers was slated to take over the position of chair to the JCS about one month later.) DCI Tenet was in Washington breakfasting with former Senator

Boren. Finally, Attorney General Ashcroft was bound for Milwaukee, Wisconsin; FBI Director Mueller, Ashcroft's subordinate, was in his headquarters near Capitol Hill — Mueller had just replaced his predecessor a week earlier. In short the president was on his own, left twisting in the wind and being spirited around by his Secret Service detail. He was cut off from information and advice though, as will be seen, he improvised enough to be able to bounce ideas off key aides. (Balz and Woodward, Part II, *ad passim*). Clearly the president was surprised by the event, whether he and his predecessor, President Clinton, should have been is another matter entirely. DCI Tenet had "declared war" on bin Laden and his terrorist network in 1998 and had received increased budgets every year, save one, since he had made his declaration. Inexplicably, we have subsequently learned that the CIA tasked only some five persons in response to Tenet's declaration of alarm.[5]

Thirteen hours after the attacks, President Bush convened "his most senior national security advisors in a bunker beneath the White House grounds." They met in the so-called Presidential Emergency Operations Center, deep in the bowels of the White House complex, designed to withstand a nuclear attack. Though Bush had encountered several foreign-policy advisors earlier that evening and had informed each of his intentions, he now announced and thereby memorialized the basis of what would become the Bush Doctrine, thence U.S. foreign policy. He informed those convened that "this is the time for self-defense," and that "we have made the decision to punish whoever harbors terrorists, not just the perpetrators" (Balz and Woodward, Part I, 2002, p. A-1).

Bush's "war cabinet" was taking shape. Each president is mandated by Congressional statute to designate NSC members and advisors — the principal foreign-policy decision-making locus. Though each president does so, *pro forma*, it is also the case that each president is close to certain advisors and cabinet members and less close to others. Consequently, whom the president trusts and in whom he confides can often be seen over time by the composition of his NSC meetings, particularly the so-called "principals meetings," and cabinet meetings. In President Bush's case, the "war cabinet" — the effective equivalent of the "principals meeting" — was comprised of Secretary of State (by tradition, diplomat in chief) Powell, Secretary of Defense Rumsfeld, Vice President Cheney — all statutory members — as well as Condoleezza Rice and DCI Tenet. The latter two are statutory advisors to the NSC. National Security Council members with the NSC advisor have become increasingly important in U.S. foreign-policy decision-making at least since the Kennedy administration.

This happened to be the second of the day's "war cabinet" meetings. A discussion ensued with the agenda having already been set broadly by the president's pronouncements. It revolved around how to operationalize Bush's already-made decisions. Rumsfeld talked of it taking some sixty days to prepare the military for major military strikes. Tenet spoke soberly of the dimensions of al Qaeda, by then identified as the likely culprit. DCI Tenet, for instance, noted that al Qaeda was a sixty-country problem, not just Afghanistan. As noted in an epigraph to this chapter, the war cabinet began "on the road to war that night without a map," and largely on the president's "visceral reactions" to 9/11 (ibid., pp. 1–2).

Previously, while the president was being moved around from base to base, Bush made several phone calls in an attempt, wisely, to get the reins of his government under his control. He spoke to Cheney two to three times by phone; after the second phone conversation with Cheney, Bush called his wife, Laura, to ensure all was well with her and his family. At one of the air force bases where the president was placed by the Secret Service, he established secure video links with Washington, effectively convening his first NSC principals or war cabinet meeting. Between the meeting and phone calls, a couple of immediate, practical issues arose.

First, as was previously noted, the FAA was tracking a plane that had changed course and appeared to be headed toward Washington. Bush and Cheney determined that the combat air patrols—which Cheney had ordered and Bush had okayed, *ex post facto*—would have the permission to shoot down the plane should it continue toward the Capital. Cheney essentially controlled the decision's implementation. As the plane neared the Capital an aide asked those assembled in the bunker: "Should we still engage?" Rice stood by with Andrew Card's deputy, Joshua Bolten, and Cheney's chief of staff, Lewis "Scooter" Libby. The vice president quickly responded, "Yes." As it got even closer the aide repeated in slightly different words, "Does the order still stand?" "Of course it does," snapped Cheney (ibid., p. 5).

A second issue arose, somewhat more political in nature. News agencies were portraying the government as inoperable, in chaos. Cheney and others began to worry about the effects of such portrayals. Cheney asked one of his top wordsmiths, Mary Matlin and Bush's counselor and confidante, Karen Hughes, to work on a speech for Bush to give upon his return. Drafts were given the president and his on-plane White House press secretary, Ari Fleischer. Back and forth went deletions, and additions. All agreed that Bush, not Cheney in Bush's absence, give the speech. They were all familiar with former secretary of state Al Haig's "I'm in control," speech when President Reagan was shot. Perhaps Cheney should have given it after all; the president had been taken aback by the attacks and had been continually spirited around the country by his Secret Service detail. He must have felt the weight of the day's events as no one else could possibly feel, not even the vice president. At one of his stops he managed to give a brief speech. Unfortunately, it was delivered with a less-than-stellar performance.

> When Bush finally appeared on television from the base conference room, it was not a reassuring picture. . . . When he got to the last sentence, he seemed to gain strength. "The resolve of our great nation is being tested," he said in even tones. "But make no mistake: We will show the world that we will pass it." (ibid., p. 8)

One cannot blame the administration for improvising. Bush had been seen publicly twice that day in less-than-flattering circumstances (ibid., p. 6). Thus, later that day it was determined that presidential advisor Karen Hughes would be deputized and would speak to the public. She seemed self-assured. Her message was simple and reassuring to the public. She described a government that was still functioning and in control. That evening once Bush returned to Washington, he dressed and spoke to the nation from the Oval Office for a brief seven minutes. He had pressing business to conduct and intended to conduct it.

In an interesting anecdote, one finds additional backing for the view that the government was taken by surprise. As the president declared the United States to be at war, as he was hustled out of Florida on a day of flying from secure base to secure base, others in Washington were taking initial actions. As noted among those in town while the president was in Florida were Rice and Cheney. Additionally, the cabinet head of the Federal Aviation Administration, Norman Mineta, clearly not typically associated with U.S. foreign-policy decision-making, was in the Capital. While Vice President Cheney—no stranger to foreign-policy *or* domestic crises—functioned as the temporary head of government awaiting the president's return, he summoned Mineta to the bunker beneath the White House. Cheney wanted updates on how many airplanes might possibly be involved; were more attacks en route, waiting to take place? No one knew. As Mineta attempted to determine the dimensions of the potential threat, he requested radar tracks from his agency. A "report came that [a] plane was 50 miles out [from the Capital]," then thirty, then ten. Mineta, improvising, yelled into a phone at his acting deputy administrator at the FAA, Monte Belger, "Monte, bring all the planes down." There were some 4,600 planes in the air at the time. Belger apparently responded, using FAA standard-operating procedures (SOPs) and routines, that the FAA was then "bringing them down per pilot discretion." Mineta "yelled back" at Belger: "[Expletive] pilot discretion; get those goddamn planes down" (Balz and Woodward, Part I, p. 4). Improvisation trumped SOPs and routines.

Bush's second war cabinet meeting actually began as a full NSC meeting after his brief seven-minute speech. At 9:00 P.M. he convened his first, full face-to-face NSC meeting (recall the earlier NSC meeting convened by Bush via video link, this actually constituted his second NSC meeting). The meeting was short: about thirty minutes. It had been a long day already, a day of tremendous consequence, and a day during which decisions had been made by individuals, rather than the larger government bureaucracy. For the most part, politics did not enter the equation, unlike typical routine foreign-policy decisions. As noted, Bush's visceral instincts set the broad outline for the government, essentially forestalling other possibilities, including studying the issue to death. A response would come; it would include military power and every tool that one could show to be efficacious; it would come soon; there would be follow-up; and finally, the president had changed from the president whose father's shadow had plagued him to George W. Bush the president during war with a new *raison d'être* for his administration.

Powell had managed to return from Lima by the evening's NSC meeting. As it broke up, Bush reconvened his smaller "war cabinet." Powell began with his view of an immediate diplomatic imperative: "dealing with Afghanistan and its ruling Taliban, which harbored bin Laden, and neighboring Pakistan, which had closer ties to the Taliban than any other nation." Pakistan had a restive Muslim public, had previously tested nuclear weapons, and was in an almost constant state of near war with India over Kashmir. "We have to make it clear to Pakistan and Afghanistan this is showtime," Powell said. Bush noted that this horror actually provided an opportunity for the administration to improve relations with Russia and China, both of which had so-called Muslim problems. Cheney raised Afghanistan's history, how both the British and the Soviets had become bogged down there in quagmires that occurred about a century apart. Bush returned to bin Laden and the idea that Afghanistan was giving him sanctuary. Tenet said the United States must deny the terrorists Afghanistan by targeting the Taliban as well. The discussion turned to whether the Taliban and al Qaeda were the same. Tenet believed they effectively were the same as bin Laden had "bought his way into Afghanistan, supplying the Taliban with tens of millions of dollars." Rumsfeld pointed out that countries that supported terrorism were the problem just as al Qaeda itself was the problem. Rumsfeld, in other words, went on record in support of Bush's already announced policy, the so-called Bush Doctrine. The president closed what was apparently a short meeting with the following warning: "We have to force nations to choose" (ibid., pp. 10–12). The die had been cast and cast primarily by President Bush. Thus process was relatively simple: The president reacted and his top advisors were left with little choice but to follow his lead. It still remained to provide specific operational details and to formulate a roadmap of how to accomplish Bush's objectives.

PROCESS SINCE 9/11: DAY TWO

Day Two of America's 9/11 national trauma began with Bush rising early and heading to the Oval Office. By 7:30 A.M., the president phoned Tony Blair, the British prime minister and one of America's staunchest allies. He talked over his decisions with Blair who, unsurprisingly, agreed with them. Blair was relieved that America was not simply going to start striking out, though he believed it had every right to do so, but that the United States was instead thinking through the response systematically, carefully, and consulting with allies. Blair offered his "total support." "Blair told Bush he had to make a choice between rapid action and effective action" (Balz and Woodward, Part II, 2002, p. A-1). As was his habit, Bush had Tenet in his office early with his daily intelligence briefing. His father (Bush 41) had warned him that it was one of the most important aspects of his day. Bush had accepted his father's advice and tended to pay attention to his daily briefing. That Tenet himself gave them is indicative of the import accorded the briefings by Bush. (Clinton had enjoyed, by contrast, reading his daily briefings. Unlike the Bush White House, the Clinton White House was less enamored with the DCI hanging about the Oval Office and other presidential redoubts.) Thus at around 8:00 A.M., Tenet and a top aide arrived to brief the president. Cheney who had an office close by, and Rice, similarly close in proximity (the Old Executive Office Building is where most of the NSC is located and is next door), joined the briefing. Bush learned, among other things, that the 9/11 attacks had been in the planning and implementation stages for some two years. Tenet also tied al Qaeda conclusively to the attacks. He told

Bush of Abu Zubaydah, his connection to 9/11, to the USS *Cole*, and to al Qaeda (Balz and Woodward, Part II, 2002). Zubaydah remains in U.S. custody, in an "undisclosed location" as of this writing (2003).

The briefing lasted about thirty minutes. After concluding that the attacks had bin Laden's fingerprints on them the war cabinet turned to another matter. Since 1998, President Clinton had authorized the CIA to send covert operatives in and out of Afghanistan to gather intelligence and they had apparently gone unnoticed. Over the previous few months Bush had tasked Rice and Tenet as well as others to undertake a review of the administration's terrorism policy. They had been at it but had yet to finish. Into the void jumped Tenet proposing a greatly expanded covert program in Afghanistan. It would be "expensive" warned Tenet but having additional eyes and ears would prove "indispensable." Again demonstrating how influential individuals—albeit playing specific roles—can be, Tenet simply used the briefing and 9/11, accurately plumbing the president's mood, to expand the CIA's role in the oncoming war. (At the NSC and war cabinet meetings on the previous day, Rumsfeld had been caught unawares. He had endorsed Bush's stated objectives, scarcely a risky position, and had talked about how many months—six—it would be before the military could be ready.) While one cannot be certain of his motivations, Tenet clearly took advantage of the situation and wrested a larger piece for the CIA. (Note, at this early point, potential intelligence failures had yet to be disclosed.) Bush simply responded: "Whatever it takes" (ibid., Part II, p. 3).

Demonstrating that he had his priorities about right, Bush's next meeting was a political one with Karen Hughes, his counselor. In addition to being his lawyer, Hughes was the *de facto* communications czar. Since the administration's fiasco with the Chinese over a spy plane, Bush had determined to keep focus on a daily-weekly message. The American public (societal variable) had to be coached along. Bush and Hughes discussed the message Hughes was to create and that Bush wished the public to hear. Bush told Hughes that he wanted her to capture "the big picture," and that "A faceless enemy had declared war on the United States of America. So we're at war." He continued that the administration needed a plan, a vision. "Americans needed to know that combating terror would be the main focus of the administration—and the government—from this moment on." Hughes left for her office to begin working on the message and was immediately interrupted by Bush calling her. "Let me tell you how to do your job today," Bush began, in an unusual flight of micromanagement quite atypical of Bush.

> This is an enemy that runs and hides, but won't be able to hide forever.
> An enemy that thinks its havens are safe, but they won't be safe forever. No kind of enemy that we are used to—but America will adapt. (Balz and Woodward, Part II, pp. 3–4)

Next Bush convened his second full NSC meeting since 9/11 where he basically repeated the message he had given Hughes to his NSC advisors. In full NSC meetings not only are the war cabinet members included but their deputies are too, as well as other persons of particular expertise. FBI Director Mueller, for instance, was included as was his boss, Attorney General Ashcroft. At one point in the meeting—perhaps demonstrating petty bureaucratic maneuverings—Mueller waxed on about the investigation the FBI was undertaking. (That is, after all, what the FBI traditionally does.) Ashcroft interrupted Mueller: "Let's stop the discussion right here," he said. "The chief mission of U.S. law enforcement," he added, "is to stop another attack and apprehend any accomplices or terrorists before they hit us again. If we can bring them to trial, so be it" (ibid., p. 4). Whether petty bureaucratic politics or not, it was clearly an instance of improvisation apropos the situational context.

Rather much as had Tenet's maneuverings, Ashcroft's maneuverings were designed to accomplish one of three things: (1) follow the desire of his president; (2) leap into a potential void, thereby carving out a larger portion of the potential governmental largesse for the Justice Department; or (3) achieve some combination of the two. It will be recalled that for the first couple of months after 9/11, Ashcroft held weekly and sometimes daily news briefings, something fairly unusual for former attorneys general of the United States. In fairness, Ashcroft was partially foisted into the spotlight by several issues that accompanied the attacks: the POW issue, the Guantanamo Bay issue, and the anthrax panic of October through December. That does not mean, however, that he did not fight for position in terms of U.S. foreign-policy decision-making: Both motivations are compatible.

As was becoming his custom, the president met with the truncated war cabinet after the full NSC meeting concluded. While the details of the meeting are very interesting, the outcome is more relevant for present purposes.

> Bush said he knew the military would resist committing forces to an ill-defined mission. "They had yet to be challenged to think on how to fight a guerrilla war using conventional means," he said. "They had come out from an era of strike from afar—you know, cruise missiles into the thing." (ibid., pp. 4–5)

Bush knew that the service chiefs have historically resisted military intervention, at least initially. They are, understandably, a cautious bunch having been burned in the past. They want to know goals, end-game strategies, and other necessary information before committing their troops. Once committed, however, the military typically approaches the task with guns a-blazin'. Bush seemed innately to understand this.

Bush met with the press that day in the Cabinet Room. He repeated the mantras that were becoming the foundations of U.S. foreign policy for the Bush administration. He told the media that yesterday's attacks "were more than acts of terror." "They are acts of war." He "described the enemy as one America had never before encountered." In a minor miscue, Hughes mistook Bush's handwritten notes, mistranslating havens as harbors. As Bush read off his script, he read, "This enemy is an enemy who thinks its harbors are safe." Continuing, however, he ended with a strong peroration: "We will rally the world. We will be patient, we will be focused, and we will be steadfast in our determination." Finally, "This will be a monumental struggle between good and evil. But good will prevail" (ibid., pp. 5–6).

Though Powell was the chief diplomat for the United States, Bush's improvisation had included Bush taking it upon himself to make some diplomatic phone calls initially. As noted elsewhere, he called Blair and Putin in the early hours following the attacks. He also contacted French President Chirac, German Chancellor Schroeder, Canadian Prime Minister Chretien, and Chinese President Jiang Zemin. Meanwhile Powell—who was rumored to have been eclipsed by others in the administration,[6] continued to work with his deputy (Richard Armitage) and his staff to create new diplomatic approaches. On the other hand, Powell's biggest potential rival, Rumsfeld, had not come forward with new thinking for a new kind of enemy and the president was getting frustrated (ibid., p. 9). Powell had managed to buy some time, bureaucratically. Thus Powell and his deputy Armitage focused on South Asia under the theory that Pakistan would be crucial to U.S. success. As Bush continued to phone and meet with various persons and groups on Wednesday, he instructed the NSC "deputies committee" to meet and to take a run at defining the scope of the war, that is, a run at resolving the differences remaining from the earlier NSC meeting that morning. At 4:00 P.M. Bush convened another NSC meeting. The language defining the scope of the war was unsatisfactory and Bush pushed the deputies to keep at it. Rumsfeld, seemingly catching up to his bureaucratic rivals, took up the cause of his deputy, Mr. Wolfowitz. Rumsfeld revisited a point that he and his deputy had made before. He asked, "Are we going against terrorism more broadly than al Qaeda? Do we seek a broader basis for support?" Powell argued that it would be far easier initially to rally the world against al Qaeda. They could win approval of a broad U.N. resolution by keeping it focused on al Qaeda. But Cheney, seemingly joining ranks with Wolfowitz and perhaps pushing Rumsfeld farther in that direction, brought the focus of the NSC to "state sponsorship of terrorism. . . . In some ways states were easier targets than shadowy terrorists." Seeming to lean toward Powell, Bush worried about their targets getting too diffuse creating operational headaches (ibid., pp. 8–9).

Powell brought the group back to the area on which he and his deputy had been working: coalition building.

> As the discussion turned to the shape of the international coalition, several things became clearer. Everyone believed that a coalition would be essential, particularly to keep international opinion behind the United States. But Bush was prepared, if necessary, to go it alone. The United States had the absolute right to defend itself, he believed, no matter what others thought; although he believed that the rightness of the cause would bring other nations along. (ibid.)

As one might expect, bureaucratic posturing would begin to evidence itself eventually, as the crisis situation became more routine, over time. The following paragraphs are therefore instructive, coming as they did late on Day Two.

> Cheney argued that the coalition should be a means to wiping out terrorism, not an end in itself. . . . [Was this a swipe at Powell? Clearly no one thought coalitions were an end in themselves.]

In that case, Rumsfeld argued, they wanted coalition partners truly committed to the cause, not reluctant participants. Powell offered what a colleague later described as the "variable geometry" of coalition building.

Rumsfeld *then raised the question of Iraq, which he had mentioned in the morning meeting.* [Bush had effectively pooh-poohed the ideas as making America's targeting too diffuse.] Why shouldn't we go against Iraq, not just al Qaeda? he asked. Rumsfeld was not just speaking for himself when he raised the question. His deputy, Paul Wolfowitz [frequently identified as a neoconservative], was even more committed to a policy that would make Iraq a principal target of the first round of the war on terrorism and would continue to press his case. Arrayed against the policy was the State Department, led by Powell, and among those who agreed with [Powell] was Shelton, chairman of the Joint Chiefs. (ibid., p. 9; italics added)

Powell began a counteroffensive:

> Powell countered that they were focused on al Qaeda because the American people were focused on al Qaeda, and the president agreed. "Any action needs public support," Powell said. "It's not just what the international coalitions support; it's what the American people want to support. The American people want us to do something about al Qaeda.
>
> Bush made it clear that it was not time to resolve the issue. And he underscored again that his principal goal was to produce a military plan that would inflict real pain and destruction on the *terrorists*. (ibid.; italics added)

Powell's argument temporarily held the day. Nonetheless, Wolfowitz, Cheney, and Rumsfeld would be heard from again.

Importantly, by the end of Day Two, some of the concepts and objectives were finally taking firm shape. "The war would be comprehensive." All the instruments of foreign policy that could be shown to be useful would be employed. Coalition building "was essential, but other nations would not dictate terms of battle. *The war would begin in Afghanistan* where al Qaeda and its assets would be the first ring of targets." Finally, the next task that the Bush administration would need to address was a plan of action (ibid.; italics added).

PROCESS SINCE 9/11: DAY THREE

The next morning, the president took his intelligence briefing, per his custom. After his briefing the president met yet again with his war cabinet. DCI Tenet spoke for some time about the assets the CIA had on the ground and their previous successes. His expanded plan included sending in more covert missions. Interestingly, perhaps reflecting his own bureaucratic shrewdness, Tenet suggested that U.S. special forces be inserted with CIA paramilitary persons to give the military and intelligence agencies "eyes on the ground." He spoke of linking up with anti-Taliban elements in the north and south of Afghanistan. In the north, they could work with the so-called Northern Alliance. In the south they would work others.

The CIA had been on the ground in Afghanistan for years and had engaged in developing a more aggressive approach toward bin Laden and the Taliban prior to September 11. The Pentagon, by contrast, had not been asked or encouraged to do any new planning as part of this pre-September 11 process. As a result, Pentagon thinking about fighting bin Laden was far more conventional—to the frustration of [Secretary Rumsfeld]—at a time when Bush was looking for the unconventional. (ibid., Part III, pp. 2–3)

DCI Tenet was leaving the door open for the military and for Rumsfeld. It is unclear what motivated him to do so. Was it that he disagreed with Powell and sought to help Rumsfeld? Or was it that he knew that negative coverage would soon be released showing manifold intelligence failures and Tenet saw a potential ally in Rumsfeld as someone who could ultimately cover Tenet's flank? Tenet was less likely to find such an ally in Powell, who would be far less vulnerable to any taint of supposed intelligence failures.

In the meantime, Powell was making the best of his earlier successes: getting Bush's blessing for the State Department's actions, forestalling the neoconservatives, and so forth. By now the war cabinet was humming with activities and "moving in many different directions." The State Department, under Powell's stewardship, was busy getting an action plan together for Pakistan. Powell had already told Bush that Pakistan would be critical. Powell thought they might have to do some major arm-twisting, or to use his metaphor, a pitcher's "brushback." Bush told Powell to do whatever he needed to accomplish drawing Pakistan into America's firm grip.

To Powell and his deputy Armitage, this was heady stuff: Bush had just given them a blank check. In consequence, the two set about creating a wish list of what they hoped to get from Pakistan. First, Pakistan needed to intercept arms shipments at its border, stop al Qaeda, and end all logistical support for bin Laden. Second, they wanted Pakistan to give the United States blanket over-flight and landing rights. Third was access to Pakistan's naval and air bases and to its borders. Fourth, Pakistan would be expected to share intelligence and immigration information immediately. Fifth, Pakistan needed to condemn the 9/11 attacks and constrain domestic expression of support for terrorism against the United States and its allies. Sixth, Pakistan needed to cut off the Taliban's fuel shipments, most of which were a lucrative black market operation run between Pakistan and Afghanistan. Seventh, the big one as far as Powell was concerned, break diplomatic relations with the Taliban government, if the evidence demonstrated that bin Laden and al Qaeda continued to be given safe haven by the Taliban regime. By phone, Powell got Musharraf—a fellow general—to agree to all seven points (ibid., pp. 5–6).

PROCESS SINCE 9/11: THE CAMP DAVID MEETING

Over the next couple of days a flurry of activities occurred. The president met with his cabinet on Friday. He had his normal intelligence briefing each morning. Bush gave a beautifully written and delivered speech at the National Cathedral in Washington that served to bring the nation together and began the bonding-healing process of a nation. Bush also visited ground zero where, in an unscripted, improvised manner, the president spoke to the workers, and jumped up on a wrecked vehicle and spoke with a bullhorn. His words—"they'll be hearing from us soon"—resonated with most Americans' post-9/11 mindset, arguably playing to the American exceptionalism ethos. Finally, Bush invited several members of his NSC and other advisors to Camp David for the weekend. Powell, Rumsfeld, and others were to head up early, take advantage of the president's temporary absence, and toss around ideas. Bush would join them shortly. One might easily view this turning point as the end of the foreign-policy crisis and the beginning of the much more deliberative, frustrating period of routinized, foreign-policy decision-making.

Much came out of the two days at Camp David, but for present purposes, the focus shall remain on decision-making and process. Tenet appears to have been a major focus at the retreat. He arrived with a briefcase full of top-secret documents—the culmination, in a sense, of four years of work—on bin Laden and al Qaeda. He took advantage of the setting, with persons there who had not yet been privy to the internal war cabinet debates, to re-present his earlier points and augment them. Several documents were the dazzling variety: a worldwide attack matrix outlining counterterrorist campaigns against potentially eighty countries. Tenet brought up Iraq as a potential target—something he had not suggested previously, thus seeming to side more with Rumsfeld and the neoconservatives, at least for the time being. He talked about expanding covert programs to other countries. Tenet even talked about the Predator surveillance plane: an unmanned aircraft that had been operating in theater for more than a year out of Uzbekistan. Tenet also reminded those assembled of the difficulties of aligning U.S. policy with disparate groups like the Northern Alliance and warlords in the south. In short, he gave the president a good deal to consider.

Secretary of the Treasury Paul O'Neill talked about freezing assets and how the incipient coalitions would help. Mueller spoke for some time but disappointed some who considered the FBI still too focused on perfecting a legal case to prosecute terrorists rather than to prevent future attacks. General Shelton, whose days were numbered as we remarked previously, talked of a three-tiered military approach. The most aggressive of the three scenarios included bombers and, rather quickly thereafter, "boots on the ground," a military phrase that has gained currency since 9/11.

Iraq came up again. The president appeared to waffle back and forth a bit on whether Iraq should be handled concomitant with Afghanistan or left for another time. For a time he appeared to be leaning toward including Iraq. At one point, Deputy Secretary Wolfowitz latched onto Bush's ambivalence. "Wolfowitz argued that the real source of all the trouble and terrorism was probably Hussein." Rumsfeld carried on with Wolfowitz's argument wondering if this were the "opportunity" the United States had been waiting for to get at Hussein? Powell objected on the basis that if Iraq could not be tied to 9/11, it would be better to focus on those who could; that was what Americans and coalition allies expected; that was what each had signed onto. Bush seemed to encourage the debate (ibid., Part V, pp. 5–7).

Finally Bush again came down on Powell's side of the Iraq issue. At one point Wolfowitz "persisted in making his arguments about Iraq and other issues, and annoyed some of his colleagues by showing up at meetings called for NSC principals only—not for deputies." During the morning session, Wolfowitz interrupted Rumsfeld "and repeated a point he had made earlier in the discussion. There was an awkward silence around the table." Bush apparently flashed a pointed look at Card, his chief of staff. Card took aside Wolfowitz and informed him that "[t]he President will expect one person to speak for the Department of Defense" (ibid.). In an afternoon session the Iraq later–Iraq now scorecard was "4 to 0 with Rumsfeld abstaining . . . against Iraq now" (ibid., p. 10). Homeland security came up in the afternoon session. Homeland security and other issues discussed previously took on new urgency after 9/11 and particularly after the weekend at Camp David.

Saturday's sessions were critically important because Bush had made initial decisions on his own—circumstances demanded he do so. Through the NSC and the more truncated principals or war cabinet meetings, the principal players in U.S. foreign-policy decision-making were involved in the decisions and were allowed the opportunity to sway the president—vetting options, once the broad outline had already been set. Camp David allowed others—new eyes in effect—to look at what decisions had been made and what decisions had not yet been made. It permitted others to scrutinize decisions and their underlying assumptions. Finally, an action plan was produced at Camp David with the CIA and special forces leading the way for America's "boots on the ground" approach. That air power would be used initially had become America's *de facto* first step in a military campaign; thus the decision was more or less *pro forma* (ibid., p. 10).

By Sunday's sessions, President Bush knew what the United States was doing, was going to do, and where and when. He prepared to sign a memorandum of notification (often called a finding) authorizing the CIA "to undertake a far-reaching and unprecedented worldwide war against terrorism. He also approved Tenet's proposal for CIA paramilitary teams to go into Afghanistan" (ibid., Part VI, p. A-1). Bush's quick decision to allow the CIA access hastened the military operations that would soon follow. The president knew what the State Department was doing and would be doing over the next several weeks and months. And he knew when and how the military would integrate with the early waves of action that he could put in motion immediately. Even the political, public-relations message was shaped and solidified by the process. The question was whether Bush could stay on script himself.

PROCESS SINCE 9/11: BEYOND THE CAMP DAVID MEETING

Upon returning to the White House on Sunday, alas, the president's first public faux pas escaped him and his managers. As he was walking from the helicopter to the White House an impromptu news conference began. Asked about the weekend and the planning for a response to the 9/11 terror, the president characterized the new U.S. policy as a "crusade." One does not necessarily think that the president meant *crusade* in the sense that Christians killed Muslims during the Crusades. One suspects, rather, that the president was feeling relatively heady given the wringer through which he had been put over the past few days. Likely, his "crusade" remark was simply the president feeling good about what had been accomplished over so little time. Further, the president, as already seen, appears to think in relatively simple terms, partially a function of his strongly held religious beliefs: right versus wrong, good versus evil, freedom versus tyranny, and so forth. Combine that with the president's own announcements regarding being judged by this war, the war bringing purpose to his administration, and so on, and it is not difficult to imagine how the utterance escaped him with little thought to its symbolic meanings. Later, White House Press Secretary Ari Fleischer and others would cover the president and help to extricate him from his unfortunate remark and the anger it caused in some circles.

Following the return from Camp David, process followed a more routine trajectory with various governmental bureaucracies implementing decisions that had been made in their absence and presented to them as a *fait accompli*. Camp David therefore provides a natural demarcation point between crisis and routine decision-making.

So what inferences can one make about process, from the aforementioned account? First, process *was* crucial. Suppose the president had been in Washington when the attacks occurred? Would process have followed the same course? He would have had access to more information, to face-to-face talks with Rice, Tenet, and Rumsfeld during the earliest hours without Powell as a counterbalance. That the early days comprised a foreign-policy crisis clearly affected policy output. This is not to say the president would not have used the military option at some subsequent point; on the contrary, it seems likely that role alone would necessitate *any* president responding militarily. Rather, it illustrates that U.S. foreign policy is a dynamic process where, presumably, learning and maturation occur; thus even under different circumstances a simple cruise-missile attack may have been ruled out as too Clintonesque. There *is* evidence that Bush and his advisors believed as much and were not going to repeat what they viewed as Clinton's mistakes. During the crisis, however, Bush was virtually untethered from the large foreign-policy bureaucracy he normally has at his disposal. This forced/allowed Bush a freer hand (individual input) as he considered his options, always bearing in mind that most Americans would demand some response (role input). Had the Defense Department and Rumsfeld been more prescient, would they have developed unconventional, guerrilla-type contingency plans earlier? Clearly, that they were caught somewhat flat-footed allowed the CIA nearly unprecedented maneuvering room. If Bush's cabinet included Wolfowitz or Cheney as secretary of state, would the outcome have differed? Would Iraq have been part of the U.S. initial response?

While these questions are rhetorical, it is worth considering them and any number of others one might wish to pose. What is not questionable, what we know with some sense of certainty, is that process proved crucial, particularly so early on in the foreign-policy crisis atmosphere, which lasted from Tuesday (9/11) through the weekend. Process sets the table, more or less, to each phase of decision-making: convocation of decision-makers, presentation and selection of options, implementation of options, and feedback or evaluation of actions taken thus far. In this case we have seen special-interest groups, for instance, whose effect on initial stages of decision-making was minimal; yet over time such interests have, increasingly, affected policymaking (societal inputs). The media initially rallied around the flag much like most of the country; only over time have media reports become more jaded. Still there have been more progovernment reports than negative ones. It will be interesting to observe media coverage over the long term as the administration expands its war against the global-terrorist hydra.

Indeed, it remains to be seen how the war on terror evolves over time. Many of the questions posed previously—as well as any number of additional questions one might wish to ask—are a function of whether the policy directions Bush set the United States on following 9/11 will endure. Put differently, only if policy truly and fundamentally changes (i.e., it has shifted its direction in some new ways and said shifts or changes continue as U.S. foreign policy) will one know 9/11's full import. Though beyond the current scope, compelling evidence of demonstrable change exists. The United States has fought a war in Iraq and continues to occupy that country to date. The Bush administration has issued veiled and not-so-veiled threats against Syria, Iran, and North Korea. The defense budget has significantly exceeded the estimates presented earlier. The once latent bureaucratic machinations have moved to cable news channels and the punditocracy. And President Bush remains remarkably popular. Thus we end by considering the research question yet again. Did 9/11 affect U.S. foreign policy? If so, how? Finally, do we expect said change(s) to be a harbinger of U.S. foreign-policy future? Or should we expect the past to be prologue?

NOTES

1. M. Kent Bolton, Ph.D. Dissertation, "How Decision Time and Degree of Anticipation Affect Decision-Making as U.S. Decision-Makers Confront Various Foreign-Policy Challenges." (Ph. D. diss., Ohio State University, 1992).
2. Surprise is not without controversy. Others have argued that Hermann's definition need not include surprise. See special edition of *International Studies Quarterly* 21 (March 1977). However, empirical evidence of surprise's synergism with high threat and short decision time has been published. See M. Kent Bolton, "Pas de Trois," *Conflict Management and Peace Science* 18, no. 2 (2001), pp. 175–212.
3. Charles Hermann, *Crises in Foreign Policy* (New York: Bobbs Mevrill, 1969).
4. Dan Balz and Bob Woodward, "America's Chaotic Road to War," *Washington Post*, 27 January 2001, p. A1.
5. See Michael Isikoff and Daniel Klaidman, "The Hijackers We Let Escape," *Newsweek*, 10 June 2002, p. 20. For details of what information went unnoticed by virtually the entire U.S. intelligence bureaucracy, see Greg Miller, "U.S. Overlooked Terrorism Sign Well before 9/11," *Los Angeles Times*, 19 September 2002.
6. *Time*, cover story, "Where Have You Gone, Colin Powell?" 10 September 2001.

CONCLUSION

Defending our Nation against its enemies is the first and fundamental commitment of the Federal Government. Today, that task has changed dramatically. Enemies in the past needed great armies and great industrial capabilities to endanger America. Now, shadowy networks of individuals can bring great chaos and suffering to our shores for less than it costs to purchase a single tank. Terrorists are organized to penetrate open societies and to turn the power of modern technologies against us.

> —President George W. Bush, West Point, New York, June 1, 2002.

George W. Bush's report on "The National Security Strategy of the United States of America," released on September 17, 2002, has stirred controversy, though, and will surely continue to do so. *For it's not only the first strategy statement of a new administration; it's also the first since the surprise attacks of September 11, 2001. Such attacks . . . prepare the way for new grand strategies by showing that old ones have failed.*

> —John Lewis Gaddis, "A Grand Strategy," *Foreign Policy*, November–December 2002; italics added.

Freedom is the non-negotiable demand of human dignity; the birthright of every person—in every civilization. Throughout history, freedom has been threatened by war and terror; it has been challenged by the clashing will of powerful states and the *evil designs of tyrants.* . . . The United States welcomes our responsibility to lead in this great mission.

> —President George W. Bush, Preamble to "National Security Strategy of the United States of America," September 17, 2002; italics added.

The "Bush Doctrine" unveiled this week will dominate discussion of U.S. foreign policy for years. . . . *The part that advocates "preemption" and explains the demise of such long-held concepts as "containment" and "deterrence" will, after a period of uncomfortable adjustment, hold up under scrutiny and reorder the world for the new century.*

—Jonathan J. Alter, "Loud and Clear,"
Newsweek, 20 September 2002; italics added.

This text's central research question centers on whether and if the direction of U.S. foreign policy has changed in demonstrable and enduring ways since 9/11. The tentative answer is *yes!* Though the evidence for concluding "yes" rests largely on circumstantial evidence—though, some empirical data are examined—the evidence is quite compelling. Clearly, according to the president's own words memorialized in his speeches since 9/11, Bush perceives himself as a president who will be judged ultimately on the outcome of the war on terror. Further, the president has taken every opportunity to caution Americans—the masses, attentive public, and elites—that the effort will be a long-term endeavor requiring patience. Taking the president at his word, Bush clearly views the war on the global-terrorist hydra as a turning point in U.S. foreign policy—and one that will last, in all likelihood, well beyond his tenure in office.

Since 1986, Congress has mandated that each administration submit its national-security strategy, known unsurprisingly, as The National Security Strategy of the United States of America. In President Bush's 2002 version, one finds a good deal of evidence of how Bush envisions U.S. foreign policy over the next generation. A compilation of speeches and assertions as well as a letter of transmittal (a "preamble") are included in the thirty-plus-page document. Using it and the president's own words, some highlights of the president's vision of U.S. foreign policy for the foreseeable future may be analyzed. Included among the president's plans for U.S. foreign policy, is his decision to expand substantially the U.S. national security bureaucracy: the Transportation Security Administration (http://www.tsa.gov/public/index.jsp), The Department of Homeland Security (http://www.dhs.gov/dhspublic/), as well as some adjustments in the standard operating procedures for extant foreign-policy agencies and/or bureaucracies. An important indicator that the president's vision is more than mere rhetoric is the dollars he has been willing to put behind America's new direction in foreign policy. An assessment of the appropriation of monies to expand America's national-security bureaucracy as well as their relationship to "America's unique internationalism," will therefore be analyzed in this concluding chapter.

THE PRESIDENT'S VIEW OF U.S. FOREIGN POLICY FOLLOWING 9/11

Let us begin with the president's "National Security Strategy."[1] In President Bush's 2002 edition, several indicators exist regarding how the Bush White House views the New World (dis)Order versus the Cold War and the decade following the Cold War. It is clear that Bush and his top advisors view the world as having changed dramatically since 9/11. It is therefore less than surprising that the administration appears prepared to supplant some fifty years of U.S. foreign-policy goals and/or strategies—deterrence and Containment—for what the principal foreign-policy decision-makers see as a new world. Henceforth, the United States will forego containment in favor of proactive, preventive intervention (something President Bush erroneously continues to label "preemption"). If the administration does, in fact, continue these new policies, it will constitute a major change in U.S. foreign policy from the past half century.

As noted earlier, U.S. foreign policy rested on three pillars prior to the twentieth century: (1) economic liberalism-commercialism; (2) the 1823 Monroe Doctrine; and (3) isolationism. With the Cold War's commencement, isolationism was replaced by internationalism (globalism). As the Cold War continued in earnest, U.S. foreign-policy objectives—the conventional or orthodox view held by most decision-makers if not most of the public—revolved around economic liberalism, the Monroe Doctrine, and internationalism.[2] Some of the values that gave rise to these objectives were based in America's origins as a federalism-based, representative democracy. Notably, those émigrés who fled Europe to America's shores avoided the feudal history of Europe as well as Europe's lack of political and religious freedoms. The tenets of U.S. Cold War foreign-policy objectives came to include anti-Communism (what one might more generally label antityranny), anti-Soviet Union, internationalism, interventionism, and deterrence.[3]

During the Cold War these objectives were operationalized as containment of the USSR and nuclear deterrence. Despite the fact that the USSR ceased to exist in 1991, U.S. foreign policy continued to reflect those same goals through the 1990s. Beyond deterring the Soviets from launching a potential first strike against America, U.S. policymakers extended their deterrence policy to America's closest allies (known as *extended deterrence*). Bureaucratic inertia/momentum and general anxiety concerning what new threats might emerge equated to a continuation of Cold War foreign-policy trends well beyond the existence of a Soviet "threat." Indeed, during much of the 1990s it seemed as though the U.S. government was unable to change fifty years of momentum. The result was that the government appeared incapable of focusing on anything other than Communism as the world's foremost tyrannical threat. There were, to be sure, flirtations with other presumed global tyrants (i.e., other *-isms*): drug-lordism, nationalism and separatism, terrorism, fundamentalism, and so on. However, in each instance the focus was short-lived; neither the government (i.e., its decision-making elites) nor the attentive public nor the general public could ever quite equate these seemingly abstract threats with the threat of Soviet-directed Communism.

Drug-lordism was threatening but its impact was felt largely in inner-city urban centers; therefore, the threat from drugs in America seemed rather abstract to suburbanites—that is, those most likely to vote. Nationalism and separatism both seemed menacing—witness the amount of coverage in places like former Yugoslavia—but, again, the threat seemed directed away from most voting Americans and thus abstract. No constituency among likely voters ever appeared that could pressure policymakers to alter Cold War goals. Fundamentalism, clearly, caught the attention of many Americans and the attentive public. With the exception of the 1993 World Trade Center attack, however, fundamentalism appeared a foreign threat. Moreover, articles in major newspapers detailed the 1993 "terrorists" as comical figures more than as threatening ones. Recall the stories of one of the perpetrators returning to the establishment from which he had rented the truck used to deliver and detonate the bomb in order to retrieve his deposit. How threatening could such amateurish behavior be? To most Americans, apparently, the answer was not very. The result: Once more, a potential threat seemed abstract to most Americans and U.S. foreign-policy goals and/or objectives remained those of the Cold War era.

The events of 9/11, in contrast, dramatically propelled the global-terrorist hydra (i.e., *Jihadism*) to the forefront of America's collective consciousness. An emerging new enemy, possibly the equal of Soviet Communism became fixed, instantaneously, as a tyrant set on upsetting America's balance of stability. The sheer horror of the Twin Towers collapsing, the Pentagon burning, and listless faces roaming the streets of New York made 9/11 anything but an abstraction. Not only could Americans perceive the seriousness of the threat, most could scarcely think of anything else for months. What with the subsequent anthrax scare accompanied by frequent alerts of additional forthcoming attacks, American society's collective psyche has been severely scarred. The U.S. government as well as the public were collectively traumatized out of their former complacency by the magnitude of 9/11 and subsequent events. The events of 9/11, importantly, presented the U.S. government with a new "big thing" on which to set its focus. If nothing else, the 1990s was a decade during which U.S. foreign policy flailed about searching for the next "big thing" (i.e., a new global tyranny) needing to be thwarted. As the U.S. government sought the next tyranny (*-ism*) during the 1990s, public complacency grew. Following 9/11, neither governmental lack of direction nor public complacency could continue.

Furthermore, U.S. foreign policy's new tyranny had real villains personified by Osama bin Laden, Dr. Ayman al Zawahiri, Mullah Omar, the faces of the nineteen hijackers who carried out 9/11, Saddam Hussein, and others. Similarly, anti-American Muslims protesting in the streets of Karachi, Baghdad, and the West Bank served further to make tangible the ominous new threat to America's security. No threat since the insidious ways of Soviet Communism ("brainwashing," police-state tactics, and so forth), has affected such a broad cross-section of Americans. Decision-making elites, the attentive public, and the average American experienced the fear of a global tyranny, bent on reversing America's preeminence, repeatedly and frequently on television news programs following 9/11. As had been the case with Soviet Communism, *Jihadism* was widely perceived as an existential threat. Flirtations with potential global tyrants during the 1990s, replacing Soviet Communism, produced no such villains nor did they provide a similar collective focus. Policymaking circles instantly stopped flailing about for the next "big thing": rather a virulent form of Islamic fundamentalism, *Jihadism* nicely fit the bill. *Jihadism* presented Americans with a real villain and a global tyrant *par excellence* requiring America's complete foreign-policy attention for the foreseeable future.

Consider the following questions. First, has *Jihadism* replaced Communism—once and for all—as the world's oppressive tyranny against which the United States must defend itself and its allies in order to protect American political freedoms and way of life? President Bush has answered in the affirmative. The president has spoken repeatedly to the question while comparing it to former tyrannies and the Cold War:

> The great struggles of the twentieth century between liberty and totalitarianism ended with a decisive victory for the forces of freedom—and a single sustainable model for national success: freedom, democracy, and free enterprise.
>
> . . . .
>
> Today, the United States enjoys a position of unparalleled military strength and great economic and political influence. In keeping with our heritage and principles, we do not use our strength to press for unilateral advantage. We seek instead to create a balance of power that favors human freedom.
>
> . . . .
>
> The gravest danger our Nation faces lies at the crossroads of radicalism and technology. . . . We will cooperate with other nations *to deny, contain, and curtail our enemies'* efforts to acquire dangerous technologies. . . . *America will act against such emerging threats before they are fully formed. . . . In the new world we have entered*, the only path to peace and security is the path of action. (President George W. Bush, *National Security Strategy for the United States of America,* "Preamble," September 17, 2002; italics added)

The answer, then, if one is to take the president at his word is an emphatic *yes*!

Second, have America's foreign-policy objectives consequently changed to meet the new threat? The president appears to have answered that question as well when he spoke to West Point cadets on June 1, 2002.

> Our Nation's cause has always been larger than our Nation's defense. We fight, as we always fight, for a just peace—a peace that favors liberty. We will defend the peace against the threats from *terrorists and tyrants*. We will preserve the peace by building good relations among great powers. And we will extend the peace by encouraging free and open societies on every continent. (President Bush's West Point Speech, New York, June 1, 2002; italics added)

Clearly some objectives and values have not changed: liberal commercialism, political freedom, antityranny, and so forth. What has changed, however, is revealing. Opposing what it perceives as a tyranny is a bedrock U.S. value. The Bush administration has equated *Jihadism* with global tyranny—quite similar to the way previous administrations (Truman, Eisenhower, Kennedy, Johnson, Nixon) equated Soviet Communism with global tyranny. Indeed, before Truman, FDR's administration equated global tyranny with Fascism and Nazism. In his own words, Bush gives justification for America's new found focus on *Jihadism*. He notes:

> The United States of America is fighting a war against terrorists of global reach. The enemy is not a single political regime or person or religion or ideology. The enemy

is terrorism—premeditated, politically motivated violence perpetrated against innocents. (President George W. Bush, Washington, D.C., National Cathedral, September 14, 2002)

To be sure, the president—and if the polling data cited earlier are indicative—and the public see *Jihadism* as a "clear and present danger" threatening America and its allies. *Jihadism* has attacked American sovereign territory (New York and Washington but also the embassy buildings in Africa and the *USS Cole*). The threat is no mere abstraction that the government is conjuring up to justify defense budgets. It is real. It is tangible. It is antithetical to America's Century. It is antithetical to America's preeminence. And it is antithetical to America's notion of political freedom. What is more, said tyranny has begun a war against America with a view toward supplanting American primacy with its own view of world order: the reestablishment of a caliphate in the twenty-first century. That an ominous tyranny has raised its head is not in doubt among most Americans. As was the case in the 1940s and 1950s, the question is whether America proactively attacks it or, rather, sets itself up as a counterexample (the shining light on the hill). Put differently, the question is whether American foreign policy sets a course as a new internationalist power or returns to its earlier years of isolationism.

How is one to view America's post-9/11 internationalism? This text's thesis—that 9/11 changed U.S. foreign-policy—would seem to be consistent with the United States returning to isolationism after some fifty years of internationalism. A return to isolationism would obviously constitute change. Indeed, a consistent if small faction of isolationism continues to exist in American foreign-policy circles. Pat Buchanan comes to mind as one who argues that America's existence in Islamic holy sites exacerbates anti-American *Jihadism*. For those who find Mr. Buchanan's views exceptional, on the fringe, and out of the mainstream of conventional wisdom, it should be noted that the highly-respected (certainly among Libertarian circles) CATO Institute takes a similar if less polemic stance.[4] Short of complete isolationism, however, is another view that America can and should refocus its energies internally. Remember, for instance, the heady talk of a "peace dividend" for a brief time in the early 1990s. The origins of this view date back to the end of the Cold War. A "peace dividend" was predicted. It was predicated on America having won the Cold War and, therefore, being able to bring many of its troops home and discontinue persistent growth in the military and intelligence budgets. (It should be noted, however, no such "dividend" ever materialized; rhetoric changed, but defense spending remained relatively constant.)

Thus, a third question must be addressed: Is the United States going to return to isolationism or at least redirect its monies and energies inward? The simple answer is no. On its face, this answer appears to challenge this manuscript's thesis. That is, how can a continuation of America's internationalist past represent change in U.S. foreign policy? The answer is this: America is beginning a new era characterized by a new level of internationalism as a result of 9/11. Since 9/11, U.S. decision-makers have forsaken "humble" internationalism for "a distinctly American internationalism."

The U.S. national security strategy will be based on a *distinctly American internationalism* that reflects the union of our values and our national interests. *The aim
of this strategy is to help make the world not just safer but better.* (President Bush,
West Point, New York 2002; italics added)

Bush continues, fleshing out what he meant by a distinctly American internationalism. His speech highlighted, among other things, the following points. Today's
"distinctly American internationalism" will (1) champion the aspirations for human
dignity; (2) strengthen alliances to defeat global terrorism; (3) work with others to
diffuse regional conflicts; (4) prevent our enemies from threatening us, our allies,
and our friends with weapons of mass destruction; (5) build the infrastructure of
democracy; and (6) transform America's national-security institutions to meet the
challenges and opportunities of the twenty-first century (ibid).

Actually, this was not the first time the president had hinted of his vision of a
distinctly American internationalism. Speaking to the Inter-American Development Bank, he said: "In World War II we fought to make the world safer, then
worked to rebuild it. As we wage war today to keep the world safe from terror, we
must also make the world a better place for all its citizens."[5] Clearly, American foreign policy is not returning to its earlier days of isolationism. Rather, distinctly
American internationalism—a new internationalism that, for lack of a better word,
one might call neointernationalism—and neointerventionism are emerging to
take the place of the past fifty years of internationalism. There can be little doubt
that 9/11 at least created the conditions for neointernationalism if not directly
causing it.

If internationalism has historically reflected a fundamental value and/or goal
of U.S. foreign policy over the past fifty years, it too has consistently been operationalized in containment and deterrence. Therefore, what can one deduce regarding the past fifty years of containment and deterrence, as operational plans to
ensure U.S. goals, spanning some eight or more presidents? Since the president
gave his provocative, thoroughly discussed "axis of evil" speech, outlines of a new
U.S. foreign-policy strategy have emerged. While there is no need to rehash all the
leaks, speeches, and rumors since then, it is worth considering a recent iteration of
Bush's new strategy. The *Los Angeles Times* reported the following in its September 2002 edition:

President Bush served notice today that the United States will *shift its strategy
away from the deterrence* that characterized the Cold War and *toward pre-emptive*
[*sic*] *action against terrorists.*

"The United States can no longer rely on a reactive posture as we have in the
past," Bush wrote. "We cannot let our enemies strike first."

That means taking action against hostile forces *like Iraq,* he said, even when
multinational groups like the United Nations balk.

[H]e made clear that the *military will be broadly reformed* in part to ensure that
U.S. interests are never again threatened the way they were in the Cold War.[6]

The attacks of 9/11 have apparently changed U.S. foreign policy demonstrably, one can infer, based on the president's words as well as budget priorities released by the administration.

By their very nature deterrence and containment are principally defensive, re-active policies. President Bush intends to turn those two policies on their heads. For some fifty years, U.S. policy was that the United States would not be the first to use weapons of mass destruction (albeit an implicit policy more than an explicit one). At least since JFK's administration (with the advent of MAD), deterrence has been premised on having a second-strike capability. America's enemy, namely the Soviets, would be deterred from using their nuclear weapons in a first strike since they could be assured that the United States would maintain enough nuclear weapons, through its strategic triad, to launch a second strike so devastating that no rational enemy of America could reasonably consider launching a first strike. Clear-ly, 9/11 is causing that policy to undergo dramatic change. The administration's po-sition is that deterrence cannot be counted on to work in today's post-9/11 environment.

Similarly, during the Cold War, containment was a defensive policy. A flexi-ble perimeter was erected around the Soviet Union. Some 300,000 American troops were stationed in Europe to contain, deter, and to act as a trip-wire defense. That is, had the Soviets attempted an invasion of America's Western Allies in Europe, America's trip-wire defense was intended to assure the Soviets that they would ini-tially encounter hundreds of thousands of U.S. and NATO troops and firepower. The stratagem guaranteed that such offensive Soviet forays would lead to huge in-creases in American troops and firepower forthwith.

For a short period of time, during Reagan's first term, there was talk of actual-ly fighting and winning such a war, including the use of theater-nuclear weapons. The Nuclear Utilization Theory (appropriately known as NUT) quickly died of its own absurdity and the United States predictably returned to its twin strategies of con-tainment and deterrence. It should be noted that President Reagan never liked de-terrence; he found it reprehensible for humanity. Thus while accepting it as U.S. strategy, he continued to seek a comprehensive nuclear defense: the Strategic De-fense Initiative or, as it was derisively known, Star Wars. Nonetheless, even during Reagan's two terms U.S. strategy remained that of his predecessors: deterrence and a return to containment. (Reagan, in fact, was the first president to successfully implement "reductions" in nuclear weapons rather than simple limitations on fu-ture deployments, perhaps reflecting his ambivalence regarding MAD.)

The United States uncomfortably continued the policy of containment fol-lowing the demise of the USSR in the early 1990s and beyond even as George W. Bush was inaugurated. Put simply, no creative alternative managed to work its way up through the foreign-policy bureaucracies. No new grand strategy was envisioned by U.S. policymakers and, therefore, bureaucratic inertia dictated a continuation of former policy. President Clinton, it will be remembered, managed to call con-tainment by another name: "enlargement." But a rose by any other name is still a rose. While the current administration openly called for a version of Reagan's Star

Wars, it too continued to rely on deterrence. Following 9/11, however, it appears that a new direction will prevail and old strategies will be replaced to match what the Bush team views as a new foreign-policy world.

It would be difficult to characterize post-9/11 changes simply as subtle adjustments. Substantively, they constitute very real differences. Recognizing the enormity of the task of redirecting a foreign-policy bureaucracy, whose procedures, routines, and mission have remained constant for some fifty years, the administration wisely sought to create public, media, and elite momentum behind its intended changes in direction. An article in May (2002) characterized the administration's thinking. The piece argued that the executive branch and its various foreign-policy agencies were issuing a plethora of terrorist warnings in order to rally American society behind the administration. Beyond the obvious political benefits, rallying American society creates pressure on the media and policymakers alike. Over time, societal pressures translate to movement in an otherwise resistant bureaucracy. Similar to Truman's experience at the outset of the Cold War with crisis upon crisis providing the administration with impetus to change, the article noted that 9/11 has given the Bush administration new direction. It further noted the effects of the administration's cheerleading efforts. "Everywhere, the national security establishment is humming with new missions, new funds, new offices with esoteric names and no publicly stated duties." In another similarity to the once-frugal Truman administration, said pressures permitted President Bush (elected as a conservative and tax cutter) to unlock "the federal Treasury to combat global terrorism,"[7] giving the administration tremendous latitude to shape its new war on the global-terrorist hydra.

Perhaps more indicative of America's new direction in foreign policy, newspapers that were often critical of new presidents—especially outsiders—and "changes" in policy generally found themselves applauding the administration's effort. (Truman, one would imagine, would love to have had such encouragement.) The *Washington Post*, for example, approved of Bush's "axis of evil" speech and intentions.

President Bush has been steadily expanding his vision of America's role in the world since September 11. Over the weekend he offered a rhetorical outline that, if realized in practice, would make him *one of the most aggressive of internationalists among presidents.*

The presidential candidate who once suggested that America approach the world with greater humility now argues that "moral truth is the same in every culture," and so "America will call evil by its name . . . and we will lead the world in opposing it." Given the threat the country faces, such presidential determination is essential, and welcome. The challenge is preserving the clarity and focus Mr. Bush speaks of.

Most U.S. allies have yet to accept the president's position that the threat of Saddam Hussein's weapons of mass destruction are such *that traditional deterrence no longer applies* and that "the only path to safety is the path of action"; *he needs to keep making the argument.*

The United States has no choice but to intervene in said conflicts.[8] This editorial, it should be stressed, was well after the initial reactions to 9/11, published some six months later. Moreover, the newspaper was not the *Washington Times*, a paper noted for its conservative editorial policies. This was an editorial in the *Washington Post*, a paper that prides itself on being a government gadfly.

When the president of the United States repeatedly makes speeches over the course of a year's time in which he identifies himself and his success with the war on terror; when the Congress gives the executive branch significant increases in appropriations to fight said war as well as to reform the government for its newly defined mission to thwart terror; when the public continues to reflect its confidence in the president's actions vis-à-vis the war on terror; and when the punditocracy nearly uniformly embraces the proposed changes not simply as a *fait accompli* but, rather, as appropriate; one may properly conclude that U.S. foreign-policy change is in the air. Whether said changes persist over time, say a generation or longer, remains to be seen. But early indications are that they will. Let us briefly consider some quantitative indicators of the thesis that 9/11 affected U.S. foreign policy in demonstrable ways.

EMPIRICAL INDICATORS

Though few, some empirical indicators exist that are suggestive of change in U.S. foreign policy since 9/11. Obviously, with 9/11 having occurred so recently, one cannot make generalizable statements regarding new "trends" in defense spending. Instead, one must rely on fairly basic descriptions and comparisons. In and of itself, defense spending may be indicative of changes in U.S. foreign policy; beyond "change," however, defense appropriations may be illustrative of executive–legislative consensus — inasmuch as the legislature appropriates via bills the executive ultimately signs — both of which, in turn, are demonstrative of America's emerging consensus regarding neointernationalism/neointerventionism.

Defense spending increased dramatically at the beginning of the Cold War, as one would expect given America's previous history of isolationism. The Cold War is frequently dated as beginning in the 1946–1947 period with the Turkey and Greece predicaments. In both cases the United States perceived Soviet behavior as a betrayal of Soviet's commitments made at Yalta and Potsdam. It was not these events alone, however, that led to dramatic increases in defense spending. It took a series of events — events that the United States viewed as proof of Soviet-Communist expansionism — coupled with a natural bureaucratic time lag before the executive branch and the legislative branch began to appropriate dramatic increases in defense spending for the Cold War.

Reconsider the following chronology. Following Turkey-Greece, the Berlin Airlift began in 1948. In 1949, America's ally in China's civil war (namely, the KMT) lost to America's Communist enemy, the PRC, with Mao Zedong at its head. The KMT fled to Taiwan. In June 1950, North Korea invaded South Korea, pouring across the 38th parallel *en masse*. North Korea, as will be recalled, represented the expansion of Communism: its Supreme Leader, Kim Il Sung, headed the State and the Korean Communist Party. What is more, by fall of 1950 troops from the newly created PRC entered the fray coming to North Korea's assistance. Collectively these events, coming in rapid succession as they did, resulted in the United States fielding American troops in perpetuity, something the United States had never done in its history. Consequently, U.S. defense spending dramatically increased, then more or less leveled out, with a gradual slope indicating gradual increases in defense spending from 1950 through the 1990s. (See Table 7.1 on page 179 and Figure 7.1 on page 180.) The change in America's defense appropriations clearly reflected America's new commitment to thwarting Communism, that is, America's new foreign-policy direction that became known as "containment." A direct relationship between America's then emerging foreign policy (containment) and its defense spending is observable. For present purposes, the question is: What do the most recent appropriations data demonstrate? Can one observe increases in defense spending indicative of the "Bush Doctrine," America's neointernationalism/neointerventionism and specifically a growing consensus concerning America's war on global terrorism?

On the one hand, several presidents have often declared "Doctrine" typically bearing their names whose declarations *appear* to signal changes in U.S. foreign policy—the "Reagan" and "Carter" doctrines have already been discussed as examples. On the other hand, said doctrines have, more often than not, signaled rhetorical flairs rather than substantive change in the direction of U.S. foreign policy. For fundamental change in foreign policy to be observable, something beyond simple rhetorical flair is required. The Truman Doctrine, for example, clearly signaled more than rhetoric. Preventing the expansion of Communism and jettisoning isolationism were accompanied by foreign-policy bipartisanship, public approbation, and measurable changes in spending priorities. (As noted, the NSC, the unified command structure of the military, the creation of the CIA, and an array of additional foreign-policy bureaucracies paralleled Truman's declaration of a fundamental redirection of U.S. foreign-policy.) If 9/11 fundamentally affected U.S. foreign policy, one would properly expect to see similar bureaucratic changes followed by measurable changes in relevant appropriations.

Let us consider defense-spending priorities since 9/11 and the resulting implementation of the "Bush Doctrine." We have amply demonstrated that a host of new bureaucracies have been created. Alone, the redirection of foreign-policy bureaucracies and the new bureaucracies created specifically to accomplish the redirection is suggestive of fundamental change. Further, we have seen, albeit over a relatively short time frame, extraordinary bipartisanship in favor of the president's war on terror. Do the appropriations data support the thesis that 9/11 redirected U.S. foreign policy? In Table 7.1 and Figure 7.1, the reader will find defense-spending data that were presented in Chapter 4. Additional data obtained from the Department of Defense—though limited to fiscal years 2001–2007 only—is also presented.

TABLE 7.1 **OMB DoD Defense Estimates**

Fiscal Year	OMB Data in Constant $1996	OMB Data in Constant $2002	Fiscal Year	OMB Data in Constant $1996	OMB Data in Constant $2002	DoD, 2003 Data Estimates, March '02
1947	$99.40	$114.67	1978	$230.60	$266.02	
1948	76.50	88.25	1979	236.70	273.06	
1949	109.10	125.86	1980	245.30	282.98	
1950	113.90	131.40	1981	259.30	299.13	
1951	186.10	214.69	1982	282.30	325.66	
1952	352.40	406.53	1983	305.00	351.85	
1953	372.10	377.34	1984	309.20	356.69	
1954	341.40	398.84	1985	330.50	381.27	
1955	285.40	329.24	1986	353.70	408.03	
1956	265.30	306.05	1987	360.50	415.87	
1957	270.40	311.93	1988	364.50	420.49	
1958	267.20	308.24	1989	369.70	426.49	
1959	267.70	308.82	1990	354.70	409.18	
1960	273.00	314.93	1991	310.10	357.73	
1961	274.20	316.32	1992	327.40	377.69	
1962	287.30	331.43	1993	314.30	362.58	
1963	281.50	324.74	1994	298.10	343.89	
1964	286.50	330.51	1995	282.00	325.32	
1965	264.50	305.13	1996	265.80	306.63	
1966	292.30	337.20	1997	264.80	305.47	
1967	346.90	400.18	1998	259.90	299.82	
1968	379.10	437.33	1999	260.50	300.51	
1969	361.00	416.45	2000	270.80	312.40	
1970	338.50	390.49	2001	278.50	321.28	$309.90
1971	308.50	355.89	2002	306.90	354.04	*329.90
1972	282.60	326.01	2003	328.00	378.38	*378.60
1973	255.30	294.51	2004	335.00	386.46	*387.40
1974	244.90	282.52	2005	346.50	399.72	*408.30
1975	240.70	277.68	2006	353.00	407.22	*429.20
1976	231.60	267.17	2007	358.40	413.45	*450.90
1977	230.20	265.56				
			Averages	$284.39	$327.30	$384.89

*Represents "estimates." Department of Defense, *National Defense Budget Estimates*, Fiscal Year 2003; Office of the Under Secretary of Defense (Comptroller), March 2002 (only 2001–2007 available). Percentages computed using OMB figures in constant 1996 dollars. All figures represent US$ billions.

Source: Office of Management and Budget (OMB), *Budget of the U.S. Government*, "Historical Tables," Fiscal Year 2003. Tables 3.1, 3.2, and 4.1 (Washington, D.C.: U.S. Government Printing Office, 2003).

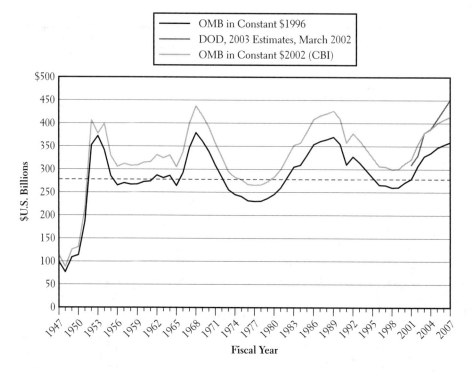

FIGURE 7.1   DEFENSE APPROPRIATIONS PLOTTED OVER TIME

OMB Figures—from Table II—with Fiscal Year Plotted on the X-axis and $US Billions in Defense Spending Plotted on Y-Axis. (Horizontal dotted line represents average.)

Presidential Terms: Harry S Truman (1945–1953); Dwight D. Eisenhower (1953–1961); John F. Kennedy (1961–1963); Lyndon B. Johnson (1963–1969); Richard M. Nixon (1969–1974); Gerald R. Ford (1974–1977); Jimmy Carter (1977–1981); Ronald W. Reagan (1981–1989); George Bush (1989–1993); William J. Clinton (1993–2001); George W. Bush (2001–present)

Clearly a limited decrease in defense spending is observable with the end of the Cold War (fiscal years 1991–1998). Two points are worth reiterating. First, there is always a time lag between the election of a new president and his first defense budget—or domestic budget for that matter. This is understandable as presidents are elected in November of an even year and inaugurated the following January (an odd year). To illustrate, consider Presidents George H. W. Bush and William Jefferson Clinton. Former President Bush (41) was elected in November 1988 taking office in January 1989; former President Clinton was elected in November 1992 but inaugurated in January 1993. Second, there is an additional time lag as each new administration faces a learning curve that varies according to the experience of the incoming president and his advisors, making a precise time lag all but impossible to specify.

Keeping these points in mind, some observations are clear. As may easily be seen, the early Cold War years comprise the most dramatic increases over the entire time frame. Still, the estimates for President Bush's war on the global-terrorist hydra are illustrative of a change of direction in U.S. foreign-policy priorities and are quite suggestive of Bush's declaration of a distinctly American internationalism. While the data presented represent descriptive comparisons, they are nonetheless supportive of the text's principal thesis. Namely, that 9/11 affected U.S. foreign policy in demonstrable ways. If the estimates presented prove accurate—and there is little reason to doubt that they will at this point—it would similarly appear that the new course will persist over time. As noted earlier, bureaucratic inertia alone could obviate a rapid return to pre-9/11 U.S. foreign policy. The next steepest increase is found by plotting the Department of Defense (DoD) fiscal years 2001–2007 data. The Vietnam buildup, however, appears quite close by comparison. In a general sense, the data are supportive of the thesis that 9/11 has demonstrably changed the direction of U.S. foreign policy. As noted, defense data can be seen as reflecting consensus among the executive and legislative branches. In the case of DoD's own data—and to a slightly lesser extent the The Office of Management and Budget (OMB) data—if using defense instruments as the principal instruments of U.S. foreign policy is assumed, said data do represent America's neointernationalism that President Bush has promised.

Some additional observations are worth noting. The average for Clinton's Defense Appropriations, for example, for fiscal years 1994–2001 was $272.55 billion. Recall that during Clinton's earliest years, talk of a "peace dividend" was prevalent. By contrast, President George W. Bush's actual and estimated defense appropriation—assuming he is reelected—for fiscal years 2002–2007 is $329.47 billion. Thus, on the one hand, Clinton's decreases in defense budgets are rather less steep than is often thought. Indeed, the decline began under his predecessor and continued under Clinton. (President Clinton's single-largest percentage decrease was 5.74 percent while President George H. W. Bush's comparable decrease equaled a 12.57 percent decrease.) On the other hand, President George W. Bush's military budget represents a rejection of—albeit one that had already begun—any notion of a peace dividend. Indeed, President Bush's average is roughly a 20 percent increase over the Clinton years, a rather substantial increase. In actuality, George W. Bush's increases have exceeded OMB estimates. (See Chapter 4 for actual appropriations that exceed earlier estimates.) In addition to his actual fiscal year 2003 defense appropriation, the president requested, and Congress readily supplied, a supplemental appropriation ($78 billion) for the war in Iraq. (See Chapter 4.)

All the more dramatic is the 20 percent increase in President Bush's actual and projected increases given essentially twelve years of decline prior to the George W. Bush's inauguration. Clearly, there is a significant increase in President Bush's actual and projected budgets indicative of the global war on terror. The average defense spending for George H. W. Bush and Clinton combined is about $292 billion annually. For George W. Bush, his actual and projected post-9/11 defense budgets average about $338 billion annually.[9] More dramatic, however, are the Department of Defense's estimations given the dollars already appropriated and signed into law by President Bush. The Department of Defense explains the differences between their figures and OMB's as a function of rounding.[10] Rounding differences, notwithstanding, the DoD's estimates represent an even steeper increase in projected defense budgets over the next several years.

Thus we conclude where we began. The events of 9/11 have exerted a profound effect on the machinery of U.S. foreign policy and on foreign-policy decision-making. Since 9/11 Americans have seen a recurrence of threat alerts indicative of additional attacks by the global-terrorist hydra. We have seen societal influences compelling the current administration (and doubtless future administrations) to take relatively extreme actions in order to protect the homeland. We have noted relatively mute criticism by media "watchdogs" and civil liberties groups of the accompanying limits these actions potentially place on civil liberties of all Americans, much less on foreign students studying in the United States (Muslims and Arabs in particular.) Indeed, quite similar to the first ten years of the Cold War, neither the public nor the Congress have demonstrated much concern over civil liberties — certainly little over Muslim Americans but, more surprisingly, very little over the general public's. Put simply, the global-terrorist hydra appears to strike a broad cross-section of Americans and Congress as so menacing that both have acquiesced in favor of the relatively extreme actions taken and contemplated by the executive branch (including Iraq in 2003). We have seen the budget spigot open up with new streams of money available to a host of new governmental commissions, agencies, and bureaucracies that may well parallel the growth in government resulting from the Cold War. Only time will tell the story definitively. Finally, we have seen a president who was widely perceived as a foreign-policy lightweight prior to 9/11 exhibit surprising determination to be judged in history according to how well his administration confronts the global-terrorist hydra. In its totality, the evidence is, in fact, compelling.

POSTSCRIPT

Since finishing the bulk of the work on this manuscript, ample additional evidence of demonstrable change in U.S. foreign policy as well as a commitment has appeared, by the Bush administration, to continue to follow said change in direction. While examination of Operation Iraqi Freedom is beyond the scope of this text, it is worth recalling that the administration has fought and won a war in Iraq, occupies Iraq — and will for the foreseeable future — and has issued varying degrees of threats to Syria, Iran, and North Korea. At present it would appear that the victory of the neoconservatives is complete. Thus, with a caveat about the comprehensiveness of the following presentation, some of the evidence is worth brief consideration.

First and foremost, President Bush decided that Iraq is integral to defeating the global-terrorist hydra, further demonstrating the administration's trajectory toward neointernationalism/neointerventionism. The president gave a speech on October 8, 2002, in which he presented a case for "regime change" in Iraq. In what the president characterized as the "Iraqi regime's own actions, its history of aggression and its drive toward an arsenal of terror," Bush laid out the criteria for the specific case of Iraq, which, if applied more generally, might well necessitate additional interventions in the future. Briefly, the criteria are possessing-producing-seeking weapons of mass destruction, though he seemed to distinguish between chemical and biological weapons versus nuclear; sheltering and/or supporting terrorism; using terror against its own people; and a record of ignoring the will of the international community, particularly as specified in UN resolutions.[11] If applied universally, America's neointernationalism/neointerventionism may well commit the United States to future interventions in Iran, N. Korea, Syria, Libya, Pakistan and Indonesia, to name only the most obvious.

As for the governmental agencies evolving to address the war on the global-terrorist hydra, bureaucratic squabbling, as one might expect more than a year after 9/11, has come into high relief. In testimony before Congress former director of the FBI, Louis Freeh, defended supposed intelligence failures that had been laid at his agency's doorstep, "bristling" at his would-be critics. Seeking to lay the blame elsewhere, Freeh "complained that both the Clinton and early Bush administrations—as well as Congress—had failed to provide adequate funding for the FBI's expanding counter-terrorism mission," prior to the 9/11 tragedies.[12] Freeh was engaging, however genuinely, in a bureaucratic maneuver known as covering one's flank.

Additional governmental inputs to U.S. foreign policy appeared in late 2002. Two articles are particularly noteworthy and may reflect disparate motivations. At the very least, Secretary Rumsfeld is exceptionally busy in positioning the Defense Department for its new role in America's war on terrorism. For instance, a Rumsfeld-appointed board, described as an "influential Pentagon advisory board," has apparently reported back to Rumsfeld its findings. Not surprisingly, the board calls for "a major expansion of the U.S. special forces' role in combating terrorism," so that it may be better prepared to deal with "'preemptive' covert operations across the globe." (Note: Rumsfeld, a talented bureaucrat, cleverly uses the word "preemptive," following Bush's lead, though it is difficult to imagine Rumsfeld does not know the difference between a preemptive and a preventive strike or war. Further, he wisely links covert actions to it, as we will see shortly, bracing the Defense Department for a turf battle with the intelligence community.) Though classified, parts of the board's findings include that global terrorism must be taken as seriously as a major theater of war. In an ominous caution, the board notes that its goals include "signaling to countries harboring terrorists 'their sovereignty will be at risk.'" The article continues, noting that some "of the proposals would appear to push the military into territory that has traditionally been the domain of the CIA, raising questions about the extent to which such missions would be subject to legal restraints imposed on CIA activity."[13]

Similarly, an article appeared fleshing out the board's proposal and attributing it less subtly to the Pentagon's expansion.

> In what may well be the largest expansion of covert actions by the armed forces since the Vietnam era, the Bush administration has turned to what the Pentagon calls the "black world" to press the war on terrorism and weapons of mass destruction.

The author notes that there exists increasing "frustration" at the "highest levels" of the Pentagon with the intelligence community, law enforcement, and the Department of Homeland Security "apparatus." "*It also reflects the desire of Secretary of Defense Donald Rumsfeld to gain greater overall control of the war on terror*" (italics added).[14]

While little has been written about the CIA's role in defeating the global-terrorist hydra—not surprisingly given its covert nature—it is worth noting a few points. Just weeks before the article on the Pentagon's "frustration" with the intelligence community (and others) as well as Rumsfeld's attempt to grab a bigger piece of the war was published, Congress held hearings in which DCI George Tenet and others were criticized for intelligence failures. Though Tenet strongly defended his agency's role, the Congressional rebuke was doubtless an embarrassment for the intelligence community generally. Thus it came as no surprise when the CIA made headlines fewer than two weeks after the "Rumsfeld frustration" article. On November 5, 2002, the *Los Angeles Times* reported a dramatic headline: "CIA Missile in Yemen Kills 6 Terror Suspects." One could reasonably infer that DCI Tenet and his peers in the intelligence community were fighting a rearguard bureaucratic turf battle.

> A missile fired from an unmanned CIA surveillance aircraft over Yemen killed six suspected al Qaeda operatives, including one of the terrorist network's most senior figures—a man the United States has hunted for years.

Rumsfeld was named in the article as "declining to discuss the details." In a fairly terse characterization of the CIA's apparent success, Secretary Rumsfeld was quoted as saying that one of the al Qaeda members was wanted in connection with the USS *Cole* attack: "So it would be a very good thing if he were out of business." The same article quoted an FBI official as suggesting the FBI had been after one of the al Qaeda members for some time, perhaps unwittingly lending a bureaucratic leg-up to its CIA rival.[15] Whether the timing was simply serendipitous or whether the CIA was countering Rumsfeld's designs on CIA's budget and mission is unclear. The effect was that the CIA came out of the bureaucratic fray smelling like a rose after some ten days of less than flattering news coverage.

Despite looming elections—in which the balance of power in both the House and the Senate were at stake—bipartisanship reminiscent of the beginning of the Cold War appeared in the first federal spending bills to become law in the new fiscal year (2003), a gift for the president. (Such bipartisanship is reflective of consensus among foreign-policy decision-making elites, if not the attentive and mass public.) The defense bill was sent to the president's desk for his signature. He signed it the following day, according to the article, some $356 billion plus an additional $10 billion for upgrading the military.[16] Thus whatever actual partisanship exists on domestic politics, the Congress has largely given the Bush administration what it has requested in order to defeat the global-terrorist hydra.

In fact, the midterm elections were held while this postscript was being written. Making the punditocracy and pollsters look rather amateurish and bucking a trend of losses in midterm elections that goes back to Franklin Roosevelt, the president's party made gains in the House and retook the majority in the Senate. If anything, one could plausibly argue that this will make the president's agenda (*viz.*, the war on terrorism, homeland security, and so on) easier to fulfill. It should be noted that President Bush actively campaigned for Republicans across the country reversing another axiom of midterm elections: Presidents do not risk their political capital by campaigning given the history of losses for the incumbent's party and the embarrassment said losses are presumed to cause the president in midterm elections. Put differently, one can plausibly expect the defense appropriation trends lines to continue increasing past fiscal year 2007.

As noted earlier, the Cold War did not begin due to one "crisis" or event. Rather, a series of actions by the Soviets or their presumed proxies confronted the Truman administration. That is, over a relatively short period of time, the "other shoe" kept dropping. A series of Soviet-sponsored moves led to what became containment and the significant increases in U.S. defense spending that endured for some fifty years.

For the war on global terrorism to represent a similarly dramatic and sustained change in direction for U.S. foreign policy, additional "shoes" will likely need to drop—that is, additional terrorist attacks on America, its worldwide assets, and/or its allies. Such attacks prevent complacency from returning to American public opinion, among the attentive public, and within decision-making circles. President Bush has continued to make clear that his administration will suffer no such complacency, frequently revisiting the themes of the new-world context of global terror as well as the patience that will be required to win it. Moreover, the recent defense bill (fiscal year 2003) signed into law by the president (late October 2002) suggests that other decision-making elites remain cognizant of the ongoing threat. The American public, by contrast, have demonstrated creeping complacency as indicated by late-2002 polling in which more Americans are reported to be more worried about the economy than the war on terror.

Should it happen that additional terrorist attacks on America and Americans occur in the relatively near future, terrorism will surely move again to the forefront of the public's priorities. Unfortunately, there is good reason to believe that attacks have been and are being planned by the global-terrorist hydra and that Americans *may* soon be reminded of the way they felt following 9/11 and for several months thereafter. In October (2002), an eerily reminiscent report was issued by the Council on

Foreign Relations. The authors begin with a quote from DCI Tenet's recent testimony before the Select Committee on Intelligence (October 17, 2002):

> When you see the multiple attacks that you've seen around the world, from Bali to Kuwait, the number of failed attacks that have been attempted, the various messages that have been issued by senior al-Qaeda leaders, you must make the assumption that al-Qaeda is in an execution phase and intends to strike us both here and overseas; that's unambiguous as far as I am concerned.[17]

The report continues noting that "generally salutary" measures have been taken since 9/11. The authors boldly state: "[T]here is still cause for concern. After a year without a new attack, there are already signs that Americans are lapsing back into complacency." The authors also note that a similar report was published months before the 9/11 attacks and that it went largely unheeded. Nonetheless, the authors attempt to warn Americans of coming dangers and make a plea for "six critical mandates that deserve the nation's immediate attention." Their critical mandates are (1) empower frontline responders, (2) take measures to ensure trade security, (3) protect America's vital infrastructure, (4) prepare America's public-health system to respond to biological and/or chemical attacks, (5) establish private-public sector security partnerships (understanding the special needs of the private sector for copyright protections and access to information as well as addressing how the Freedom of Information Act [FOIA] might be addressed with respect to said partnerships), and (6) fund and train the National Guard to be the frontline in homeland security (ibid., pp. 13–14). Though beyond the scope of this text to delve into the report, suffice it to say that if Americans—decision-making elites and the public alike—were to read the current report, there would be little likelihood of a complacency problem. Its gist is ominous.

The report provides a critically important service. It makes clear that another "shoe" will drop. It is a matter of when, not if. Rather like in the early years of the Cold War, Americans can expect additional terrorist attacks both in America and abroad. Hence, quite similar to in the early Cold War years, policymakers will have justifiable reasons to increase defense spending, to continue to create and strengthen new agencies for homeland security, and to keep America on its new course of foreign policy. In short, it makes it clear that the global-terrorist hydra continues to exist, plan, implement, and prepare to initiate new and horrendous threats against America's security. As President Bush eloquently said, America did indeed wake up to a new world following 9/11. One can only hope that the apparent changes in U.S. foreign policy documented in this text are indicative of an America (the public, the elites, the decision-makers) prepared to withstand the onslaught that will surely come—and come sooner than later.

NOTES

1. *National Security Strategy of the United States of America*, the White House, September 17, 2002, http://www.whitehouse.gov/nsc/nsc.pdf.
2. Walter S. Jones, *The Logic of International Relations*, 8th ed. (New York: Longman, 1997).

3. Charles W. Kegley, Jr. and Eugene R. Wittkopf, *American Foreign Policy: Pattern and Process*, 5th ed. (New York: St. Martin's Press, 1996).
4. Ivan Eland, "Does U.S. Intervention Overseas Breed Terrorism? The Historical Record," CATO Institute, December 1998, http://www.cato.org/pubs/fpbriefs/fpb50.pdf.
5. President George W. Bush, "Expand the Circle of Development by Opening Societies and Building the Infrastructure of Democracy," March 14, 2002, at the Washington, D.C. forum on Inter-American Development Bank.
6. Associated Press, "President Outlines New First-Strike Strategy," *Los Angeles Times*, 20 September 2002.
7. William M. Arkin, "A Policy in from the Cold," *Los Angeles Times*, 26 May 2002.
8. *Washington Post*, editorial, "Taking the Offensive," 4 June 2002, p. A-16.
9. The OMB data were converted to 2002 dollars using the U.S. Department of Labor (http://stats.bls.gov/), Bureau of Labor Statistics CPI calculator. Doing so more accurately reflects the current defense appropriations recently published in major newspapers. For instance, see Associated Press, "Bush Signs Big Boost in Defense Spending," *Los Angeles Times*, 24 October 2002, p. A-26, where the president is reported to have signed a $355.5 billion bill for defense and another $10.5 billion supplemental for "financing the building and upgrading of the military. . . ." See Postscript in this chapter.
10. See Department of Defense, *National Defense Budgets for FY 2003*, Office of the Under Secretary of Defense (Comptroller), March 2003, Calculation Methodology, p. 3.
11. President George W. Bush, "Iraq: Denial and Deception," 7 October 2002: www.whitehouse.gov/2002/10/2002/007-8.html. The invasion/liberation of Iraq actually began in March 2003. See James Gerstenzang, "New Air Strikes Hit Targets in Baghdad," *Los Angeles Times*, 20 March 2003.
12. Bob Drogin, "Freeh Bristles at Critics of FBI Efforts to Fight Terrorism," *Los Angeles Times*, 9 October 2002.
13. Greg Miller, "Wider Pentagon Spy Role Urged," *Los Angeles Times*, 26 October 2002.
14. William M. Arkin, "The Secret War," *Los Angeles Times*, 27 October 2002.
15. Greg Miller and Josh Meyer, "CIA Missile in Yemen Kills 6 Terrorist Suspects," *Los Angeles Times*, 5 November 2002.
16. Jennifer Loven, "President Boosts Defense Spending," *Los Angeles Times*, 24 October 2002, p. A-26; Associated Press, "Bush Signs Big Boost in Defense Spending: The $355.5-Billion Bill Is the Largest Increase since the Reagan Era, amid Threat of Terrorism and War," in *Los Angeles Times*, 24 October 2002 p. A-2.
17. See the recent report of an independent task force sponsored by the Council on Foreign Relations, "America Still Unprepared—America Still in Danger," Gary Hart and Warren B. Rudman, co-chairs (Project Director: Stephen E. Flynn), released publicly in October 2002. It is eerily reminiscent in that the same authors released a report predicting terrorist attacks on the American heartland some two years before 9/11.

BIBLIOGRAPHY

SECONDARY SOURCES

Alterman, Eric. *Sound and Fury: The Washington Punditocracy and the Collapse of American Politics.* New York: HarperPerennial, 1998.

Bamford, James. *Body of Secrets.* New York: Doubleday, 2001.

Bolton, M. Kent "How Decision Time and Degree of Anticipation Affect Decisionmaking As U.S. Decisionmakers Confront Various Foreign-Policy Challenges." Ohio State University, Ph.D. diss., 1992.

——. "Vietnam Crucible: The Political Economy of Normalization in the Post-Cold War World." Abbas Grammy and Kaye Bragg, eds. *United States Third World: Relations in the New World.* Nova Science Publishers. New York, 1996.

——. "Domestic Sources of Vietnam's Foreign Policy: Renovation, Reform, and Normalizing Relations with the United States." In *Vietnam's Foreign Policy in Transition,* edited by Carlyle Thayer and Ramses Amer. Singapore: Institute of South East Asia Studies, 1999.

Chomsky, Noam. *The Fateful Triangle: The United States, Israel, and the Palestinians.* Boston: South End Press, 1983.

Chomsky, Noam, and Edward S. Herman. *Manufacturing Consent: The Political Economy of the Mass Media.* New York: Pantheon, 2002.

Gaddis, John Lewis. *Strategies of Containment.* Oxford: Oxford University Press, 1982.

Gelb, Leslie H., and Richard K. Betts. *The Irony of Vietnam: The System Worked.* Washington, D.C.: Brookings Institution, 1979.

Hermann, Charles F. "International Crisis As a Situational Variable." In *International Politics and Foreign Policy,* edited by James Rosenau. New York: The Free Press, 1969, pp. 409–421.

——. *Crises in Foreign Policy.* New York: Bobbs Merrill, 1969.

Jones, Walter S. *The Logic of International Relations.* 8th ed. New York: Longman, 1997.

Kegley, Charles W., Jr., and Eugene R. Wittkopf. *American Foreign Policy: Pattern and Process.* 5th ed. New York: St. Martin's Press, 1996.

Melanson, Richard A. "Reconstructing Consensus." New York: St. Martin's Press, 1991.

———. *American Foreign Policy since the Vietnam War: The Search for Consensus from Nixon to Clinton.* New York: M. E. Sharpe, 1996.

Prados, John. *Keeper of the Keys: A History of the National Security Council from Truman to Bush.* New York: Morrow, 1991.

Rashid, Ahmed. *Taliban: Militant Islam, Oil and Fundamentalism in Central Asia.* New Haven: Yale University Press, 2000.

Rosenau, James N. "Pre-Theories and Theories of Foreign Policy." In *Approaches to Comparative and International Politics,* edited by R. Barry Farrell. Evanston, IL: Northwestern University Press, 1996.

Wittkopf, Eugene R., Charles W. Kegley, and James M. Scott. *American Foreign Policy: Pattern and Process.* 6th ed. New York: Wadsworth, 2002.

Woodward, Bob. *The Commanders.* New York: Pocket Books, 1991.

Primary Sources

Allen, Mike. "President Has Tough Words for N. Korea." *Washington Post.* February 20, 2002, p. A-1.

———. "White House Angered at Plan for Pentagon Disinformation." *Washington Post.* February 25, 2002, p. A-17.

———. "Questions Swirl around Bush over 9-11 Attacks: Administration Knew of Bin Laden Threat in May." *Washington Post.* May 16, 2002.

Allen, Mike, and Clay Chandler. "Bush Says U.S. Will Pursue Campaign: Japan's Help Urged in Defusing Threats." *Washington Post.* February 19, 2002, p. A-1.

Allen, Mike, and Amy Goldstein. "Security Funding Tops New Budget: Bush Plan Marks Return to Deficit." *Washington Post.* January 20, 2002, p. A-1.

Alonso-Zaldivar, Ricardo. "Cost of Fortifying Airports May Top $6 Billion in 2002." *Los Angeles Times.* May 26, 2002.

Anderson, John Ward. "Iranian Courts Target Reformist Legislators: Hard Line Clerics Pursue Political Changes." *Washington Post.* February 18, 2002, p. A-19.

Anderson, John Ward, and Peter Baker. "Killers Likely Never Intended to Free Pearl: Abduction and Videotaped Slaying of Reporter Meant to Send Message, Pakistani Police Say." *Washington Post.* February 23, 2002, p. A-16.

Argetsinger, Amy, and Valerie Strauss. "Schools Translate Terror into Curricular Changes." *Washington Post.* February 8, 2002, p. A-1.

Arkin, William M. "A Policy in from the Cold: The Bush Administration Has Returned to Cold War-Style Secrecy and an End-Justifies-Means Attitude." *Los Angeles Times.* May 26, 2002.

———. "The Secret War: Frustrated by Intelligence Failures, the Defense Department Is Dramatically Expanding its 'Black World' of Covert Operations." *Los Angeles Times.* October 27, 2002.

Assadi, Mohammed. "Arafat Pledges Elections Soon: Palestinian Cabinet Meets." *Washington Post.* June 14, 2002, p. A-20.

Associated Press. "U.S. General Says Enemy Is Regrouping." *Los Angeles Times.* March 20, 2002.

———. "Al Qaeda Plot Revealed in Sarajevo." *New York Times.* March 23, 2002.

——. "U.S. Citizens Warned of Threats in Italy." *Los Angeles Times*. March 27, 2002.

——. "Italy Says Warnings Unfounded." *Los Angeles Times*. March 29, 2002.

——. "Text of Arafat's Terrorism Statement." April 13, 2002.

——. "F.B.I. Says Suicide Bombers Likely in U.S." May 20, 2002.

——. "Bush Urges Congress to Move Quickly on Cabinet Post." *New York Times*. June 7, 2002. *New York Times*: http://www.nytimes.com/aponline/national/AP-Attacks-Bush.html.

——. "Mineta Says Spending Bill 'Undermines' Airline Security." July 23, 2002.

——. "President Outlines New First-Strike Strategy Defense: President Bush's Doctrine Amounts to the Official Declaration of the Death of the Cold War Strategy That Pushed the Superpowers to Stockpile Nuclear Weapons As a Way of Ensuring Peace." *Los Angeles Times*. September 20, 2002.

——. "Bush Signs Big Boost in Defense Spending." *Los Angeles Times*. October 24, 2002.

Baldauf, Scott. "Musharraf Takes on Spy Agency: The Pearl Case and a Foiled Bomb Plot May Be a Response to Pakistan's Crackdown." *Christian Science Monitor*. February 22, 2002.

Balz, Dan, and Bob Woodward. "America's Chaotic Road to War: Bush's Global Strategy Began to Take Shape in First Frantic Hours after Attack." *Washington Post*. January 27, 2002.

——. "'We Will Rally the World': Bush and His Advisers Set Objectives but Struggled with How to Achieve Them." *Washington Post*. January 28, 2002.

——. "Afghan Campaign's Blueprint Emerges." *Washington Post*. January 29, 2002.

——. "A Pivotal Day of Grief and Anger: Bush Visits Ground Zero and Helps Move the Country from Sorrow to War." *Washington Post*. January 30, 2002.

——. "At Camp David, Advise and Dissent: Bush, Aides Grapple with War Plan." *Washington Post*. January 31, 2002.

——. "Combating Terrorism: 'It Starts Today.'" *Washington Post*. February 1, 2002.

——. "A Presidency Defined in One Speech: Bush Saw Address As Both Reassurance and Resolve to a Troubled Nation." *Washington Post*. February 2, 2002.

——. "Bush Awaits History's Judgment: President's Scorecard Shows Much Left to Do." *Washington Post*. February 3, 2002.

——. "Daschle Defends Challenge of Bush on War." *Washington Post*. March 2, 2002. p. A-13.

——. "Bush Doctrine Begins to Blur." *Washington Post*. April 3, 2002, p. A-1.

Bearak, Barry. "Unknown Toll in the Fog of War: Civilian Deaths in Afghanistan." *New York Times*. February 10, 2002.

——. "Kabul Rushes 1,000 More Men to Join G.I.'s on Battle's Sixth Day." *New York Times*. March 8, 2002.

Becker, Elizabeth, and James Dao. "Hearts and Minds: Bush Will Keep Wartime Office Promoting U.S." *Christian Science Monitor*. February 19, 2002.

Belluck, Pam. "With Patriotism Renewed, July Hits a Deeper Chord." *New York Times*. July 4, 2002.

Bennet, James. "Israel Acts to Seize Palestinian Land after 19 Die in Blast." *New York Times*. June 19, 2002.

——. "Arafat Says Elections in January Will Decide His Leadership."*New York Times*. June 26, 2002.

Bennett, Philip, and Steve Coll. "Prince Reaffirms Saudi U.S. Alliance: Ruler Denounces Stance on Palestinians." *Washington Post*. January 29, 2002. p. A-1.

Blanford, Nicholas. "Palestinian Ties to Iran, Hizbullah Look Firmer." January 18, 2002.

——. "Emboldened by U.S. Jibes, Hizbullah Prepares for War." *Christian Science Monitor.* February 8, 2002, p. 7.

Blustein, Paul. "Unrest a Chief Product of Arab Economics." *Washington Post.* January 26, 2002, p. A-1.

Bolton, M. Kent. "Pas de Trois: The Synergism of Surprise, Threat, and Response Time and Its Effects on U.S. Foreign-Policy Behavior." *Conflict Management and Peace Science* 18, No. 2 (2002): pp. 175–212.

Bonner, Raymond, and Jane Perlez. "Finding a Tepid Ally in the War on Terror. U.S. Presses Indonesia to Arrest 2 Clerics." *New York Times.* February 17, 2002.

Bourdreaux, Richard. "Italy Convicts 4 Linked to al Qaeda." *Los Angeles Times.* February 23, 2002.

Brezezinski, Zbigniew. "Moral Duty, National Interest." *New York Times.* April 7, 2002.

Broder, David S. "The Democrats Punt." *Washington Post.* April 7, 2002, p. B-7.

Brookings Institute. Foreign Policy Studies Chronology. http://www.brook.edu/dybdocroot/fp/projects/terrorism/chronology.htm.

Brownstein, Ronald. "New Era Means Trimming Tax Cut." *Los Angeles Times.* January 14, 2002.

——. "Debating War's Sway over Voters." *Los Angeles Times.* January 24, 2002.

Bumiller, Elisabeth. "Jiang Is to Visit the U.S. in October: No Date Was Given for Hu's Visit," *New York Times.* February 21, 2002.

Bumiller, Elisabeth, and David E. Sanger. "Bush, As Terror Inquiry Swirls, Seeks Cabinet Post on Security." *New York Times.* June 7, 2002.

Burns, John. "U.S. Commander Predicts End to Afghan Battle but Not to War. *New York Times.* March 18, 2002.

Burns, Robert. "Rumsfeld Warns of Deadlier Threats." *Los Angeles Times.* January 31, 2002.

——. "Speech on Iraq." *Washington Post.* October 8, 2002, p. A-20.

Canadian Press. "Bin Laden and Mullah Omar Are Still Alive, Says Al-Qaida-Linked Organization." February 19, 2002.

Chaddock, Gail Russell. "Soft Debate Surfaces on Terror War: Democrats Raise Doubts, Risking 'Unpatriotic' Label." *Christian Science Monitor.* March 4, 2002.

Chaddock, Jessica. "The Wrong Target." *Washington Post.* March 4, 2002, p. A-19.

Chandrasekaran, Rajiv. "Al Qaeda Feared to Be Lurking in Indonesia." *Washington Post.* January 11, 2001, p. 1.

Chen, Edwin, and Henry Chu. "U.S. and China to Broaden Contacts." *Los Angeles Times.* February 21, 2002.

Chivers, C. J., and David Rhode. "Afghan Camps Turn out Holy War on Guerrillas and Terrorists." *New York Times.* March 18, 2002.

Chu, Henry. "China Says Radicals Led Attacks and Colluded with Bin Laden: Asia: Report Blames Muslims in Restive Xinjiang for 162 Deaths." *Los Angeles Times.* January 22, 2002.

Clymer, Adam. "Ex-Operative Writes of the Decline at C.I.A." *New York Times.* January 26, 2002.

——. "European Poll Faults U.S. for Its Policy in the Mideast." *New York Times.* April 19, 2002.

CNN. "Inside Politics." March 20, 2002.

CNN. *Wolf Blitzer Reports.* June 27, 2002.

CNN and MSNBC. Reference to grumbling at the Pentagon. Mid-October 2002.

Cohen, Richard. "Flunking Foreign Affairs." *Washington Post.* April 18, 2002, p. A-21.

——. "Born on the Fourth of July." *Washington Post.* July 4, 2002.

Colomgant, Nicolas. "Mali's Muslims Steer Back to Spiritual Roots: Leaders Say a Decade of Western Aid Has Brought with It Materialistic Western Values." *Christian Science Monitor.* February 26, 2002.

Constable, Pamela. "Karzai's Charges Raise Doubts; Controversy Highlights Governments Fragility." *Washington Post.* February 17, 2002, p. A-16.

——. "Behind Confident Front, Karzai's Control often Illusory." *Washington Post.* February 25, 2002, p. A-16.

——. "Afghan Assembly Elects Karzai: Overwhelming Win by Interim Leader Opens a New Phase." *Washington Post.* June 14, 2002, p. A-1.

Cooper, Richard T., and Josh Meyer. "CIA-FBI Feuding Relentless. Intelligence: Unending Battles between the Agencies over Sept. 11 Revelations Lead Reformers to Consider Major Changes." *Los Angeles Times.* May 26, 2002.

Council on Foreign Relations. *Report of an Independent Task Force.* "America Still Unprepared—America Still in Danger." Gary Hart and Warren B. Rudman, Co-Chairs (Project Director: Stephen E. Flynn). October 2002.

Crossette, Barbara. "Study Warns of Stagnation in Arab Societies." *New York Times.* July 2, 2002.

Curtius, Mary. "Violence Unabated Amid U.S. Envoy's Mideast Visit Conflict: A Maimed Statue in Bethlehem Symbolizes the Carnage Zinni Seeks to End." *Los Angeles Times.* March 15, 2002.

Dao, James, and Eric Schmitt. "Pentagon Readies Efforts to Sway Sentiment Abroad." *New York Times.* February 19, 2002.

Demick, Barbara. "Is N. Korean Threat Overstated?" *Los Angeles Times.* February 6, 2002.

——. "Visit Stirring up Anti-Americanism." *Los Angeles Times.* February 18, 2002.

Dewar, Helen. "Lott Calls Daschle Divisive." *Washington Post.* March 1, 2002, p. A-6.

Dextre, Finn. "Pakistan Says It Seized Americans Tied to al Qaeda." *New York Times.* June 13, 2002.

Diamond, John. "Al Qaeda Menace Believed Dispersing: Network Hobbled but Harder to Hunt." *Chicago Tribune.* February 20, 2002.

Diehl, Jackson. "Pakistan's Thorny Transition." *Washington Post.* February 18, 2002, p. A-23.

Drew, Christopher, and Judith Miller. "Though Not Linked to Terrorism, Many Detainees Cannot Go Home." *New York Times.* February 18, 2002.

Drogin, Bob. "Missiles Not Biggest Threat, Report Says. Terrorism 'Ships, Trucks, Airplanes, and Other Means' Are Called Likely Methods of Conveyance for Chemical, Biological, or Nuclear Attack on U.S." *Los Angeles Times.* January 12, 2002.

——. "Freeh Bristles at Critics of FBI Efforts to Fight Terrorism. Intelligence: Ex-Director Defends His Own Actions and Says Bureau Lacked Money and Staffing." *Los Angeles Times.* October 9, 2002.

Eggen, Dan. "'Carnivore' Glitches Blamed for FBI Woes." *Washington Post.* May 29, 2002, p. A-7.

Eland, Ivan. "Does U.S. Intervention Overseas Breed Terrorism? The Historical Record." CATO Institute. December 1998. http://www.cato.org/pubs/fpbriefs/fpb50.pdf.

Erlanger, Steven. "German Officials Deny Knowing Location of an Important Figure in Hamburg Plot." *New York Times.* June 13, 2002.

Fineman, Mark. "Defense: Ex-President and Other Washington Elites Are Behind the Carlyle Group." *New York Times.* January 10, 2002.

Finn, Peter. "Macedonian Police Kill 7 Suspected Terror Cells." *Washington Post.* March 3, 2002, p. A-1.

——. "Arrests Reveal al Qaeda Plans." *Washington Post.* June 16, 2002, p. A-1.

——. "Syria Interrogating al Qaeda Recruiter: Sept. 11 Plot Details Shared with U.S." *Washington Post.* June 19, 2002, p. A-1.

Firestone, David, and Allison Mitchell. "Congress Gets Bill Setting up Security Dept." *New York Times.* June 19, 2002.

Ford, Peter. "Cold War Won, Can NATO Fight Terror?" *Christian Science Monitor.* May 28, 2002.

Friedman, Thomas L. "Blunt Question, Blunt Answer." *New York Times.* February 10, 2002.

——. "An Intriguing Signal form the Saudi Crown Prince." *New York Times.* February 17, 2002.

——. "The Hard Truth." *New York Times.* April 3, 2002.

Garvey, Megan, and Carl Ingram. "Terrorism Grants Go to States, Cities." *Los Angeles Times.* February 1, 2002.

Gellman, Barton. "Struggles inside the Government Defined Campaign." *Washington Post.* December 20, 2001, p. A-1.

——. "Struggles inside the Government Defined Campaign." *Washington Post.* December 20, 2002, p. A-1.

Gellman, Barton, and Thomas E. Ricks. "U.S. Concludes Bin Laden Escaped at Tora Bora Fight." *Washington Post.* April 17, 2002, p. A-1.

Gerstenzang, James. "Cheney Finds Israeli Issue Trumps Iraq." *Los Angeles Times.* March 18, 2002.

——. "Mideast: Leader Predicts 'Grave Consequences' if the U.S. Does Not Do More to Halt the Violence but He Pledges That Oil Will Not Be Used As a Weapon." *Los Angeles Times.* April 26, 2002.

Ghattas, Sam F. "Arab Leaders Endorse Peace Plan." *Los Angeles Times.* March 28, 2002.

——. "Al Qaeda: Bin Laden Still Alive." Associated Press. June 23, 2002.

Goldern, Tim. "Young Egyptians Hearing Call of 'Martyrdom.'" *New York Times.* April 26, 2002.

Goldstein, Amy, and Juliet Eilperin. "Congress Not Advised of Shadow Government: Bush Calls Security 'Serious Business.'" *Washington Post.* March 2, 2002, p. A-1.

Goodman, Ellen. "Deluded Bombers." *Washington Post.* April 6, 2002, p. A-21.

Gopalakrishnan, Raju. "Facing Criticism, Philippines Backtracks on U.S. Troops." Reuters. January 18, 2002.

Gordon, Michael R. "As Threat Eases, U.S. Still Sees Peril in India Pakistan Buildup." *New York Times.* January 20, 2002.

——. "No Easy Victory Is Seen in Fierce Strategy." *New York Times.* March 5, 2002.

——. "Saudis Warning against Attack by U.S. on Iraq." *New York Times.* March 17, 2002.

——. "U.S. Says It Found Qaeda Lab Being Built to Produce Anthrax." *New York Times.* March 23, 2002.

——. "A Top Qaeda Commander Believed Seized in Pakistan." *New York Times.* March 31, 2002.

Graham, Bradley. "Afghan Tape Helped Lead to Singapore Terror Cell." *Washington Post.* January 12, 2002, p. A-1.

——. "Bush to Propose Sustained Rises in Military Spending." *Washington Post.* February 3, 2002, p. A-6.

——. "Pentagon Seeks Own Foreign Aid Power." *Washington Post.* April 8, 2002, p. A-1.

Graham, Bradley, and Vernon Loeb. "U.S Forces Gain Edge in Afghan Attack." *Washington Post.* March 6, 2002, p. A-1.

Grier, Peter. "Mideast Fractures Cause Global Stress." *Christian Science Monitor*. March 29, 2002.

——. "Security Shuffle: Is Nation Safer? President Bush Establishes a Cabinet-Level Homeland Security Post, the Latest in a Series of Agency Shakeups." *Christian Science Monitor*. June 7, 2002.

Hafezi, Parisa. "Karzai Pledges Good Relations with 'Brother' Iran." Reuters. February 24, 2002.

Haven, Paul. "As Operation Anaconda Winds Up, War Goes On." Associated Press. March 18, 2002.

Hendren, John. "U.S. Took Time for This Afghan Raid." *Los Angeles Times*. March 4, 2002.

Hendren, John, and John Daniszewski. "Navy SEAL Was Captured and Killed." *Los Angeles Times*. March 6, 2002.

Henneberger, Melinda. "Rome Embassy May Have Been Bomb Target." *New York Times*. February 24, 2002.

Hiatt, Fred. "A Flinch on Chechnya." *Washington Post*. February 25, 2002, p. A-23.

——. "Bush's Comparison of Convenience." *New York Times*. July 1, 2002.

Hitchens, Theresa. "Press Release, CDI." Washington, D.C., January 31, 2002.

Hoagland, Jim. "Assessing the War Honestly." *Washington Post*. February 14, 2002, p. A-33.

——. "No Easy Exit." *Washington Post*. March 3, 2002, p. B-7.

——. "Pakistan: Pretense of an Ally." *Washington Post*. March 28, 2002, p. A-29.

Holbrooke, Richard. "Rebuilding Nations." *Washington Post*. April 1, 2002, p. A-15.

Hulse, Carl. "Terror Inquiry Shines Light on Senator Seeking Stage." *New York Times*. June 21, 2002.

Hussain, Zahid. "Musharraf Wants Pearl Killers Caught." *Los Angeles Times*. February 22, 2002.

Ignatius, David. "France's Constructive Critic." *Washington Post*. February 22, 2002, p. A-25.

International Studies Quarterly. "Special Edition." March 21, 1977.

Isikoff, Michael, and Daniel Klaidman. "The Hijackers We Let Escape." *Newsweek*. June 10, 2002, pp. 1–11.

Jehl, Douglas. "Pakistan Cutting Its Spy Unit's Ties to Some Militants." *New York Times*. February 20, 2002.

Johnston, David, and Elizabeth Becker. "C.I.A. Was Tracking Hijacker Months Earlier Than It Had Said." *New York Times*. June 3, 2002.

Johnston, David, and Don Van Natta, Jr. "Congressional Inquiry into 9/11 Will Look Back As Far As 1986." *New York Times*. June 5, 2002.

Johnston, David, Don Van Natta, Jr., and Judith Miller. "Qaeda's New Links Increase Threats from Global Sites." *New York Times*. June 16, 2002.

Kaiser, Robert G., and David B. Ottaway. "Saudi Leader's Anger Revealed Shaky Ties." *Washington Post*. February 10, 2002, p. A-1.

Kaufman, Marc. "Wondering if This Man Can Pull It Off." *Washington Post*. February 17, 2002, p. B-1.

Keller, Bill. "The Soul of George W. Bush." *New York Times*. March 23, 2002.

Kessler, Glenn, and Walter Pincus. "Bombing Link Swayed Bush: Reported Arafat Payment to Terror Group Shifted Stance." *Washington Post*. June 26, 2002, p. A-1.

Keyser, Jason. "Bombing Injuries 29 in Tel Aviv." *Los Angeles Times*. March 30, 2002.

Khan, Kamran, and Karl Vick. "FBI Joined Pakistan in Staging Raids." *Washington Post*. March 30, 2002, p. A-13.

Kiefer, Francine. "Medicare, Social Security Reform, and His Energy Plan Face Tough Prospects: 'Softer Initiatives' Look Better." *Christian Science Monitor*. February 1, 2002.

King, Colbert I. "Saudi Arabia's Apartheid." *Washington Post*. January 19, 2002, p. A-27.

Kinsley, Michael. "Lying in Style." *Washington Post*. April 19, 2002, p. A-25.

Krauthammer, Charles. "Saudi Peace Sham." *Washington Post*. March 6, 2002, p. A-19.

Krauthammer, Henry, Darin Briscoe, and Mitchell Landsberg. "A Changed America: Civil Liberties Take a Back Seat to Safety." *Los Angeles Times*. March 10, 2002.

Kristof, Nicolas D. "Let Them Be P.O.W.'s." *New York Times*. January 29, 2002.

———. "Sleeping with Terrorists." *New York Times*. February 12, 2002.

———. "The Wrong War." *New York Times*. February 19, 2002.

———. "Devils and Evil Axes." *New York Times*. February 26, 2002.

———. "The Angola Mirror." *New York Times*. March 5, 2002.

———. "Anthrax? The F.B.I. Yawns." *New York Times*. July 2, 2002.

Kunkle, Fredricke. "At Pentagon, Healing and Rebuilding." *Washington Post*. January 22, 2002, p. A-1.

Kurtz, Howard. "Patriotism Comes under Attack," *Washington Post*, January 4, 2002.

———. "War Coverage Takes a Negative Turn." *Washington Post*. February 17, 2002, p. A-14.

———. "A Leaky Ship Goes Under: Press Sinks Pentagon Propaganda Boat." *Washington Post*. February 27, 2002.

———. "The Second-Guessing Syndrome." *Washington Post*. June 13, 2002.

LaFranchi, Howard. "Public Sees New Global Role for U.S.: Among Americans, One Lesson of Terror Attack Is That the U.S. Needs to Look Outward." *Christian Science Monitor*. January 11, 2002, p. 1.

———. "U.S. Seeks Right Equation to Topple Saddam." *Christian Science Monitor*. March 1, 2002.

Lichtblau, Eric. "Terrorists Noted Flaws in Security, Report Says." *Los Angeles Times*. February 1, 2002.

———. "Bias against U.S. Arabs Taking Subtler Forms." *Los Angeles Times*. February 10, 2002.

Lichtblau, Eric, and Josh Meyer. "U.S. Seeks Public's Help in Search for 5 from al Qaeda. *Los Angeles Times*. January 18, 2002.

Loeb, Vernon, and Bradley Graham. "Democrats Criticize Budget, Anti-Terror War." *Washington Post*. February 28, 2002, p. A-8.

Los Angeles Times. "A War without Congress." March 7, 2002.

———. "Justice Dies in the Dark." April 3, 2002.

Loven, Jennifer. "House Passes Defense Spending Bill." *Associated Press*. May 10, 2002.

———. "President Boosts Defense Spending. Bush: $355.4 Billion Bill Allows Military 'to Defend Freedom around the World.'" *Los Angeles Times*. October 23, 2002.

Lumpkin, John J. "CIA: Al Qaeda Poses Largest Threat to U.S." *Los Angeles Times*. February 6, 2002.

———. "Pakistan Hands over Senior al Qaeda." *Los Angeles Times*. April 1, 2002.

Lynch, Colum. "U.S. Postpones Plans to Reveal Findings on Iraq: Mideast Crisis Delays Campaign at U.N. to Expose Alleged Efforts to Obtain Prohibited Weapons." *Washington Post*. April 7, 2002, p. A-22.

MacFarquhar, Neil. "Saudi Arabia Arrests 13 Men Tied to Attack on a U.S. Base." *New York Times*. June 19, 2002.

———. "Al Qaeda Says Bin Laden Is Well, and Was behind Tunis Blast." *New York Times*. June 23, 2002.

Mallaby, Sebastian. "And Their Armies." *Washington Post*. April 1, 2002, p. A-15.

Malnic, Eric, William C. Rempel, and Ricardo Alonso-Zaldiver. "EgyptAir Co-Pilot Caused '99 Jet Crash, NTSB to Say." *Los Angeles Times.* March 15, 2002.

Margasak, Larry. "U.S. to Seek Death Penalty." *Los Angeles Times.* March 28, 2002.

Marlantes, Liz. "Fragile Freedoms." December 13, 2001.

——. "Bioterror: All the Rules Change." *Christian Science Monitor.* December 17, 2002.

Mashal, Lutfullah, and Philip Smucker. "An Assassination Attempt This Week Highlights a Divide between Pashtuns and the Northern Alliance." *Christian Science Monitor.* April 12, 2002.

——. "The Afghan King Returned to Kabul Yesterday, While near Kandahar, an Errant Bomb Killed Four Canadian Troops." *Christian Science Monitor.* April 19, 2002.

Marshall, Tyler, and John Hendren. "U.S. to Leave Philippines Despite Hostage Situation." *Los Angeles Times.* May 27, 2002.

McDermott, Terry. "A Perfect Soldier." *Los Angeles Times.* January 27, 2002, p. A-1.

McLaughlin, Abraham. "Secret Service Dons New Role for a New Era." *Christian Science Monitor.* February 6, 2002.

——. "Homeland Security: Pork or Protection?" *Christian Science Monitor.* March 6, 2002.

——. "Bush Plans Super-Agency to Improve U.S.-Border Control." *Christian Science Monitor.* March 25, 2002.

——. "East Theft: Radioactive Bomb Parts, Stolen Commercial Radioactive Devices Could Be Used to Make 'Dirty Bombs.'" *Christian Science Monitor.* April 10, 2002.

——. "Pressure Mounts to Overhaul the FBI: Missteps Could Lead Agency to Change Focus. but Are Americans Ready for More Domestic Intelligence Gathering?" *Christian Science Monitor.* May 8, 2002.

McLaughlin, Abraham, and Gail Russell Chaddock. "Christian Right Steps in on Mideast: A Strong, New Pro-Israeli Voice Muscles into the Traditional Jewish-Arab Political Dynamic in Washington." *Christian Science Monitor.* April 16, 2002.

Meyer, Josh, and Aaron Zitner. "Troops Uncovered Diagrams for Major U.S. Targets, Bush Says." *Los Angeles Times.* January 30, 2002.

Milbank, Dana. "Bush Seeks $27.1 Billion More for Military, Security, Relief Efforts." *Washington Post.* March 22, 2002, p. A-7.

——. "Plan Was Formed in Utmost Secrecy." *Washington Post.* June 7, 2002, p. A-1.

Miller, Bill. "Ridge Close to Unveiling New Terror Alert System: Tiered Warnings, Flexibility Sought." *Washington Post.* March 9, 2002, p. A-13.

Miller, Eric. "More Money Won't End the War." *Boston Globe.* February 5, 2002, p. A-11.

Miller, Greg. "U.S. Overlooked Terrorism Sign Well before 9/11: "Inquiry, a House-Senate Panel Report Says al Qaeda Was Focusing on a Domestic Attack and the Use of Planes As Weapons As Far Back As Mid-90s." *Los Angeles Times.* September 19, 2002.

——. "Wider Pentagon Spy Role Urged: Influential Panel Wants Special Forces More Active in Counter-Terrorism, Entering CIA Domain." *Los Angeles Times.* October 26, 2002.

Miller, Greg, and Josh Meyer. "CIA Missile in Yemen Kills 6 Terrorist Suspects: Unmanned Plane Fires at Car Carrying Alleged al Qaeda Operatives, Marking an Aggressive Shift in the Bush Administration Tactics." *Los Angeles Times.* November 5, 2002.

Miller, Judith. "U.S. Plans to Act More Rigorously in Hostage Cases." *New York Times.* February 18, 2002.

Mitchell, Allison, and Carl Huse. "Congress Seeking to Put Own Stamp on Security Plan." *New York Times.* June 12, 2002.

Mohan, Geoffrey. "Radical School Reform: Pakistan Seeks to Stamp out Extremist Training Grounds by Revamping the Curriculum of Madrassas." *Los Angeles Times.* March 23, 2002.

Mohan, Geoffrey, and Esther Schrader. "Back at Base, U.S. Troops Say Afghans Failed Them." *Los Angeles Times*. March 11, 2002.

Monmaney, Terence. "Living with 9/11 State of Mind Mood: Many Search for Meaning and Reinforce Ties to Loved Ones, but Will It Last?" *Los Angeles Times*. February 26, 2002.

Moore, Molly. "6 Die in Shootout at Settlement: Palestinian Raid Sparks Battle; Mother, 3 Children among Victims." *Washington Post*. June 21, 2002, p. A-1.

Morin, Richard, and Claudia Deane. "Poll: Strong Backing for Bush, War." *Washington Post*. March 11, 2002, p. A-1.

Morin, Richard, and Dana Milbank. "Bush and GOP Enjoy Record Popularity: Poll Finds Broad Support Despite Doubts on Economy." *Washington Post*. January 29, 2002, p. A-1.

Mufson, Steven. "The Way Bush Sees the World." *Washington Post*. February 17, 2002.

Murphy, Dan. "'Activated' Asian Terror Web Busted." *Christian Science Monitor*. January 23, 2002, pp. 1, 4.

Murphy, Dean E., and David M. Halbfinger. "9/11 Bridged the Racial Divide, New Yorkers Say, Gingerly." *New York Times*. June 16, 2002.

Nauman, Michael. "Why Europe Is Wary of War with Iraq." *New York Times*. February 18, 2002.

Neilan, Terrance. "Pentagon Faces More Questions on Afghan Raid, Plus C.I.A. Role." *New York Times*. February 12, 2002.

——. "8 Killed As Bomb Goes Off Near U.S. Consulate in Pakistan." *New York Times*. June 14, 2002.

Neuman, Johanna. "Flood of Wartime Spending Keeps Nation's Capital Flush with Capital." *Los Angeles Times*. January 22, 2002.

New York Times. Editorial. "Lawmakers to Investigate U.S. Intelligence Failures." February 12, 2002.

——. "The Uses of American Power." March 3, 2002.

——. "Afghanistan's Marshall Plan." April 19, 2002.

——. "Handling Foreign Visitors." June 6, 2002.

——. Editorial. "Back to the Drawing Board." June 7, 2002.

——. "The New Politics of Antiterrorism." June 16, 2002.

——. "Battle Plans for Iraq." July 6, 2002.

Newsweek. "The Hijackers We Let Escape." June 10, 2002. Internet, http//:www.msnbc.com/news/760647.asp.

O'Harrow, Robert, Jr. "Intricate Screening of Fliers in Works: Database Raises Privacy Concerns." *Washington Post*. February 1, 2002. p. A-1.

Orme, William. "U.S. Alleges Iraq's Army Is Rebuilding." *Los Angeles Times*. March 7, 2002.

Ottaway, David B., and Robert G. Kaiser. "Military Presence Seen As Political Liability in Arab World." *Washington Post*. January 18, 2002, p. A-1.

Paddock, Richard C. "Singapore Says Terror Ring Planned Attacks on Americans." *Los Angeles Times*. January 12, 2001.

——. "Asia Group Broken up Last Month Had al Qaeda Training, Officials Allege." *Los Angeles Times*. January 18, 2002.

——. "Southeast Asian Terror Exhibits al Qaeda Traits." *Los Angeles Times*. March 3, 2002.

Paddock, Richard C., and Bob Drogin. "A Terror Network Unraveled in Singapore." *Los Angeles Times*. January 20, 2002.

Pasternak, Judy, and Stephen Braun. "Emirates Looked Other Way While al Qaeda Funds Flowed: For Years the Persian Gulf Country Shrugged Off Warnings about Money Laundering." *Los Angeles Times*. January 20, 2002.

Pereira, Brendan, and Luz Baguiro. "Terror Sweep in Region Stepped Up: Malaysia Mounts Big Operation, Netting 14 Suspects, While the Philippines and Indonesia Move to Jail Militants." *The Strait Times Interactive*. April 9, 2002.

Perlez, Jane. "Botched Siege under Scrutiny in Philippines." *New York Times*. February 9, 2002.

Peterson, Scott. "Special Ops Tackle Aide Mission: Afghanistan Is a Laboratory for a New Kind of U.S. Military Humanitarian Mission." *Christian Science Monitor*. March 1, 2002.

———. "An Uneasy Iraq Awaits U.S. Move." *Christian Science Monitor*. March 25, 2002.

———. "U.S. vs. Iraq: Saddam May Have Fired the First Shot." *Christian Science Monitor*. April 9, 2002.

Pianin, Eric, amd Bill Miller. "For Ridge, Ambition and Realities Clash." *Washington Post*. January 23, 2002, p. A-1.

Pianin, Eric, and Bob Woodward. "Terror Concerns of U.S. Extend to Asia: Arrests in Singapore and Malaysia Cited." *Washington Post*. January 18, 2002, p. A-18.

Piller, Charles. "U.S. to Curb Computer Access by Foreigners." *Los Angeles Times*. March 7, 2002.

Pincus, Walter. "Al Qaeda Leader Talked of Plot against U.S. Embassy." *Washington Post*. January 23, 2002, p. A-9.

———. "Congress to Postpone Revamping of FBI, CIA." *Washington Post*. June 13, 2002, p. A-1.

Pincus, Walter, and Colum Lynch. "Wolfowitz Had CIA Probe U.N. Diplomat in Charge." *Washington Post*. April 15, 2002, p. A-1.

Pomfret, John. "China Sees Interests Tied to U.S.: Change Made Clear in Wake of Sept. 11." *Washington Post*. February 2, 2002, p. A-1.

Price, Niko. "Rival Militias Battle outside Kabul." *Los Angeles Times*. April 12, 2002.

Priest, Dana, and Thomas E. Ricks. "U.S. Units Attacking al Qaeda in Pakistan: Covert Operation Straddles Border." *Washington Post*. April 25, 2002, p. A-1.

Priest, Dana, and Walter Pincus. "Strife, Dissent Beset Hill's Sept. 11 Panel: Bipartisan Group Disagrees on Mission." *Washington Post*. May 20, 2002, p. A-1.

Prusher, Ilene R. "Local Afghan Commander Says bin Laden and His No. 2 Have Been in the Khost Area." *Christian Science Monitor*. March 26, 2002.

Purdum, Todd. "Democrats Starting to Fault President on the War's Future." *New York Times*. February 28, 2002.

Pyes, Craig, and Geoffrey Mohan. "Grenade Attack in Pakistan Kills Two Americans." *Los Angeles Times*. March 18, 2002.

Raymond Bonner, and Jane Perlez. "Asian Terror: Al Qaeda Seeks Niche in Indonesia, Officials Fear." *New York Times*. January 23, 2002.

Reid, T. R. "Britain Set to Bulk Up Its Afghan Deployment." *Washington Post*. March 19, 2002, p. A-16.

Reitman, Valerie, and David Zucchino. "Slaying of Afghan Minister Shakes Faith in Government." *Los Angeles Times*. February 17, 2002.

Reuters. "War on Terror Should Not Include Iraq, Russia Tells U.S." February 3, 2002.

———. "Violence Flares in India Kashmir: 19 Killed As Separatist Violence Escalates." March 5, 2002.

———. "Saudi Prince Accepts Bush Invitation after Snub." March 17, 2002.

———. "Purported Bin Laden E-Mail Attacks Saudi Plan for Mideast." *Washington Post*. March 28, 2002, p. A-22.

———. "Nepal Kills 90 Maoist Rebels in Crackdown." *New York Times*. May 3, 2002.

Rhode, David, and C. J. Chivers. "Al Qaeda's Grocery List and Manuals of Killing." *New York Times*. March 17, 2002.

Rice, Condoleezza. "Text: National Security Adviser." September 19, 2002. *eMediaMill Works*, http://www.cnn.com/2001/us/09/ret.rice.security/.

Rich, Frank. "Freedom from the Press." *New York Times*. March 2, 2002.

Richey, Warren. "Terror Could Tilt High Court on State Rights." *Christian Science Monitor*. February 11, 2002.

——. "U.S. Debating Wider Assault on Columbian Rebels." *Los Angeles Times*. February 23, 2002.

——. "U.S. Works Up Plan for Using Nuclear Arms: Administration, in a Secret Report, Calls for a Strategy against at Least Seven Nations." *Los Angeles Times*. March 9, 2002.

Richter, Paul. "U.S. Shift Clouds Arms Deal." *Los Angeles Times*. January 13, 2002.

Ricks, Thomas E. "European Security Leaders Alarmed by Bush's Stance." *Washington Post*. February 3, 2002, p. A-16.

——. "Defense Dept. Divided over Propaganda Plan: Critics Fear 'Information Operations' Could Backfire, Hurt Pentagon's Credibility." *Washington Post*. February 20, 2002, p. A-10.

——. "Rumsfeld Kills Pentagon Propaganda Unit: News Reported As Damaging, Inaccurate." *Washington Post*. February 27, 2002, p. A-21.

——. "Battle Sends Broader Message of U.S. Resolve." *Washington Post*. March 5, 2002, p. A-15.

Ricks, Thomas E., and Vernon Loeb. "Rumsfeld and Commanders Exchange Briefings." *Washington Post*. March 3, 2002, p. A-19.

Risen, James. "Rifts Plentiful As 9/11 Inquiry Begins Today." *New York Times*. June 4, 2002.

Risen, James, and David Johnston. "Intercepted al Qaeda E-Mail Is Said to Hint at Regrouping." *New York Times*. March 6, 2002.

Risen, James, and Judith Miller. "Bin Laden's Trail Is Lost but Officials Suspect He Is Alive." *New York Times*. February 4, 2002.

Rosenblatt, Robert A., and Warren Vieth. "White House Sees Shrinking Budget Surplus." *Los Angeles Times*. August 23, 2001.

Rubin, Alissa J. "U.S. Bombers Pound al Qaeda Mountain Lair." *Los Angeles Times*. March 4, 2002.

Rubin, Alissa J., and David Zucchino. "Sense of Urgency Grows over Afghan Security." *Los Angeles Times*. February 25, 2002.

Safire, William. "The Great Unwatched." *New York Times*. February 18, 2002.

——. "The Inspection Ploy." *New York Times*. March 4, 2002.

——. "Ending the War Process. *New York Times*. March 11, 2002.

——. "Sharon on Survival." *New York Times*. April 4, 2002.

——. "Saddam's Offensive." *New York Times*. April 8, 2002.

Sander, Thomas H., and Robert D. Putman. "Walking the Civic Talk after Sept. 11." *Christian Science Monitor*. February 19, 2002.

Sanger, David E. "Bush Renews Pledge to Strike First to Counter Terror Threats." *New York Times*. July 20, 2002.

Schmidt, Susan. "Mueller Announces a New Focus for FBI: Agency Shifts Priorities to Anti-Terror Work." *Washington Post*. May 29, 2002.

Schmidt, Susan, and Walter Pincus. "Al Muhajir Alleged to Be Scouting Terror Sites: U.S. Says al Qaeda Had Instructed Suspect." *Washington Post*. June 12, 2002, p. A-1.

Schmitt, Eric. "Vote in House Strongly Backs an End to I.N.S." *New York Times*. April 26, 2002.

——. "Wolfowitz, in Philippines, Looks to a Greater U.S. Role." *New York Times*. June 4, 2002.

Schmitt, Eric, and James Dao. "A 'Damaged' Information Office Is Declared Closed by Rumsfeld." *New York Times.* February 27, 2002.

Schneider, Howard. "Abdullah Appeals for Broad Mideast Peace." *Washington Post.* March 27,
2002.

———. "Saudi Puts Faith in Iraqi Pledge: Crown Prince Says He Trusts Vow to Respect Kuwait's
Borders." *Washington Post.* March 30, 2002, p. A-12.

———. "Arab Ministers Urge Action against Israel: Palestinian Violence Is Called Justified."
Washington Post. April 7, 2002, p. A-19.

Schneider, Howard, and Walter Pincus. "Bin Laden Video Includes Sept. 11 Praise."
Washington Post. April 16, 2002, p. A-12.

Schneider, William. "A Reagan Echo: Bush's Version of Cowboy Diplomacy Has Our Allies
Reeling, but the 'Axis of Evil' Is Running Scared." *Los Angeles Times.* February 24, 2002.

Schrader, Esther. "Iran Helped al Qaeda and Taliban Flee, Rumsfeld Says." *Los Angeles Times.*
February 4, 2002.

———. "Military Fuses Old, New to Create a Lethal Force." *Los Angeles Times.* February 10,
2002.

———. "War, on Advice of Council." *Los Angeles Times.* February 15, 2002.

———. "Pentagon Closes Besieged Strategy Office: The Agency Stirred Misinformation Claims;
Attempts to Mislead the Enemy Wartime Will Continue, Officials Claim." *Los Angeles
Times.* February 27, 2002.

Seelye, Katharine Q. "TV Drama, Pentagon-Style: A Fictional Terror Tribunal." *New York
Times.* March 31, 2002.

———. "War on Terror Makes Odd Twists in Justice System." *New York Times.* June 23, 2002.

Seelye, Katharine Q., and David E. Sanger. "Bush Reconsiders Stand on Treating Captives of
War." *New York Times.* January 29, 2002.

Serrano, Richard A. "Detainees in Cuba Refuse to Eat after Cell Incident: Most of the 300 Prisoners from Afghanistan War Being Held at the U.S. Naval Base Stage a Protest after a
Guard Disrupts One Muslim's Prayers." *Los Angeles Times.* March 1, 2002.

Shaker, Thom. "The Military: U.S. to Send Special Forces to Train Army for Kabul." *New
York Times.* March 26, 2002.

Shenon, Philip, and James Risen. "Qaeda Deputy Reported to Plan New Attacks." *New York
Times.* February 14, 2002.

Spires, Alan. "Jordan Advises U.S. against a Military Campaign in Iraq." *Washington Post.*
March 13, 2002, p. A-24.

———. "Cheney Meets with Yemeni President." *Washington Post.* March 14, 2002.

———. "Saudis Rebuff U.S. Plan to Confront Iraq." *Washington Post.* March 17, 2002, p. A-22.

———. "Peacekeepers Won't Go Beyond Kabul, Cheney Says." *Washington Post.* March 20,
2002.

———. "Policy Divide Thwarts Powell in Mideast Effort." *Washington Post.* April 26, 2002, p. A-1.

Spires, Alan, and Dan Balz. "U.S. Seeks Arab Role in Reviving Peace Talks." *Washington Post.*
April 6, 2002, p. A-1.

Smucker, Philip. "After the War, Fighting Begins." *Christian Science Monitor.* February 1,
2002, p. 6.

———. "Blast May Mark Shift in Terror: Two Tunisian Officials Were Ousted Saturday in the
Wake of a Bombing." *Christian Science Monitor.* April 29, 2002.

Soo-Jenong Lee. "N. Korea Resume Talks with U.S." *Los Angeles Times.* April 8, 2002.

Streitfeld, David, and Charles Piller. "A Changed America: Big Brother Finds Ally in Once-
Wary High Tech." *Los Angeles Times.* January 19, 2002.

Stevenson, Richard W. "Bush Budget Links Dollars to Deeds with New Ratings." *New York Times.* February 3, 2002.

Stout, David. "C.I.A. Director Defends Agency and Warns of al Qaeda Threat." *New York Times.* February 6, 2002.

Strauss, Valerie, and Emily Wax. "Where Two Worlds Collide: Muslim Schools Face Tensions of Islamic, U.S. Views." *Washington Post.* February 25, 2002, p. A-1.

Taylor, Catherine. "Taliban-Style Group Grows in Iraq: In the Kurdish North, a New Islamist Group with Ties to al Qaeda Has Killed Women without Burqas, Seized Villages." *Christian Science Monitor.* March 15, 2002.

Telhami, Shibley. "Why Suicide Terrorism Takes Root." *Los Angeles Times.* April 4, 2002.

Tempest, Rone, and Rone Daniszewski. "U.S. Forces Gain Ground in Afghan Mountain Battle." *Los Angeles Times.* March 7, 2002.

Theodoulou, Michael. "Arab Press Finds Roots of Terrorism Closer to Home." *Christian Science Monitor.* January 28, 2002, p. 7.

Time Magazine. "Where Have You Gone, Colin Powell?" Cover Story. September 10, 2001.

Tyler, Patrick E. "White House Acts to Regain the Initiative." *New York Times.* June 7, 2002.

Tyson, Ann Scott. "Does bin Laden Matter Anymore? In the Pentagon Corridors, the 'Evil-Doer' Is No Longer the Focus—Even if Most Americans Think He's Supposed to Be." *Christian Science Monitor.* March 1, 2002.

————. "U.S., Allies in a Riskier Kind of War." *Christian Science Monitor.* March 5, 2002.

VandeHei, Jim, and Dan Eggen. "Hill Eyes Shifting Parts of FBI, CIA: Homeland Security Department Would Get Own Operatives." *Washington Post.* June 13, 2002.

Vick, Karl. "Pakistani Leader Accused of Trying to Grab Power: Restructuring Plan Is Broadly Condemned." *Washington Post.* June 28, 2002, p. A-18.

Von Drehle, David, and Susan Schmidt. "Mueller May Be Stronger after Tough Week." *Washington Post.* June 2, 2002, p. A-1.

Wain, Barry. "A Questionable Strategy." *Far Eastern Economic Review.* January 31, 2002.

Washington Post. "Bush Cites CIA-FBI Breakdown: House-Senate Panel Starts 9/11 Intelligence Failure." June 5, 2002, p. A-1.

————. "Bush to Propose Security Cabinet Position: Major Restructuring Needs Congressional Approval." June 6, 2002.

————. "Mueller Says Criticism Underscores Need for FBI Changes: Director Wants More Agents, Money and Time." June 6, 2002.

————. "U.S. to Track Visitors Deemed a Security Risk. June 6, 2002, p. A-1.

Washington Post. Editorial. "The Present Danger." January 19, 2002, p. A-26.

————. "Cross Talk among Allies." February 20, 2002, p. A-14.

————. "Debating the War." March 3, 2002, p. B-6.

————. "Annapolis Takes on Terrorism." March 30, 2002, p. A-16.

————. "Taking the Offensive." June 4, 2002, p. A-16.

————. "Bush to Propose Security Cabinet Position: Major Restructuring Needs Congressional Approval." June 6, 2002.

————. "Signs of Drift." June 16, 2002, p. B-6.

Watson, Paul. "Deadly Shooting in Calcutta May Be Linked to al Qaeda." *Los Angeles Times.* January 23, 2002.

Watson, Paul, and Sidhartha Barua. "Somalian Links Seen to al Qaeda." *Los Angeles Times.* February 25, 2002.

Weir, Fred. "A New Terror-War Front: The Caucasus." *Christian Science Monitor.* February 26, 2002.

———. "Chechnya's Warrior Tradition." *Christian Science Monitor.* March 26, 2002.

White House Press Release. "President Signs Aviation Security Legislation." November 19, 2001. http://www.whitehouse.gov.

Wilkinson, Tracy. "Israel Attacks Arafat Compound." *Los Angeles Times.* March 29, 2002.

Will, George F. "War and Then a Wall." *Washington Post.* April 3, 2002, p. A-23.

———. "Dispensing with Arafat." *Washington Post.* June 26, 2002, p. A-25.

———. "Dispensing with Arafat." *Washington Post.* June 6, 2002, p. A-25.

Williams, Carol. "U.S. Spirits 6 Terror Suspects out of Bosnia." *Los Angeles Times.* January 19, 2002.

Winfield, Nicole. "Al Qaeda Leader Convicted in Italy." Associated Press. February 22, 2002.

Woodward, Bob. "President Broadens Anti-Hussein Order: CIA Gets More Tools to Oust Iraqi Leader." *Washington Post.* June 16, 2002, p. A-1.

Wright, Robin. "Bush, Mubarak Vow to Redouble Efforts for Peace: Meeting in Washington, the Leaders Back a Recent Saudi Initiative on Arab-Israeli Conflict." *Los Angeles Times.* March 6, 2002.

———. "An Iraqi Campaign Faces Many Hurdles. Mideast: If the U.S. Opts for Military Action against Hussein, the Battle Could Prove to Be America's Toughest in Decades." *Los Angeles Times.* March 10, 2002.

Wright, Robin, and Mark Magnier. "Bush Is Dogged by 'Axis of Evil' in Visit to Japan." *Los Angeles Times.* February 19, 2002.

Wright, Robin, Mark Magnier, and Barbara Demick. "Bush Puts Asia back at Top of Agenda." *Los Angeles Times.* February 17, 2002.

Zakhilwal, Omar. "Stifled in the Loya Jirga." *Washington Post.* June 16, 2002, p. B-7.

U.S. GOVERNMENT DOCUMENTS

Bush, George W. "Remarks at National Day of Prayer and Remembrance." The National Cathedral. Washington, D.C. September 14, 2001. Released by the Office of the White House Press.

———. "Address to a Joint Session of Congress and the American People." United States Capitol, Washington, D.C. September 20, 2001. Released by the Office of the White House Press.

———. "Presidential Address to the Nation." White House Web Site: www.whitehouse.gov. October 7, 2001.

———. "Text: Bush on Homeland Security Development." *eMediaMillWorks.* January 24, 2002.

———. "Expand the Circle of Development by Opening Societies and Building the Infrastructure of Democracy." The Washington, D.C. Forum on Inter-American Development Bank. March 14, 2002.

———. "Presidential Remarks at National Day of Prayer and Remembrance." White House Web Site: (www.whitehouse.gov). September 14, 2002.

———. "Iraq: Denial and Deception." October 7, 2001. http:www.whitehouse.gov/2002/10/2002/10.f.html.

United States Constitution. Articles I and II, *ad passim.* 1776.

U.S. Congress. *The National Security Act. Congressional Record.* Vol. 93. (March 12, 1947) 80th Congress, 1st session.

——. "The National Security Strategy of the United States of America." The White House. September 17, 2002. www.whitehouse.gov/nsc/nss.pdf.

U.S. Department of Labor. Bureau of Labor Statistics CPI Calculator. http://stats.bls.gov/.

U.S. Department of Defense. "National Defense Budgets for FY 2003." Office of the Under Secretary of Defense (Comptroller). March 2003. Calculation Methodology. p. 3.

U.S. Department of Transportation. Transportation Security Administration. *The Aviation Act.* Public Law 107-71. 115 Stat. 597. November 19, 2001. http://www.tsa.dot.gov.

U.S. Congress. (1971.) *The War Powers Act.* U.S. Congress, The War Power Act of 1973, Public Law 93–148, 93rd Congress, 1st session.

U.S. Congress. House. *The Patriot Act.* HR 3162. 107th Cong., 1st sess., October 24, 2001.

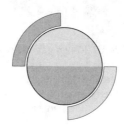

INDEX